DATI

JY 7 '82	
AP 9 '84	
AP 25 '84	
MY 3 '84	
OC 22 '84	
NO 21 '84	
AP 3 '85	
MAR 15 1993	

GAYLORD

THE PASTORAL PSYCHOLOGY SERIES,
NUMBER 7

ALIENATION:
PLIGHT OF MODERN MAN?

Edited by

WILLIAM C. BIER, S.J.

FORDHAM UNIVERSITY PRESS · NEW YORK

Printed in the United States of America

Table of Contents

Preface

A series of Pastoral Psychology Institutes, sponsored by the Psychology Department of Fordham University, was begun in 1955. With the single exception of 1967 when no Institute was given, they have been offered on an
alternate-year basis since their inception. The volumes in the Pastoral Psychology Series are an outgrowth of the Institutes, with the current volume
containing the papers presented in the 1971 Institute.

These Institutes, intended originally for the clergy and initially open only
to them, began with a series of topics in which, it was judged, the behavioral
sciences were in a position to make a contribution to clergymen in their
attempt to deal with problems encountered in pastoral work. In more recent
years the Institutes have been opened to other professional persons in addition to clergymen, and the topics selected for treatment have been broadened
accordingly.

The first two Institutes, those of 1955 and 1957, dealt rather briefly with
a series of topics and were combined for publication into a single volume,
the first in the Pastoral Psychology Series, entitled: *Personality and sexual
problems in pastoral psychology.* Subsequent Institutes were devoted to
single topics which received more extensive treatment. The 1959 Institute
concerned itself with addiction, before the drug problem assumed the proportions found today, and appeared as volume two in the series: *Problems in
addiction: Alcohol and drug addiction.* The 1961 Institute focused on the
teenager and provided the material for volume three: *The adolescent: His
search for understanding.* Marriage was the topic of the 1963 Institute and
volume four in the series: *Marriage: A psychological and moral approach.*
The 1965 Institute concerned itself with the topic of woman in the Church
and in the modern world, and quietly directed attention to a number of
features in the position of women which have subsequently been under-
scored, sometimes rather stridently, by Women's Lib. This Institute gave
birth to volume five in the Pastoral Psychology Series under the title: *Woman
in modern life.* The last previous Institute, that in 1969, addressed itself to

the question of conscience by reason of the central position which this topic had come to assume both in the Church and in the world. This Institute provided the material for volume six in the series with the title: *Conscience: Its freedom and limitations.*

A significant feature of the Institutes has been their interdisciplinary approach. From the beginning of the series there has been a consistent emphasis on the contributions of the behavioral sciences, including, in addition to psychology, particularly psychiatry and sociology. Frequent contributions have also been made by such disciplines as theology, philosophy, political science, and social work. More limited contributions, depending usually upon the particular topic under consideration, have been made to the Institute series by anthropology, the legal profession, and the judiciary.

All the Institutes have conformed to the same overall pattern of arrangement. They have been conducted from a Monday through a Friday of a week in the latter half of June. The Institute reported in the present volume ran from the 21st to the 25th of June, 1971. This time was initially selected and has been adhered to because it fits, with a minimum of inconvenience both to contributors and to participants, between the end of the academic year and the start of summer school or other summer commitments. It also has the not-inconsiderable advantage of being held at a time when the academic facilities of the campus are not taxed and hence are available for the Institute.

The Institutes have provided a concentrated week-long experience focused on a pre-selected topic, and the interchange in both formal discussion and informal conversation between the contributors, who gave the papers, and the participants, who attended, has proved to be a notably valuable feature of the Institutes. Not all the contributors were able to remain for the entire Institute, although some did; but most of them remained for at least a full day. The Institutes were planned to provide as much interaction as possible among those present. Thus, luncheons on the three middle days of the Institute, a reception following the afternoon session on one of the days, and morning and afternoon coffee breaks, were all made part of the Institute fee with the design of maximizing the opportunity for interchange and discussion.

Consistently, the discussion period after the presentation of the papers has emerged as a most valuable feature of the Institute. Invaluable, however, as discussions of this kind are for those who are present, experience with them indicates that their significance is greatly—if not indeed almost entirely—conditioned by the immediate context in which they occur. They represent a face-to-face situation, where expression, gesture, and tone of voice are important elements, and where the atmosphere of spontaneous interchange is all-important. All of this dies in the printed word. It is virtually impossible —and this is said on a basis of experience—to recapture this atmosphere afterwards, and this volume, like its predecessors, makes no attempt to do so. This experience, which is a living one, is the bonus which is reserved for those who are able to spend the week required to attend the Institute—as opposed to those who must be content with the reading of the published volume. We believe, however, that the published proceedings have a contribution to make to a far larger group than those who are able to attend the Institute sessions, especially since the topics of the more recent Institutes have been broadened beyond problems encountered in pastoral work and attendance at the Institutes has been opened to various professional persons. The reception accorded the previous volumes in the Pastoral Psychology Series would seem to attest to the validity of this conviction.

The topics chosen for the Institute series have combined an attention to the perennial, as for instance personality and sexual problems in pastoral work, and to the contemporary. With the continuation of the series more attention has been given to immediately current problems. Thus it can be said that the topics chosen for the more recent Institutes have been timely, even in a period of rapidly changing times. Indeed some of them—notably those on addiction and the place of woman in the modern world—were ahead of their time, at least if judged by the amount of attention accorded to them subsequent to their treatment in the Institute series. It has been the aim of the planners of the Institute series to select topics which are not only current, but which lend themselves to, and indeed require, the kind of interdisciplinary approach which the Institute series is in a position to provide.

In selecting *Alienation* as the topic for the 1971 Institute, the planning Committee believed that it had achieved both the above-mentioned objectives. Quite evidently, man's estrangement not only from his world but even from himself has become one of the growingly pervasive characteristics of modern man as he nears the three-quarter mark in the twentieth century. The youth culture with its subculture and its counterculture was only the most obvious manifestation of such alienation. Hardly less obvious was the sense of alienation found in minority groups in this country and in the nations of the "third world" abroad. Somewhat less obvious, but hardly less significant, was the alienation experienced—in the world and in the Church—by the older generation who felt themselves to be the victims of change and to be estranged from a world already profoundly different from the world they had known and had helped to form. Need it be said that a topic as pervasive as alienation in the modern world could be treated only in interdisciplinary perspective?

The subtitle of the volume poses a question: *Plight of modern man?* The planning Committee purposely put this as a question rather than as an affirmation, a question which it was the function of the Institute to explore. One of the contributors to the volume, Dr. Samuel Z. Klausner, points out at the beginning of his paper the *double-entendre* contained in the question. "The question mark," he writes, "may turn on the word 'alienated' or, alternatively, may turn on the word 'plight.' " All our contributors would be in at least general agreement that alienation is one of the problems besetting modern man, if not indeed one of his predominant characteristics. There would be less agreement, however, whether alienation is necessarily a plight. As some of the contributors point out, some degree of alienation is perhaps an inevitable accompaniment of adolescence and may even be necessary for the development of personal independence and maturity. Similarly, some degree of alienation may be a necessary ingredient for achieving social and political reform, even of a constructive variety. Less constructive and less redeeming features are discernible in the alienation of the older generation.

A glance at the table of contents reveals that the material presented in this volume is divided into eight sections. The first two sections provide the background for a consideration of alienation. Quite evidently, alienation, as a concept, has its more remote roots in philosophy and in religion, and then, more recently and more pointedly, in the writings of such political and social theorists as Hegel and Marx. This is the historical background provided in Section I. It is only a general background, however. Equally needed to bring modern man's sense of estrangement to the peak experienced today was the confluence of events of the present century, particularly those during and after the Second World War and the long cold-war atmosphere of the past thirty years. These more contemporary influences are explored in Section II.

It seemed to the planning Committee that there were three focal points of alienation which deserved special and reasonably extended treatment in the Institute. These were: alienation in the political and social order (Section III), the alienation of youth (Sections IV and V), and religious alienation (Section VI). Section VII gives attention to several additional, selected manifestations of alienation. Finally, in Section VIII representatives from several differing disciplines suggest what, from their respective points of view, might be modern man's response to his sense of estrangement.

Some reviewers of previous volumes in the Institute series have commented upon the lack of an index in the respective volumes. Attention was given to this point in preparing the present volume for publication, but, on consideration, it did not seem that an index in a volume of this kind would have anything substantially to contribute to the orientation of the reader beyond what is already provided in the Table of Contents, with its eight sections and with its sub-topics under each section. Hence, this volume, like its predecessors, appears without an index.

As editor of the Proceedings and chairman of the Institute Committee, I am pleased to pay grateful tribute to my fellow Committee members, all of whom are Fordham University faculty members and all of whom shared with me the responsibility for the planning and conduct of the Institute out of which these Proceedings came. They are: Rev. Francis P. Canavan, s.j., Associate Professor of Political Science; Dr. Ewert H. Cousins, Associate

Professor of Theology; Rev. Joseph G. Keegan, s.ɪ., Associate Professor of Psychology; Rev. Quentin Lauer, s.ɪ., Professor of Philosophy; Rev. Edwin A. Quain, s.ɪ., Professor of Classics and Director of Fordham University Press; and Dr. Gerald H. Shattuck, Associate Professor of Sociology.

January, 1972   WILLIAM C. BIER, s.ɪ.

ALIENATION
PLIGHT OF MODERN MAN?

I
ALIENATION IN
HISTORICAL PERSPECTIVE

Alienation and Reconciliation in the Judaeo-Christian Experience

JOSEPH A. BRACKEN, S.J.

Father Joseph A. Bracken, S.J., received an M.A. degree from Loyola University (Chicago) in 1960, and the Dr. phil. degree from the University of Freiburg (Germany) in 1968. At the present time he is an assistant professor of dogmatic theology at St. Mary of the Lake Seminary, Mundelein, Illinois. Father Bracken is a contributor to philosophical and theological journals, and is a member of the American Catholic Philosophical Association and the American Theological Society.

Alienation is a complex term which can have various shades of meaning, according as it is used to explain human behavior from different points of view. In Judaeo-Christian experience, i.e., as a specifically religious phenomenon, alienation is perhaps best understood within the general theological context of sin and redemption. Even if, as Paul Tillich points out, sin and alienation are not identical in their meaning, they are closely related on the level of religious experience, especially if the notion of sin be allowed to include both "original" or hereditary as well as personal sin. As Tillich himself says in his *Systematic theology*, "man's predicament is estrangement, but his estrangement is sin. It is not a state of things, like the laws of nature, but a matter of both personal freedom and universal destiny" (Tillich, 1957, p. 46). In my treatment I shall describe alienation, therefore, in terms of sin and redemption through the saving action of Jesus Christ. For this purpose I

3

shall draw upon some pertinent reflections of the American philosopher Josiah Royce, in his book *The problem of Christianity*. I have chosen Royce over Tillich and other modern theologians who have likewise analyzed the alienation of modern man, first of all, because Royce's position is quite succinct and thus more readily comprehensible to the ordinary reader, and secondly, because I believe that Royce's solution to the problem of alienation is especially pertinent to institutional Christianity in this final third of the twentieth century. There follows therefore first a summary of Royce's doctrine on alienation and reconciliation, as it is set forth in *The problem of Christianity*, and then my comments on its relevance to the contemporary scene.

ROYCE'S VIEW ON ALIENATION AND RECONCILIATION

In Royce's judgment, the doctrine of Christianity can be summarized in three leading ideas: 1.) "The salvation of the individual man is determined by membership in a certain spiritual community—a religious community and, in its inmost nature, a divine community, in whose life the Christian virtues are to reach their highest expression and the spirit of the Master is to obtain its earthly fulfilment." 2.) "The individual human being is by nature subject to some overwhelming moral burden from which, if unaided, he cannot escape. This burden is at once a natural inheritance and a burden of personal guilt." 3.) "The only escape for the individual, the only union with the divine spiritual community which he can obtain, is provided by the divine plan for the redemption of mankind. And this plan is one which includes an Atonement for the sins and guilt of mankind. This atonement, and this alone, makes possible the entrance of the individual into a saving union with the divine spiritual community, and reveals the full meaning of what the Master meant by the Kingdom of Heaven" (Royce, 1968, pp. 72–73). In brief, therefore, the doctrine of Christianity is that mankind is called by God to life in community, that this call is inhibited, however, by the "moral burden" of the individual which makes life in community virtually impossible, and finally that only the atoning action of Jesus Christ has made possible for future generations the formation of this spiritual community, on which their salvation as individuals intrinsically depends. I will now explain each of these three ideas in succession, with special emphasis, however, on the second idea dealing with the "inescapable moral burden" of the individual, i.e., his alienation from God, his fellow man, and himself.

Royce begins by answering an implicit objection to his first thesis, namely, that God wills the salvation of mankind in and through membership in a universal spiritual community. The objection is as follows: Jesus Christ in the Gospel narratives preaches a gospel of repentance for sin and love for the neighbor, but makes little or no explicit reference to the Church, which as a matter of fact arose only after His death and resurrection and under the leadership of the apostles (Royce, 1968, p. 75). Hence, if Jesus Christ by His life and preaching represents the revealed word of God to mankind, then there is no divine plan of salvation for the individual through membership in a spiritual community. The Church, in other words, is a purely human institution and has no intrinsic connection with the Gospel message. Royce responds to this objection by taking note of the development of dogma within the primitive Christian community. That is, the early Christians came to realize that the "Kingdom of Heaven," as originally preached by Jesus, was to be realized "in and through and for the Church,—in the fellowship of the faithful who constituted the Church as it was on earth, through the divine Spirit that was believed to guide the life of the Church; and for the future experience of the Church, whenever the end should come, and whenever the purpose of God should finally be manifested and accomplished" (Royce, 1968, p. 76). Likewise, the early Christians in Royce's opinion transformed the somewhat vague precept of Christ to love one's neighbor as oneself into the more concrete and specific commandment to love one's fellow Christian as a member of the same faith-community or Church (Royce, 1968, pp. 87–95). St. Paul in his frequent references to the Church as the Mystical Body of Christ was in large part responsible for this transformation of Christianity into a religion of loyalty to one's neighbor within the Christian community (Royce, 1968, p. 95). Hence, by taking note of this doctrinal development within the early Christian community, Royce can still claim that God does indeed will the salvation of mankind through membership in a spiritual community, since Christianity, the revealed religion *par excellence,* makes membership in the Church a necessary condition of salvation for the individual.

He then goes on to the second leading idea in Christianity: namely, that "the individual human being is by nature subject to some overwhelming moral burden from which, if unaided, he cannot escape." In Royce's opinion, this moral burden is both a natural inheritance and the consequence of personal sin. It is, first of all, a natural inheritance because it is an inevitable by-product of life in society with other men. That is, the cultural environment which is the natural inheritance of every human being born into civil society has an ultimately deleterious effect on his ability to join with his fellow men in genuine community. Life in society, says Royce, tends to make the individual human being self-centered and highly competitive with respect to his fellow man (Royce, 1968, pp. 106–114). On the other hand, precisely the opposite dispositions of mutual trust and self-dedication are required to foster genuine community. Hence, one must regretfully conclude that life in society has, as mentioned above, an ultimately deleterious effect on the individual's ability and antecedent willingness to enter into true community with his fellow man.

Royce substantiates this somewhat surprising thesis through appeal to the following observable phenomena in civil life. Men become genuinely self-conscious, i.e., aware of themselves as distinct individuals, only through imitation of, or more often opposition to, their fellow men. An individual living alone on a desert island would indeed have a certain conduct or set pattern of behavior, but he would not be truly conscious of it as his own behavior, because he would have no one with whom to compare himself. Thus "play and conflict, rivalry and emulation, conscious imitation and conscious social contrasts between man and man,—these are the sources of each man's consciousness about his own conduct" (Royce, 1968, pp. 108–109). On the other hand, the self-consciousness which is thus engendered by the clash of wills and social ideals among the members of the same society becomes an insuperable burden, when the individuals seek some higher form of affective union with one another in community. Society has trained them all too well to be self-sufficient. Their self-sufficiency now effectively inhibits them from the mutual self-giving required for genuine community.

Langdon Gilkey makes almost the same point, albeit from a different point of view, in his recent book *Religion and the scientific future*. He condemns the modern myth that "awareness" or increased technical understanding of man and his environment will inevitably lead to a new social utopia. "A scientific culture can become demonic if science is not used by men whose self-understanding and thus whose public action is guided by symbols that transcend the limits of scientific inquiry and illumine the spiritual, personal, and free dimensions of man's being" (Gilkey, 1970, p. 89). Chief among those symbols to which Gilkey refers would obviously be that of life-in-community, such as Christianity espouses.

Thus far the moral burden of the individual as a natural inheritance or inevitable consequence of life in a civilized society. Royce now takes up the moral burden or alienation of the individual in terms of personal guilt. Every individual human being is at some time in his life tempted, Royce claims, to a sin against the Holy Spirit, that is, to a betrayal of his most cherished life-ideal or self-image. If for one reason or another he yields to this temptation and betrays his own "better self," then he commits an unpardonable sin. That is, he can never forgive himself for the conscious betrayal of his own higher ideals. Royce does not stipulate that every adult man or woman will inevitably sin in this way against the Holy Spirit. But, if anyone is conscious of such an act of "treason" or self-betrayal, then he will find himself making the following confession: "That fact, that event, that deed, is irrevocable. The fact that I am the one who then did thus and so, not ignorantly, but knowingly,—that fact will outlast the ages. . . . My guilt is as enduring as time" (Royce, 1968, pp. 160–161).

On this somber note, Royce takes up his third thesis—namely, that the individual human being will nevertheless be saved through membership in the Christian community, because Jesus Christ, its founder, effectively atoned for the sins of its future members by His unswerving loyalty to the ideal of a universal community of all mankind, even unto death. Hence, while the self-centered moral training of the individual in society and above all the burden of personal guilt which each individual carries in virtue of an earlier self-betrayal would normally make life in community impossible for mankind, Jesus Christ as the "Suffering Servant" of Second Isaiah (42–53) embodies in His own person a new ideal of love for and loyalty to one's fellow man which creates anew the necessary psychological conditions for human community. Christ's atoning life and death, in other words, represents a new and creative triumph of the spirit of community: "a triumph which is not so much a mere compensation for what has been lost, as a transfiguration of the very loss into a gain that, without this very loss, could never have been won. The traitor cannot thus transform the meaning of his own past. But the suffering servant can thus transfigure this meaning; can bring out of the realm of death a new life that only this very death rendered possible" (Royce, 1968, p. 181). The ideal of love for and loyalty to a universal community of mankind has thus in the person of Christ triumphed over the ever-present fact of sin and divisiveness. That is, men and women since the time of Christ have had the courage to form community, to live a life of loyalty to one another, only because it is now absolutely certain that "no baseness or cruelty of treason so deep or so tragic shall enter our human world, but that loyal love shall be able in due time to oppose to just that deed of treason its fitting deed of atonement" (Royce, 1968, p. 186).

COMMENTS ON ROYCE'S CONCEPT OF ALIENATION

So much for Royce's doctrine of alienation and reconciliation within the Judaeo-Christian experience. My own comments will be limited to Royce's analysis of alienation as the "inescapable moral burden of the individual." This moral burden, it will be remembered, is the result both of life in society and of personal sin. With regard to the first of these, I would suggest that Royce offers a thought-provoking reflection on the role of the Church in the modern world. If modern man for a variety of reasons finds himself alienated from God, his fellow man, and ultimately from himself, is the primary response of the Church to this need to consist in a new papal encyclical on the social nature of man or in an intensified effort of individual Catholics everywhere to live a life of genuine community, especially within the family and in the local parish? (see Bracken, 1971). This is not in any way to discount the value of magisterial pronouncements on the part of the pope and hierarchy. The point, however, is that modern man has had enough of theory which simply gives rise to countertheory. What he is really looking for here is the actual practice of life-in-community by people who have learned to give themselves to one another without reserve. Furthermore, only in the light of the actual experience of life-in-community does the ethical teaching of the *magisterium* on the social nature of man achieve real stature and significance.

Seen in this perspective, the recent controversy in the Catholic Church over such issues as birth control, priestly celibacy, and abortion takes on a new seriousness. Important as these moral questions are in themselves, they are still strictly secondary to the further question of loyalty to the Church as a genuine community: is it, namely, possible to dissent from the teaching authority of the Church on a specific issue without *ipso facto* calling into question one's basic commitment to the community? Elsewhere I have tried to deal with this question in terms of a new ontology of community, in which dissent from legitimate authority can play a constructive role within the Church (see Bracken, 1970). Here I would emphasize only that the immediate resolution of the specific moral issue is far less important than the threat to the unity of the Christian community which is posed by a highly controversial and acrimonious debate within the Church over that same issue. Ultimately, the true position of the Church vis-à-vis a given moral question will be worked out by men of good will, but in the meantime irreparable damage can be done to the integral unity of the Christian community and to its public image precisely as a community before the non-believer.

Moving now to the second source of alienation in Royce's eyes, namely, the irreparable guilt which arises from self-betrayal, I would have this comment. Royce has, in my opinion, given a new perspective to the old truth that man cannot be saved by his own efforts but only through the saving grace of Jesus Christ. What Royce makes clear is that this saving grace is mediated to the individual through the faith-community. That is, it is membership in the community which alone can reconcile the individual to himself, give him confidence that love is stronger than the self-alienation caused by personal sin. Here too, however, more thought must be given to the communitarian structure of the Church and, in this instance, to the communitarian dimension of the sacraments. For, if the sacraments are the normal channels of grace and if, as noted above, grace is mediated to the individual through the community, then the sacraments are clearly the divinely ordained instruments, by which community is originally created, sustained, and repaired. The Eucharist obviously retains according to this scheme its traditional significance as the sacrament of Christian unity (or community), but all the other sacraments would clearly profit from a more solidly communitarian reinterpretation. Baptism, for example, should in line with this thinking be administered, wherever possible, during the Sunday liturgy, when not only the parents and relatives, but also the entire congregation, can witness and give its approval to the rite whereby a new member is added to the local faith-community. Likewise, marriage and holy orders should be seen as special events in the life of the total community, because each sacrament is in its own way indispensable for the perpetuation of the Church as a living reality.

Admittedly, there are problems connected with this communitarian approach to the sacraments in the context of a large urban parish. The parish membership is extensive and constantly changing; furthermore, many churchgoers find it difficult to form community with a "total stranger" in the pew next to them. But precisely here lies the challenge both to church leaders and to the individual Christian. If secular man, as Royce maintains, is alienated by an insuperable moral burden, then the Christian should respond by preaching the Gospel of salvation through Christian community. To preach this Gospel without hypocrisy, however, the Christian must renew his personal commitment to the ideal of Christian community and seek to implement it in his dealings with others, above all the members of his own faith-community, on a day-to-day basis.

REFERENCES

Bracken, J. A. (s.j.) Toward a grammar of dissent. *Theological Studies,* 1970, *31,* 437–459.

Bracken, J. A. (s.j.) Salvation through community. *American Ecclesiastical Review,* 1971, *164,* 97–106.

Gilkey, L. *Religion and the scientific future.* New York: Harper & Row, 1970.

Royce, J. *The problem of Christianity.* (2nd ed.) Chicago: University of Chicago Press, 1968.

Tillich, P. *Systematic theology.* Vol. ii. Chicago: University of Chicago Press, 1957.

Alienation: Marxist Social Category

QUENTIN LAUER, S.J.

Father Quentin Lauer, S.J., received an M.A. degree from St. Louis University in 1943, a Th.L. degree from Woodstock College in 1949, and the degree Docteur ès Lettres from the Sorbonne in 1955. He is professor of philosophy at Fordham University, and he was visiting professor at the University of Texas in the spring of 1969, and at the New School for Social Research in the fall of 1969. Father Lauer is the author of four books: La phénoménologie de Husserl *(1955),* The triumph of subjectivity *(1958),* Phenomenology and the crisis of European philosophy *(1965), and* Hegel's idea of philosophy *(1971). He is also co-author (with Roger Garaudy) of* A Christian–Communist dialogue *(1968). He is a member of a number of professional and learned societies, among them the American Philosophical Association, the Metaphysical Society of America, and the Hegel Society.*

In recent years, under the impact of Karl Marx's early manuscripts on economics and politics which, although published in 1932, have been exploited only since the end of World War II, the concept of "alienation," which plays such a large part in these manuscripts, has become a favorite with those who would emphasize the "humanist" leanings of the young Marx. In the English-speaking world no one has done more than Erich Fromm to popularize the term "alienation" and, with it, the humanist interpretation of

Marxism (Fromm, 1961). In doing this, of course, Fromm and company conveniently forget that in the *Communist Manifesto* (1848) Marx himself indicated his disenchantment with the term—if not with the concept—alienation. Apparently it had become then—as it is becoming now—a sort of catch-all term designating whatever one does not like about the socio-political situation but which one is not particularly willing to do anything about (see Schacht, 1970, Ch. 4). To quote Marx: "The German literati . . . wrote their philosophical nonsense beneath the French original. For instance, beneath the French criticism of the economic functions of money, they wrote 'alienation of humanity' " (Marx, 1848, p. 39).

It would be a mistake, however, to think that in repudiating a term which had become vague and meaningless Marx was abandoning a concept which served so well to highlight the task which his revolutionary philosophy had set for itself. In capitalist society, Marx was convinced, the human individual —every human individual, rich and poor alike—had lost himself, becoming enslaved to an economic force which men had created but could no longer control. Man had become an alien in an alien world, and his only salvation lay in turning the world upside-down (or right-side up) and thus regaining (or gaining for the first time) control over his own destiny. Whatever one may think of Marx's solution to the social problems of his day, there is no disputing his extraordinary sensitivity to the truly miserable situation of the ordinary laborer and to the structures of society which seemed to make that situation irremediable.

All Marx's writings, from the early manuscripts of 1842–1843 to the unfinished *Capital* of 1873, are focused on the task of disalienating man, a task which demanded that Marx "scientifically" trace the process of alienation, in order that by his action ("praxis") man might "scientifically" reverse the process. Thus, although the term "alienation" may be absent from his most mature writings, the consciousness of the contradiction in human life signified by that term is never absent. From the beginning of his career to the end Marx's goal is the resolution of that contradiction.*

ALIENATION IN HEGEL AND FEUERBACH

The origin of the term "alienation," in the sense in which Marx employs it, can be traced to Hegel, even though Hegel gives to the term a much more

---

* Although there is no need here to enter into controversy, it would seem that the efforts of authors like Erich Fromm in America and Maurice Merleau-Ponty (*Humanisme et terreur, Les aventures de la dialectique*) in Europe to see a cleavage between the thought of the early and that of the late Marx is simply missing the point. There is a genuine logical continuity and consistency to a thought which goes from a concept of human being and living, through a consideration of the social framework which conditions that living, to an attempt to account scientifically both for the genesis of existing social structures and for the means necessary to right existing wrongs (see Avineri, 1967, p. 45).

positive (even benign) significance than does Marx.† To put it as simply as possible, alienation for Hegel signifies the estrangement of man from his essential nature as no more than a rational being. This he sees as a necessary step in the process of man's spiritual development; if man is to become more than he is merely by nature (i.e., by being rather than by acting) he cannot simply remain what he is, he must become other, and this otherness (or othering) is alienation. This is accomplished by training, by culture, by education—in short, by man's constantly becoming what his essential nature, merely as that, does not make him to be. To put it somewhat crudely, alienation is for Hegel another term for "growing-up," a process of progressive and alternating self-differentiation and self-identification, of relating to others in order to *become* what one is, and of distinguishing oneself from others in order to *be* what one is—and in order to relate.

When Marx picked up the term, however, it had already been given a new coloration by Feuerbach (1841) in *The essence of Christianity*. As the latter saw it, man has a constant tendency to project outside himself qualities which belong properly to human nature but which man idealizes and places in a God, who thus becomes all man looked for but did not find in himself. For Feuerbach, then, religion is the very essence of alienation; it is man's refusal to become all he is capable of being, his unwillingness to find the perfection of human being in being human, relinquishing that responsibility in favor of submission to an alien God, who is the idealization of those qualities which in their essence are properly human. The concept of alienation, then, has changed from the becoming-other which is essential to a developmental process; it has become a degradation of man from what he truly is or should be.*

It is the latter concept of alienation which Marx took over, and, although he extended it to include not only the religious but also—and more significantly—the economic and the political, the religious model continues to be the symbol of the alienated state in which men find themselves in society. Its roots are economic; its ramifications are political and religious; and it constitutes what human "praxis" must overcome, if man is to become what he truly is. In one sense, then, Marx is closer to Hegel in his use of the term, since he sees alienation as a moment in a dialectical process; in another,

---

† Hegel speaks of alienation in most detail in his *Phenomenology of mind* (c. VI, sect. B: "The Self-Alienated Spirit"). Actually here and elsewhere he uses two terms which, although not synonymous, refer to the same phenomenon of man's becoming other than he is naturally in order to become what he truly is. The term (along with its cognates) most frequently used in this section is *Entfremdung* (literally: "estrangement"). The second term is *Entäusserung* (literally: "exteriorization"), which emphasizes the aspect of turning outward in order to find the true inner self.

* Feuerbach did not look upon religion, particularly Christianity, as a degradation. He did, however, look upon the failure to recognize the projection involved, precisely as a projection, as degrading. Man can return himself to himself, only if he realizes that in adoring God he is adoring the ideal in man.

however, he is closer to Feuerbach in giving it only negative significance.

It can already be seen, I think, how this concept differs from the significance of the term "alienation," either in history or in contemporary usage, with which we have become familiar. We know of alienation as a term designating the transfer of property, mental disorder, interpersonal estrangement (Schacht, 1970, pp. 1–5), an estrangement from God through sin, or a withdrawal from normal social relationships. For Marx, however, alienation has a meaning much more radical than any of these. It designates, too, the process whereby man brings about this state of not being what he truly is.

As Hegel uses the term, alienation signifies the stepping outside of himself which is necessary for man, if he is not to remain simply static, simply natural. Man must, so to speak, stand off from himself and see himself "objectively" in order to realize what it is to be man. For the individual this means finding his true self outside himself in the social whole of which he is part. But, it also means estranging himself from the social whole in order to prevent his individual self from being swallowed up in the whole. We might call it the sort of distancing which is necessary, if we are to understand and thus be ourselves: distancing ourselves from ourselves in order to ask questions about ourselves; distancing ourselves from our social selves in order to ask questions about the strange society in which we have our being. In this sense alienation is a necessary element in the process of human growth. It is a ceasing to feel merely identical with oneself in order to be related to one's society and one's world; and it is a ceasing to feel at one with one's society and world in order to reaffirm one's self-identity.

There is inevitable discord between one's actual condition and one's essential nature, and each is somehow alienated from the other; willful self-assertion alienates the individual from his social reality, whereas abject surrender to the social whole alienates him from his individual self. The two must blend in man's harmonious self-realization. In the concrete this means that if the only authority the individual recognizes is himself he is condemned to isolation from his true self (Hegel, 1821, #98), and if he acts only under the guidance of an alien authority he is condemned never to find even his social self (Hegel, 1821, #26, and pp. 232–233). One can, so to speak, be so extremely individual that the only relation one has to other men is that of belonging to the same abstract general class of man (Hegel, 1807, pp. 515–516). By the same token, one can be so swallowed up in the generality that there is nothing left to relate to others (Hegel, 1807, p. 518). Sheer individualism, then, is alienation, and so is sheer collectivism; only in the alienation of men from themselves and from each other can there be a happy blending of the two.

For Feuerbach the question is at once the same and different. Like Hegel, he sees the self-realization of man situated in the reconciliation of individual self-affirmation with the affirmation of solidarity with the whole of which the individual is but a part. Unlike Hegel, however, he speaks of a whole which is not a concrete social whole but only the abstract totality of "mankind." The reconciliation, then, centers on the assertion that man's confrontation with his world reveals to him all the reality there is. So long as he does not look elsewhere for what he does not yet find he is not alienated. Since, however, no individual does find in himself all he is looking for, and since above all he does not find in himself the perfection of those qualities which make for being human, he projects all he does not find into an ideal being outside himself (outside mankind), whom he calls God. This is the essence of religion, and it is essentially alienation. Only if he can convince himself that there is nowhere to look but in this world, nowhere to find those ideal qualities but in man, can he overcome that alienation. Otherwise he is condemned to adore a God whom he himself has created and thus remain perpetually alienated, finding his true reality not in himself but in another.

According to Feuerbach the overcoming of alienation does not mean the abolition of religion, but it does mean seeing religion for what it truly is, i.e., the recognition of an immanent dimension of man, not the affirmation of a being which transcends man. He must transfer to mankind what he once gave to this alien God. Man's self-realization, then, is to be found in the love of man for man, a universal love which embraces all men (Feuerbach, 1841, Ch. 26, pp. 247–269).

Although Marx will not agree with a Feuerbach who sees the locus of true reality in the abstract totality of "mankind" (Marx, 1845a, p. 69; Easton & Guddat, 1967, p. 468), or with Feuerbach's solution to the problem of alienation in a purification of religion which permits man's genuine self-realization, he will agree with Feuerbach's contention that Hegel "spiritualizes" both the problem of alienation and its solution (Marx, 1844, p. 340; Easton & Guddat, 1967, p. 333), and that Hegel's philosophy is but the reintroduction of religious alienation (Easton & Guddat, 1967, pp. 316–317). The problem, as Marx sees it, is that Feuerbach's materialism is unhistorical, and his history is unmaterialistic (Marx, 1845a, pp. 37–38). Feuerbach, says Marx, does not go to the roots of alienation, because he fails to see its source in the productive activity of man, with the result that his solution to the problem is no more realistic then Hegel's (Easton & Guddat, 1967, pp. 435–436).

MARX'S APPROACH TO ALIENATION

What Marx will seek to do, then, will be to give a scientific (materialist–historical) explanation of and solution to man's alienated situation by showing how it came about (Marx, 1859, pp. 11–13). In so doing, in order to come to terms with the historical process of alienation, he will adopt Hegel's dialectical method of explanation (having first despiritualized it, "putting it back on its feet") and Feuerbach's description of religion, which Marx considers symbolic of man's total alienation. What is important, he is convinced, is to bring the question out of the realm of mere ideas into the real world of human action, to get beyond the stage of theoretical criticism of an existing situation to that of "real" criticism which will not only explain but also change the situation (Marx, 1859, pp. 12, 269). If man is to be disalienated, it is not enough to analyze the state he is in; it is necessary to go further and translate thought into action—better still, to recognize that thought divorced from action is not truly thought.

It would be a mistake, in seeking to follow Marx here, to think that the prime target of his polemic is religion. Religion, it is true, is a significant manifestation of man's alienation, and one has missed the point if, as so many have done, one tries to soft-pedal Marx's anti-religious polemic (e.g., Schacht, 1970). It is, however, precisely a manifestation of man's alienation, not a cause; the sources of that alienation are to be sought elsewhere, and if the uncovering of these sources will permit alienation to be eliminated, it will not be necessary to attack religion. Disalienated man will simply have no need for it (Fromm, 1961, pp. 139–140). In another sense, however, it is important for Marx to recognize religion as uniquely symbolic of alienation; in it we have, so to speak, the model of the situation in which man has created a force outside himself to which he has become subservient.

As we mentioned before, the term "alienation" occurs only in the writings of the young Marx, most of which were not published during his own lifetime. In a very important sense, however, the concept expressed by this term remains a constant in his thought to the very end of his endeavors. It was, perhaps, the vagueness and imprecision of the term, particularly when employed by the German "literati," which made it later distasteful to him, but the situation which he strives to describe and overcome in his *Critique of political economy* (1859) and his monumental *Capital* (1873) is still the one he designated as alienation in his youth. One can, in fact, see in his detailed historical analysis of capitalist society a concrete elaboration of the process whereby man becomes progressively more and more subservient to the creature he himself has produced, thus alienating himself from his true being.

It is, nevertheless, admittedly difficult to understand what the "alienation of man" can mean, if we do not at the same time know what man has become estranged from. In the case of Hegel it was easy enough to see that the progressive distancing of the human individual from his merely essential nature could be called—perhaps metaphorically—alienation, and that the same term could be applied to the individual's return to himself by refusing to be swallowed up in his "social substance." Since Marx, however, is convinced that an "essential nature" of man can belong only to the realm of ideas (Marx, 1859, pp. 11–12, 268), and since the "social substance" in which

Hegel, apparently, could feel at home was particularly unacceptable to Marx, it is less easy to see what, in capitalist society, man is alienated from.

The difficulty we encounter here may, however, be lightened, if we focus on the concept of man which emerges from Marx's overall treatment of man's history. In this history there is no antecedently inscribed "essential nature" which guides and prescribes man's process of development. Marx is, nevertheless, able to borrow an expression from Feuerbach and refer to man as a "species being" (*Gattungswesen*), by which he means not only a being characterized by a specific activity but also one who by this activity makes himself to be what he is (Marx, 1844, pp. 84–85; Fromm, 1961, pp. 100, 183). To be human is to be something more than merely a being of nature. Man distinguishes himself from beasts, says Marx, by the fact that he *produces* the satisfaction of his own needs. The beast can only take for himself what is given; man can produce for himself what is not yet given (Marx, 1845a, p. 17; Fromm, 1961, p. 200). What is distinctive of man, then, is productive activity.

If production, of course, is to be more than haphazard and minimal it requires planning, and planning requires thought (intelligence); if it is to satisfy the increasing needs which emerge as the result of its own functioning this productive activity must be more than individual, it must be cooperative, social, and this requires communication through language;* if producing the satisfaction of increasing social needs is to be economically feasible, not every man can produce everything, and this requires a division of labor. Thus, in his development man distinguishes himself more and more from the beast: he distinguishes himself by thought, by language, by social living, by specialization of activities. All these distinguishing marks, however, are subsequent to and grounded in the one basic distinguishing characteristic—productive activity. It might, of course, be objected that there are many distinctively human activities—artistic, literary, recreational—which are in no sense of the word productive. To this Marx would reply that all human activity is either contributory to or derivative from the productive process. Whatever significance other activity has is inseparable from this relationship.

It is, then, by productive activity that man is what he is and becomes what he becomes. This activity is creative in the sense that it takes what is given in nature and transforms this into what it would not be without the intervention of human action. By the same token, through this action man is self-creative, precisely in that by transforming nature he more and more distinguishes himself not only from the beast but also from what he originally was. Productivity, however, is truly human, and man is truly himself, only

* Although this is not the place to go into the intricate reasonings by which he seeks to establish it, Marx is convinced that, since consciousness is a social product, and not vice versa, language as a means of social communication somehow precedes consciousness (Fromm, 1961, p. 201). For our purposes it is sufficient to show that he sees both language and thought as issuing from human *action*.

to the extent that through the activity whereby he transforms nature he continues to create himself. But this he cannot do, if either the activity of producing or the product of the activity belongs to another than himself.

ECONOMIC ALIENATION

It is here, then, that we first come to the peculiarly Marxist concept of "alienation." If we take what is, perhaps, the most basic of the familiar meanings of the term—namely, the transferral of ownership, making one's own property belong to another—we can immediately see the analogy. If we add to this that in making one's productive activity belong to another one is alienating one's most basic human distinguishing characteristic, we should have no difficulty understanding what Marx means by the most fundamental form of alienation, the alienation of labor (Fromm, 1961, pp. 93–109). Although it is true that only in a capitalist society will Marx invest this term with the pejorative connotations it has for him and has for those who today employ it in their critique of contemporary social structures, it should be pointed out that we shall be able to grasp the full import of the developed concept only if, with Marx, we trace it back to its simplest manifestation.

We have seen, in what can be called Marx's analysis of the origins of human production, that the fulfillment of any need through productive activity inevitably results in the emergence of other needs which in their turn demand to be fulfilled (Marx, 1859, p. 13). Thus, early in the process a point is reached where the individual simply cannot fulfill all his own needs (with regard to the need for offspring, of course, this is true from the very beginning [Easton & Guddat, 1967, p. 422]). At this point, then, production becomes social, and when production becomes social, some individuals specialize in one form of activity, others in another. So far, however, we have only the inevitable division of labor which is necessary, if production is to be efficient and life is to go on. Still, a division of tasks quite readily turns into a distribution of roles, where some habitually do one sort of thing and others another. From this to an identification of individuals with the roles they play in the productive scheme is no great step, and thus a fixation of functions takes place.

Separation of Economic Roles

Where the division of labor, however, solidifies into an enduring separation of roles, a significant change in social structures has occurred. If more than one kind of work enters into the productive scheme, as indeed must be the case, quite obviously one kind of work will be valued more highly than another, if for no other reason than that one kind of talent will be rarer than another (although it is difficult to see how Marx's analysis can account for variations in talent—unless it be the luck of doing the kind of work which develops the talents in question). To put it as simply as possible, some will do mental work and others will do manual work (Fromm, 1961, p. 204)— and those who do mental work will enjoy a double advantage: (1) there will be fewer of them, and thus as individuals they will be more in demand; (2) their position in the productive scheme will be such that the manual workers will be dependent upon them for the very significance of what the latter do.

Where production is simple, however, and each man owns the instruments with which he works, the differences will still not be enormous; so far, then, it will be relatively easy to equalize the contribution which each makes to the overall process. But such a state of affairs cannot long endure; those whose contribution is at once rarer and more indispensable to the successful functioning of the process will begin to claim a larger share of the social product. It is here that the division of labor begins to have far-reaching economic and social effects.

In one sense a greater share in the product of labor simply means more wealth, greater buying power—still a somewhat superficial difference—but in another sense it means a greater capacity to gain possession, through expenditure of wealth not needed for subsistence, of those things which are necessary to the continued functioning of the productive process, i.e., the instruments of production. When this point has been reached, there will be some members of society who own not only a greater share in the social product but also the very instruments which others must use if they are to work at all. Some, then, own the means of purchasing the labor of others, of alienating that labor by owning it, and thus of bringing about the alienation of those who do the work.* With the development of production, too, those who own the means of production will acquire an ever-larger share in what is produced, and the self-perpetuating process is under way whereby some get richer and others poorer: "The worker becomes poorer the more wealth he produces and the more his production increases in power and extent" (Fromm, 1961, p. 95).

It is no mystery, then, why Marx considers the private ownership of the means of production—usually abbreviated to "private property," and thus easily misunderstood—as the real expression of the division of labor. There should be little less, if any, difficulty in understanding that this represents for Marx a state of alienation for those who have to sell their labor in order to survive. That it should ultimately represent a state of alienation of society itself and, therefore, of all its members, will not be clear, however, until we

---

* Marx is careful to point out that only in the final stage of the development of private ownership of the means of production (i.e., the capitalistic stage) does it reveal itself as thus alienating (Fromm, 1961, p. 106).

have pursued Marx's analyses further. Two elements which Marx emphasizes in the analysis up to this point are important to note here: first, that the process is natural and, therefore, inevitable; and, secondly, that the process is dialectical in the sense that the very operation of the productive activity which distinguishes man from the beast brings about the contradictory state in which he is alienated from himself (Marx, 1845a, pp. 7–28; cf. Marx, 1873, p. 15). What began simply as a dialectic of need and fulfillment, where the very existence of a need gave rise to the activity requisite to fulfill the need, has turned into a process wherein the activity of productive forces produces a cleavage between the operation of those forces and the manner in which their products are diversely allocated to them.

Marx's Notion of Historical Development

Before going on it would be well to note that the sort of analysis Marx presents, even though it purports to speak of primitive economic and social development in a way which Marx himself calls "historical," need not be historical in the accepted sense of describing an actual series of events which have occurred in the past. In Marxist terms to analyze any structure is to uncover the process which produced it—to do anything less is simply to accept it as "given." Marx's primary object of concern and the chief target of his critical attack is the economic system prevailing in his own day, which he calls "capitalism" (Marx, 1859, p. 269). He is annoyed with those political economists, chiefly British, who analyze this system as though it were simply a given, describing its functionings and determining its "laws" in such a way as to create the impression that these laws are valid for all times, all places, and all social conditions (Easton & Guddat, 1967, p. 490). Laws such as these, like the laws of physics or chemistry, are to be discovered but not changed; they enable the economist to predict what will happen when certain measures are taken, but they do not permit the system itself, which is a "given," to be questioned—let alone abolished. Within such a framework, then, the sort of human alienation which Marx describes—a universal alienation, when the system is universal—is not only inevitable but also permanent. What Marx wants to do, however, is to eliminate alienation, and this he can do only if he can show, first, that the situation is the product of identifiable human activity and, secondly, that human activity can rectify the situation (Marx, 1845b, #3; Marx, 1873, p. 14). If the situation is simply "in the nature of things," nothing can be done about it; if it is the result of historical causes at work, something can be.

The analysis, then, is "historical" only in the sense that it accounts for the kind of activity which brings about the kind of situation observable in contemporary society, not confining itself to a mere description of what the case is. If the situation has been brought about by human productive activity a number of conclusions follow. (1) Since the situation is just one stage in an ongoing historical process it need not be permanent. (2) The term "alienation," which is used to designate a given state of human relationships, should also have an active sense, indicating that it is man's activity which does the alienating. (3) The "laws" which govern economic activities—and, consequently human social and political structures—are not "natural" but "historical" laws, which determine how change comes about, not how an unchanging system functions. (4) The historical laws which have been operative in bringing about the present situation will be the laws which function in remedying the situation. (5) The situation will not be remedied, so long as the essentially alienating system continues to exist; "reform" within the system will be necessarily ineffective, since alienation is essential to the system; only "revolution" can get rid of the system itself.*

By now, we can see that the absence of the term "alienation" in Marx's later writings by no means signifies that he has dropped the concept; the situation which he seeks to account for, and eventually to remedy, in *Capital* is precisely the situation of "alienation" he has described in his earlier manuscripts. The German "literati" may have rendered the term abstract and, therefore, distasteful; they have not changed Marx's mind regarding what needs to be done. What has changed, however, is the approach to the problem. The "historical" analyses which Marx has instituted, particularly in the *Critique of political economy* and in *Capital,* have permitted him to view the present situation as having been brought about by the operation of historical laws of which no one up to his time had been conscious. The mere "logic," so to speak, of the productive process has brought about the results we now observe. For the future, however, no blind operation of historical laws will bring about different results; man must consciously take the situation in hand, make the laws work for him—as do all practical scientists—and thus actively bring about his own disalienation (Marx, 1859, p. 12).

Inevitability of Alienation within Capitalism

What, then, is the situation which needs to be changed? Here we must return to Marx's analysis of the productive process in operation, remembering, of course, that the point of departure is always the way the system functioned in his own day, chiefly as the effect of the Industrial Revolution, which is still going on. We have seen that, by working, man has produced not only the goods which satisfy his needs but also a socio-economic situation which is characterized (*a*) by a stifling division of labor which paralyzes human initiative in the vast majority, and (*b*) by the private ownership of the means of production which concentrates the control of productive forces

* Minus the term "alienation," the five points of the above analysis can be found in the Preface to Vol. I of *Capital.*

in the hands of a few. Not only is a situation such as this self-perpetuating; it also carries within itself the inherent tendency to develop in the direction of progressive depersonalization of the relationships involved. Those who control the forces of production are those who accumulate the major share of the wealth produced. Without going into the detailed and intricate analyses which Marx undertakes of the use-value, exchange-value, and surplus-value, which attach to the products of human work, we can say that those who own the means of production amass the larger share of produced value in the form of profits. As profits accumulate, however, they are not permitted to lie idle; eventually they turn into capital, which is qualitatively different from either mere profits or mere wealth in that it takes on the character of an independent force, which in a very real sense is controlled by no one; instead it becomes the driving force which controls the productive process (cf. Marx, 1873, Part VII). It was the British political economists who had so clearly shown that capital (or the capitalist economy) has laws of its own to which persons engaged in the process must simply submit. This is, in fact, precisely the criticism Marx levels at these economists: they simply take it for granted that this is the way things are and that the laws of capital operate with the same inevitability and impersonality as do the laws of nature (Marx, 1847, p. 9). Given the capitalist system, Marx admits, this is true; but, he adds, why must the capitalist system be given? Why must man relinquish control of that which has been brought into existence by his own activity?

Here, then, we are at the roots of what Marx means by "alienation," whether or not he employs the term. We have seen in regard to what he called "religious alienation" that it involved man's projection of his own human ideals into a being outside himself, to whom he then became subservient. In the economic form of alienation just described—a far more basic alienation in Marx's eyes—man has by his own activity produced a monster called capital, to which he is not only subservient but literally enslaved. By unconsciously following out the logic of the productive process, man has engendered a multiple alienation which now crushes him. By working he has alienated himself from his *work,* because he has produced a system in which his work no longer belongs to him. In the situation which productive work has brought about, man's work has ceased to be that which characterizes him as man and has become a commodity which is bought and sold in the market place (the term "labor market," incidentally, was not coined by Marx). This means that man has accomplished another, deeper alienation— he has alienated *himself,* for, as his work becomes a commodity, so does he become a commodity (Marx, 1873, Part VI, pp. 586–617; cf. Löwith, 1967, p. 271), thus alienating his very dignity as man—he no longer belongs to himself. The work which characterizes him and is his dignity has become simply a means to an end, that of producing wealth—for another—worse still, of producing money, whose only quality is its quantity (Fromm, 1961, p. 141). Thus man has turned his work into an alien force; he has lost interest in his work and is interested only in his "job," i.e., in what his work will produce for him in the form of money (see Schacht, 1970, p. 90).

By the same token, man has alienated himself from the *product* of his work, not only in the sense that he has no control over it—it simply flows into the system—but also in the sense that, given modern techniques of production, he may never even see it; it simply "stands opposed to him as an autonomous power" (Schacht, 1970, p. 85). The product has, so to speak, become divorced from the work, and the work has become divorced from the worker. The product is the "objectification" of the laborer's work, and with the alienation of the product the work is alienated (Fromm, 1961, p. 95). What is more, with the loss of control over the product of his work there ensues, according to Marx, an alienation of man from *nature* itself. In the sense that the original function of work is the transformation of what is given in nature, man and nature can be said to cooperate in production; the work of man and the work of nature are in tune with each other. When, however, the product of his work is taken from him, a cleavage is introduced between man and nature, for both man and the product of his work have lost their continuity with nature (Fromm, 1961, pp. 100–103).

Finally, within society there occurs an alienation of men from *each other*. As Marx sees it, the very fact that a man works, produces, not for himself but for another, means that the productive process results in an antagonism between those who work and those for whom they work, between those who produce capital and those who own capital. What began simply as a division of labor has become a division of classes, and the one class is alienated from the other. This sort of split can be recognized within a particular society, says Marx, but it becomes more acute and more irreconcilable in proportion as society itself becomes more universal, and a universal antagonism arises between all those who have only their work to sell and all those who alone have the means to purchase that work (Marx, 1848, Part I).

Capitalists as well as Workers are Alienated

Lest all this should seem to point to an alienation only of the worker— which would be serious enough—Marx contends that all men are alienated in the system, capitalists as well as workers. To understand how the capitalist, too, is alienated in the process of production, we must go back to an earlier characterization of capital. Precisely because capital has grown into an independent force governed by its own laws and progressively less and less subject to control by human persons, the capitalist himself is governed by the laws which govern capital, most basic of which is that it must increase. He, then, is constrained to increase it (Marx, 1873, pp. 15, 649, 680, 707).

Thus, the capitalist too is alienated in the overall depersonalization which capital engenders; like the worker he is not master of his own destiny.

If all Marx did were to paint this sombre picture of man's economic alienation, we should have to conclude to the inevitability of it and then say that to man is left the task of making the most of it. This, says Marx, is what reform seeks to do—the best that inadequate forms of socialism can aim at (Marx, 1848, Part III). If the capitalist system, with its essential alienation of man, is destined to endure, then the best we can hope for is a modification of some of the effects of alienation, but man will ever be a stranger in an alien world. The very reason behind Marx's lifework, however, and particularly behind *Capital,* was not merely to show the inevitability of alienation, if things are allowed to continue in the direction they are going, a point which political economists had either missed or deliberately covered over (Calvez, 1956, pp. 244, 262–263), but also to show that man can consciously take matters into his own hands by reappropriating what capital had expropriated and thus returning himself to himself. Only if we understand what this reappropriation means for Marx can we fully understand him when he speaks of the expropriation (or exploitation) which is alienation. Before we do this, however, we must look at two other forms of alienation of which he speaks, the political and the religious, which, although they manifest characteristics properly their own, are nevertheless, to his way of thinking, ultimately but extensions of the economic alienation we have already seen.

POLITICAL ALIENATION

The one most basic feature of all alienation, as Marx sees it, is man's loss of his true self by making it subservient to something outside himself which he himself has created. It is a relinquishing of self-determination and an allowing of oneself to be determined by an alien force. This, as we saw, is what man has done when by his own productive activity he has created capital. This is what he also does when he creates the political power which is the state and then subjects himself to it. It is not as though Marx were denying that the community, even the political community, is a necessity for human living; he was too much of a realist for that. What he does say, however, is that political power as he experienced it—let us say, the power of the nineteenth-century European nation-state—is an alienating force, or, better still, is a vehicle for man's own self-alienation. It is tempting, of course, to see in this primarily an attack by Marx on the Prussian–Lutheran deification of the state as a means of overcoming innate human corruption (Calvez, 1956, pp. 60–61). To some extent it is, of course, precisely this; Marx does fight constantly for human autonomy against such a state (cf. Calvez, 1956, pp. 61–62). But there is more to it than that. Hegel, in his discussion of alienation, had spoken of "state power" and "wealth" as two forces to which man could surrender himself in an effort to avoid the responsibility of self-determination. This sort of state power Marx takes to be characteristic of states as states. Simply living in a modern state, then, is in his view an alienation. Society is formed by the *actions* of men, not by their simply living together, and the actions of citizens in a modern state are minimal (Marx, 1847, pp. 6–7). They are not the sort of actions which really form a society; hence, man is alienated in his social being.

By his economic activity, man has brought the state colossus into being, but there his action stops; an impersonal power has taken over, and it is subject only to the laws of its own being. What is even more important, however, is that the state supports and maintains the capitalist way of life, and no matter what the participation of the citizen in the public life of the state may seem to be, he is still condemned to the economic alienation which is inseparable from political existence (Bottomore, 1963, pp. 38–39). In fact, the division of classes which puts the seal on alienation characterizes the political situation in any state, and the state itself is but the instrument of the dominant class in it, since it is inevitable that the class which controls the state will make its own interests the interests of the whole society (Bottomore, 1963, p. 63; Marx, 1845a, pp. 40–41). In contemporary states this class, the bourgeoisie, has alienated all forms of life by turning money, "the universal power of abstraction" (Calvez, 1956, p. 211), into the only recognized value. It would be stretching a point to say that Marx himself made any great direct contribution to political theory—he did not even foresee what political structures would be consequent on the revolution, other than an initial "dictatorship of the proletariat." His aim, after all, was to revise economic history in such a way as to account historically for the alienation of man in society and to provide guidelines for the sort of revolution which eliminates this alienation. It was not to provide a blueprint for the political structures which would emerge from this revolution (see Avineri, 1967). In fact, Marx has more than once been criticized for not knowing where the revolution was to go, once it had been inaugurated.

RELIGIOUS ALIENATION

On the other hand, with regard to religious alienation and what was to be done about it, there never seem to have been any doubts in Marx's mind. Despite the efforts of some who would like to make Marxism more palatable to the religious mind (e.g., Aptheker, 1968), it is quite clear that for Marx religion is a need only for alienated man (Marx & Engels, 1964, pp. 41–42). In one sense, of course, he could be tolerant toward religion, not advocating that it be directly attacked or suppressed—above all, not persecuted—precisely because he was convinced that for disalienated man religion would simply disappear as incompatible; religion and reason are so completely incompatible that when men begin to live rationally they will inevitably repudiate religion (Marx & Engels, 1964). To attack religion directly is to attack a symptom rather than the real illness. It is important to note, in this connection, that Marx's polemic against religion, unlike that of a Nietzsche, is not directed against the perversion of religion which he might have found in the Christianity of his day (which even a deeply religious contemporary like Kierkegaard could recognize). In Marx's view religion itself is a perversion; it is essentially immoral (Easton & Guddat, 1967, pp. 231–233); it is the profoundest expression of that alienated state which is inescapable so long as man's social reality has not been achieved (Löwith, 1967, p. 350). The religion of which Marx speaks is the religion of which Feuerbach (1841, 1851) speaks not only in his *Essence of Christianity* but also in his less-well-known *Essence of religion*. In religion thus understood "man vainly projects his true being outside himself and loses himself in an illusory transcendent world" (Calvez, 1956, p. 54).

If we are to understand the profound roots of Marx's distrust of religion, however, we must try to follow the thought which sees in religion not merely a form or manifestation of alienation but, more significantly, the very reason why man does nothing about his alienated state. Religion justifies that state. The celebrated dictum "religion is the opium of the people" (Marx & Engels, 1964, p. 42) refers to both the narcotic quality which religion has of rendering man insensible to his misery and its paralyzing effect of robbing him of the initiative to remedy the situation. It may very well be true that religion will be impossible for disalienated man, but it is equally true that disalienation will be impossible for religious man. Religion and alienation are inseparable. It is through religion that both antagonistic classes in society consecrate the prevailing alienated state of affairs: the worker by listening to its promises of an end to his misery in the "beyond," the hereafter; the bourgeois capitalist by finding in it a justification of the status quo. If the way things are is the way they must be, then religion which promises a transcendent remedy is the only answer. Religion, then, teaches man resignation, which is a denial of his power to create his true social being in the real world; it teaches an approval of the human condition as it is, which blinds man to what it can be; it supports the class-oppression which characterizes contemporary social and political structures (Marx, 1844, "The Jewish Question," pp. 28–66).

What it all comes down to is that Marx can see no hope for the future of man, if religion endures in any form whatever. To overcome the alienation of some while others continue to be alienated is no solution at all to the problem of society or of man as a social being, and if religion exists at all then alienation exists. It is true that the alienation manifested in religion is particularly acute in a state, like Prussia, where religion (or one religion) enjoys a privileged position (Calvez, 1956, p. 58), but the solution is not the separation of Church and State—or the declaration that religion is simply a private affair (Marx, 1844, pp. 48–50, 236–238). Religion as a private affair is an alienating force more radical even than a state religion (Marx, 1844, pp. 46, 50–51), for it promotes the false division between the public and the private existence of man (Calvez, 1956, p. 77) and thus perpetuates that false picture of the real world which is integral to the religious view. A state which has within itself an independent religious force against itself is an alienated state. As we have seen before, however, none of this means for Marx that religion should be suppressed. To suppress religion would, after all, be to ignore the root cause of alienation. What is needed is to eliminate the causes of that alienated consciousness which makes it possible (or necessary) for man to be religious. In this sense the survival or non-survival of religion could be an indicator of just how successful disalienation had been. At the same time the true Marxist will consistently denounce religion, since in so doing he will attract men's attention to both the fact of their alienation and to its true causes (Calvez, 1956, p. 91).

Once more, however, we should recall that Marx refuses to be satisfied with an abstract criticism of alienation in any of its forms or manifestations. Alienation is simply not a matter of mere consciousness, as it had been, Marx felt, for Hegel and even for Feuerbach; it is a matter of life. It is through his activity that man has come to the state he is now in; only through his activity ("praxis," for it must be fully conscious) will he overcome that state. What is more, if it is productive activity which distinguishes man as man, then it will be productive activity which brings to an end that same state of alienation and restores man to his true "species being." Neither thoughts nor words constitute real criticism of the real situation; only action is real criticism, and theory can be significant only as immanent in practice (Calvez, 1956, p. 104). Abstract philosophizing about the human situation, precisely because it is abstract, is itself a form of alienation, suppressing as it does the action wherein man realizes his true self (cf. Calvez, p. 107).

THE COMING OF DISALIENATION

What, then, is to be done? To answer this question Marx turns once more to his version of "history." By extrapolating from his analysis of the contemporary situation he finds that the dialectical process which is history has manifested certain constant characteristics and that these constitute the "laws" of historical development. To begin with, in any given situation needs arise which demand to be fulfilled, and the fulfillment of needs always gives rise to further needs which in turn demand to be fulfilled. Constant in this is that the activity of productive forces fulfills needs as the needs arise and in so doing develop precisely as productive forces. The division of labor which is inseparable from social production is one such development of the forces of production; so too are the institution of private property and the division (opposition) of classes attendant upon it. In one sense each development of productive forces makes for progress in the productive process. In another, each is destined to become outmoded, to be inadequate to the needs which demand to be fulfilled, to become, in the words of the *Critique of political economy,* the "fetters" which hold back progress (Marx, 1859, p. 12; cf. Marx, 1845a, pp. 72ff.). Whenever this occurs there is "alienation," a contradiction which is to be overcome, if progress is to continue.

By a technique of historical prestidigitation, vaguely modeled on Hegel's dialectic of "Domination and Servitude" in the *Phenomenology of mind,* Marx ties all this in with a successive recrudescence of class antagonisms, according to which history has been constantly marked by the domination of one class by another (in each instance the state serves the interests of the dominating class). This situation is dialectical, because the dominating class engenders the class which it dominates, and the dominated class is destined to turn things around and become the dominating class. This turning around —or overturning—is revolutionary and constitutes that change in the relationships of production which makes for social and political progress. The history here is unquestionably a bit flimsy, but it permits Marx to see the system of capitalist economy which characterizes his own day as but one of the stages in the overall history of the productive process. It enables him, too, to account for the origin of the economic factors which characterize the contemporary situation and to identify the revolutionary change in productive relationships which has already begun (Marx, 1873, p. 14). More than this it enables Marx to withhold any moral judgments regarding each of the successive stages in the process; the only judgment necessary (and legitimate) is an historical one, and that is concerned with judging when any given stage has outlived its usefulness, has engendered the sort of contradiction which demands that human "praxis" push on to a further stage. He detects that this is exactly what has happened in his own age. The entire world has become divided into two antagonistic classes, the bourgeoisie and the proletariat, and the former by following out the logic of its own mode of production has engendered not only the capitalist system but also the socioeconomic class which is destined to bring about its demise and put an end to alienation (Marx, 1873, p. 20).

There are differences, however, between the historical past which Marx has described and the future which he anticipates, chief of which is the fact that while all changes in the past came about automatically, simply by the operation of the "laws" which governed the process, the change which has now been inaugurated will be the result of conscious action along the lines of development which "history" has revealed (Marx, 1845a, pp. 21–22). As in other exploited classes, the proletariat's members will manifest themselves as the "grave-diggers" of the bourgeoisie—but they will do so consciously. It is for this reason that the inculcation of "class consciousness" is so important. It is for this reason, too, that Marx must make men conscious both of their alienation in society and of the need to eliminate those bulwarks of capitalist alienation—private property, the state, and religion. Another difference is that the process has reached such a point that class opposition has become totally universalized: the whole of human society is composed of only two antagonistic classes, the bourgeoisie and the proletariat (abstractly put, capital and labor). As a result, the elimination of one of these classes by the other will mean the complete elimination of class antagonisms and, thus, the complete elimination of classes, since classes exist only in opposition to each other and by virtue of their competing interests (Bottomore, 1963, p. 58).

The society which is being ushered in, then, is the classless society, in which, since there will be no classes, there will be no class interests, and the only interests left will be the interests of man as such. Man, then, will be truly disalienated, and alienation in all its forms will be at an end. Because man has reappropriated what the system had expropriated he will regain his alienated self. Quite obviously this reappropriation will not be individual—men cannot as individuals regain the ownership of a product which is social —it will be collective; the product of human activity will belong to each because it belongs to all, not merely to some.

It should not be difficult to see what an appeal such an analysis—and program—must have for those who are oppressed and, hence, alienated in our contemporary world-society. Although the exploitation of which Marx speaks is primarily the exploitation of the "workers of the world" by bourgeois capitalists, he is equally incisive in his characterization of the universal exploitation of all men by the impersonal force which is capital. Wherever men grow aware of being exploited, whether as workers, as colonials, or simply as the disadvantaged segment of a particular society, they can find in Marx's teaching not only an explanation of why things are the way they are but also an assurance that things need not be the way they are, that human beings can take the situation in hand and remedy it (Bottomore, 1963, pp. 132–133).

When they turn to Marx for a solution, however, there is a danger that they will fail to ask the questions which need to be asked. The very fact that the solution has been dignified with the magic appellation of "scientific" will preclude in many minds the need of asking these—or any—questions. But they must be asked, and they are basically two. (1) Is the "scientific" explanation of exploitation and alienation, based as it is on an analysis of the productive process and which is only superficially "historical," in fact an oversimplification which fails to take into account the infinite complexities of both human motivation and historical contingency? (2) Does a solution which finds its "scientific" justification in such an oversimplified explanation present the only viable alternative to the existing situation? There is something pathetically naïve in the assumption that to say that the state of alienation need not be permanent is equivalent to saying that Marx's solution to the situation imposes itself. To ask questions such as these is in no way to impugn the acuteness of Marx's critique of socio-economic structures, but it does open up the possibility that both the explanation and the solution are more "theoretical" than they purport to be.

REFERENCES

Aptheker, H. Marxism and religion. In H. Aptheker (Ed.) *Marxism and Christianity.* New York: Humanities Press, 1968. Pp. 29–39.

Avineri, S. The Hegelian origins of Marx's political thought. *Review of Metaphysics,* 1967, *21,* 33–56.

Bottomore, T. B. (Ed. & trans.) *Karl Marx: Early writings.* New York: McGraw-Hill, 1963.

Calvez, Y. *La pensée de Karl Marx.* Paris: Editions du Seuil, 1956.

Easton, L. D., & Guddat, K. H. (Eds.) *Writings of the young Marx on philosophy and society.* New York: Doubleday, 1967.

Feuerbach, L. *The essence of Christianity* (1841) (trans. by G. Eliot). New York: Harper & Row, 1957.

Feuerbach, L. *Essence of religion (Das Wesen der Religion)* (1851). Leipzig: Kröner.

Fromm, E. *Marx's concept of man.* New York: Ungar, 1961.

Hegel, G. W. F. *Phenomenology of mind* (1807) (trans. by J. B. Baillie). New York: Harper & Row, 1967.

Hegel, G. W. F. *Philosophy of right* (1821) (trans. by T. M. Knox). New York: Oxford University Press, 1967.

Löwith, K. *From Hegel to Nietzsche* (trans. by D. E. Green). New York: Doubleday, 1967.

Marx, K. *The Holy Family (Die heilige Familie)* (1844). Berlin: Dietz, 1953.

Marx, K. *German ideology* (1845) (trans. by R. Pascal). New York: International Publishers, 1947. (a)

Marx, K. Theses on Feuerbach (1845). In K. Marx & F. Engels *On religion.* New York: Schocken, 1964. Pp. 69–72. (b)

Marx, K. *The poverty of philosophy (Das Elend der Philosophie)* (1847). Berlin: Dietz, 1952.

Marx, K. *Communist Manifesto* (1848) (trans. by M. Mayer). Chicago: Regnery, 1950.

Marx, K. *Critique of political economy* (1859) (trans. by N. I. Stone). Chicago: Kerr, 1909.

Marx, K. *Capital* I (1873) (trans. by E. Unterman). Chicago: Kerr, 1909.

Marx, K., & Engels, F. *On religion.* New York: Schocken, 1964.

Schacht, R. *Alienation.* New York: Doubleday, 1970.

II
ALIENATION IN
CONTEMPORARY PERSPECTIVE

Alienation in
Ecological Perspective

SAMUEL Z. KLAUSNER

Samuel Z. Klausner is both a psychologist and a sociologist. His B.S. degree is from New York University and his M.A. and Ed.D. degrees (in psychology) are from Columbia University, as is his Ph.D. (in sociology). He has taught at City College of the City University of New York, the Hebrew University (Jerusalem), Columbia University, Union Theological Seminary, and since 1967 at the University of Pennsylvania, where he is the director of the Center for Research on the Acts of Man. In addition to his frequent contributions to professional journals in the areas of psychology, sociology, and religion, Dr. Klausner is the author of the following books: Psychiatry and religion *(1964),* The quest for self-control *(1965),* The study of total societies *(1967),* Why man takes chances *(1968), and, most recently in keeping with the topic of the present paper,* On man in his environment: Social scientific foundations for research and policy *(1971).*

This Institute's title "Alienation: Plight of Modern Man?" contains a *double-entendre*. The question mark may turn upon the word "alienation" or upon the word "plight." The two questions raised in this paper are, therefore, "is man alienated from his physical environment" and, if so or if not so, "is this a plight, a situation portending danger"? To judge whether man *is*

33

alienated asks for a statement of fact. Science is one prime source of statements of fact about the environment. To judge whether a scientific statement of fact describes a plight requires a judgment of value. Typically, in discussions of alienation, judgments of fact are meshed with judgments of value. When, in addition, the term "alienation" is also a call to action, it has become an ideological term—one among a series of ideological terms which have been insinuated into the ecological debate. Even the term "ecology" itself tends to become ideological.

The fundamental distinction between scientific and ideological language rests on the relation posited between the self and its object. Scientific language assumes the possibility of a break between an observer and an object. In this sense, the very method of science appears to be alienative. Meaning is defined by an object's location in a theoretical frame of reference. This meaning is shared by all who follow the same principles of observation. While the scientific frame of reference is a social product, the interpretations it offers are independent of any particular observer. Ideological language, in contrast, defines the meaning of an object in terms of its relation to the individual or collective self. Ideological meanings are not contemplative but point to the realization of future states.

More specific differences between scientific and ideological language may be derived from this general orientation. The referent of a scientific term is carefully set off from the referents of other terms. Its meaning is specified denotatively. The referent of an ideological term shares permeable boundaries with the referents of other ideological terms. The rules of inclusion and exclusion are flexible, combining both denotative and connotative elements. Scientific ecology refers to the interdependence of specific processes. Ecology as an ideological idea refers to a variety of approved, perhaps God-given, events joined in a natural, and so desirable, cluster.

Correlatively, scientific terms tend to treat phenomena analytically—separating events by the method of abstraction. Ideological terms tend to treat phenomena synthetically—drawing events together into a composite. The method of generalization, the identification of commonalities, identifies the parts to be brought together.

A scientific term refers only to cognitive aspects of an event. It guides contemplation of the object contributing to an understanding within the frame of reference. An ideological term appends an evaluation to the fact indicating an expected attitude toward the fact. The object is related to human purposes. Scientific ecology reports the eutrophication of a lake while ecology as ideology draws the conclusion that it is becoming a muddy swamp unfit for fish or man. Action is indicated against the polluters.

The solution of our environmental problems requires both the analysis of fact and an ideology for evaluation and for directing action with respect to these facts as well as to human purposes. When, however, the ideological element enters into the definition of the situation, it hinders a clear apprehension of the facts needed to plan action and may promote a spurious action. Man / environment relations are, from a societal perspective, the relations which form among men as they consider the physical environment. This is one source of the ideological component. This paper will begin by tracing some recent history of the term "alienation" as applied to man / environment relations. Then, we shall document the shift in the meaning of ecology from a scientific to an ideological term. The infiltration of ideology has imposed a sense of crisis in ecological analysis and introduced religious elements into ecological choices. Scientific analysis is a play at alienation between man and nature. This play at alienation is necessary to attain those particular understandings of man and nature which reduce the likelihood of becoming alienated from nature in reality. Thus, to answer the initial question, man does, in a playful sense, alienate himself from nature but this is not, in itself, necessarily dangerous.

ALIENATION AS IDEOLOGY

The term "alienation" has traditionally denoted a moral pejorative. The discussion of alienation has been couched in the language of despair. The basic imagery is always that of loss—whether of God, of fellow man, of nature, or of one's own technological product—the loss of self. Alienated men are recognized as alone, lonely, and deeply troubled. They find their jobs monotonous and degrading. Alienation is expressed in senseless acts of violence, thwarted self-realization, family breakdown, impersonalization, and dehumanization (Josephson & Josephson, 1962). The term, sometimes referring to a state (aloneness), sometimes to conditions producing that state (e.g., anomie) and sometimes to its sequelae (e.g., violence), has become a magnet for such a variety of negative connotations that we lose sight of its denotative underpinning. Alienation becomes almost synonymous with the notion of split personality in the analysis of schizophrenia. It appears in studies of social deviance as a near-substitute for the concept of nonconformism. It may mean social isolation or exclusion from membership in a group or even radical exclusion from the human group. As with all ideological terms, the press is to remedial action.

Man alienated from nature is depicted as destroying nature and poisoning himself. Purportedly, his alienated state allows him to pollute air and increase respiratory disease, and to introduce DDT into the food cycle, eventually poisoning birds dependent upon fish which concentrate the chemical. Because of his alienated state, he disgorges waste into the Great Lakes. No twinge of guilt appears when, as a consequence, his neighbors clear alewife carcasses from their beaches.

This view is stated in depth by Hannah Arendt. She casts *homo faber* as

the epitome of alienated man, maintaining that this creator has always been
a destroyer of nature. Violation and violence are present in all fabrication.
Erecting a man-made world implies destroying part of God's created nature
(Arendt, 1958).* This conjunction of fact and value in the concept "alienation" is not surprising. The theological–ontological concept of the alienation
of man from God implies perdition. Christian natural law weds fact and
value. As a consequence of the Fall, alienation implies a fundamental separation. A being with near-angelic status demoted to fleshly man undergoes a
change in essence.

Marx, in regenerating the concept of alienation in a materialistic context,
combined its sociological meaning as a statement of fact with the social
political consequence of the condition of alienation—the opportunity it
gave the owner of private property to exploit the producer of that property.

Marx's discussion of alienation grows out of political economists' analyses
of the division of labor. Sociologists trained in the Durkheim tradition are
accustomed to thinking of the division of labor as a basis, not for alienation,
but for organic solidarity. The very separation of occupations is the ground
of their interdependence. For Marx, this very mutual dependence is the
portal for exploitation. Marx charges that the narrow occupational participation of a person becomes the only basis of his worth. He is reduced
both spiritually and physically, says Marx, to the condition of a machine.
From being a man he becomes merely an abstract activity increasingly dependent upon fluctuations in market price. The division of labor increases
the productive power of labor. However, the product of his labor is pre-
empted by a dominant capitalist class. The worker is impoverished while
contributing to the wealth and refinement of society (Bottomore, 1963).†

Reasoning in Hegelian terms, Marx argued that labor, the activity of the
individual, becomes embodied in some object or physical thing outside him.

* Arendt reminds us that, originally, the term "culture" pointed to an attitude of
loving care in the intercourse of man and nature, the tending of nature until it became
fit for human habitation. The work of *homo faber* is not culture but an effort to subject
nature to the domination of man. The Greeks classed the artisan, an example of *homo
faber,* as a Philistine because his utilitarian mentality disabled him from judging an
item of art apart from its function (Arendt, 1954, pp. 197–226).

† MacIntyre (1968) compares the role of the division of labor in Marxist theory
with the role of the Fall in Christian theology. In theology, the Fall separated man
from God. Similarly, the division of labor creates the first real cleavage in society.
It makes of each individual a hunter, a fisherman, a shepherd, and so on. The
productive force which arises through the cooperation of different individuals appears
as an alien force, the power of the community existing outside each of them. This
conclusion is reminiscent of Durkheim's comment that social norms are experienced
in terms of exteriority and constraint. The Marxist, however, continues. To maintain
his livelihood, the worker must fulfill the demands the community makes on his
calling rather than the demands of his own nature. The interests of the individual
clash with those of the community. The state embodying the interest of the community becomes an instrument for coercion of the individual despite the fact that the
power of the state is based on the product of labor. Paradoxically, though, the class
controlling the state uses the producer's product to exploit him.

Capital itself is one such storehouse of objectified labor. As Marx put it, within capitalism, the objects produced by labor—its product—stand opposed to it as an alien being, a power independent of the producer. Capital is used to exploit its original producer. Alienation involves the loss of control of one's own product and thus, like sin, becomes alienation from the self.*

The root issue is that of control: not the analytic understanding of control but the value question of who should control. For Marx, the object of control is the self's activity and its objectified product. Control by the capitalist means that the worker's labor, his own spontaneous activity, becomes another's activity. The question of control resolves itself into the rights of ownership and is thus a matter of social rules. Under capitalist organization, these are rules pertaining to property. As producer and capitalist struggle for their respective rights, the physical object recedes into the background. It is the transfer of rights of ownership to other than the producer or group of producers which constitutes alienation. To use Marx's idiom, the worker is alienated from his species life, that is, from his nature as a member of the collective. Each man is alienated from other men. Marx writes that every self-alienation of man from himself and from nature appears in a relation which he postulates between other men and himself and nature (Bottomore, 1963, p. 130). Thus, what begins as an analysis of the relationship between man and the physical environment becomes an analysis of the relationship between man and man.† The analysis points to a course of action and is, in this respect, ideological.‡

* As Lichtheim (1968) expresses the paradox, work, man's existential activity, estranges him from nature and from himself. The image is that of slaves building the wall which prevents their escape. In general, as soon as an act is externalized, it becomes enmeshed with the acts of others. The manifest consequence does not follow simply from individual intent; it is a resultant of the interrelation of each act with all other relevant acts. Then, in some cases, the consequences of action may frustrate the intent of the original action. For Marx, structural conditions lead to loss of control over the product.

† Lynn White, Jr. (1968) illustrates the intimate relation between exploitation of nature by man and of man by man. He describes how a change in the method of tillage during the seventh century changed social relations. The method of scratch plowing would make a relatively shallow incision in the earth. This required cross-plowing to turn up enough soil for planting. Cross-plowing produced small square plots which were worked by, and in turn supported, a single farmer-family. A plow with a vertical knife to cut the lines of the furrow and a moldboard to turn it increased the power of the machine, and required oxen to pull it. Emphasis shifted from the distribution of land based on the needs of the family to the distribution of land based on the capacity of a power machine to till the earth. In Marx's terms, land could then become capital. Man's relation to the soil was changed from that of direct use to that of exploitation. The exploitation of land arose as a side effect of the exploitation of man by man.

‡ Social ideology of alienation borrows from theological ideology its sense of cruciality. Theological alienation is radical because it sunders a primal oneness. The sociological concept, however, cannot be thrown back against an initial nonalienated condition of oneness. The very definition of society is contingent, *ab initio,* upon

ECOLOGY AS IDEOLOGY

Ecology, originally introduced as a scientific term, itself becomes ideological. In the ideology of ecology, the central issue is alienation of man from the environment; again, the issue at root becomes one of control. Biologists have used the term "ecology" to refer to a system of plants and animals connected by a balanced network of processes involving transfers of matter and energy. Biological or chemical processes within plants and animals are the units of ecological thought. The oxygen cycle and the rainfall cycle, names for designated stations in the respective cycles, express the ecologic organization of natural events. The system is considered, at least theoretically, closed.

Ecology as an ideological term becomes a call to action rather than an analytic category. It joins "alienation" with a long list of scientific and speculative philosophical terms which have been impressed to serve social purposes. Its predecessors have included such terms as "surplus value," "ego strength," "cultural relativism," and "ideology" itself.

The writing of Shephard (1970), a prominent bio-ecologist, reflects the tension between the status of ecology as science and as ideology. After describing ecology as the study of organisms in an environment and the processes which link organisms in place, he avers that ecology as such cannot be studied because it is not a discipline. Rather it is a perspective on the human situation. Man is in the world and his ecology is the nature of that "inness." The members of the world, writes Shephard, are engaged in a kind of choreography of materials and energy and information.

Factual Statements Become Value Statements

Its status as a perspective would not exclude ecology from science. References to the "human situation," to "man," and to the quality of "inness" are, however, social-philosophical and as such incipiently ideological. These terms conjure up images of wholeness, concreteness, and even something of ontology and philosophical anthropology. The synthetic tendency of the ideological term wins out over the analytic tendency of the scientific term.*

---

some degree of individuation or, on the group level, of stratification. Further, radical separateness is sociologically inconceivable. *Ex definitione*, there is order among the multiplicity; otherwise, no social relation would remain to be treated sociologically. The notion of exploitation itself would evaporate since it too is a relationship. The sociological analysis must always deal with degrees of separateness or must specify aspects in which a human being is disengaged—from others, from culture, or, most fundamentally, from his self.

* This association of ecology with the ideal of the "whole" or the "totality" is not isolated. Hare (1970), for instance, assigns the total natural, social, and the built environments to ecology. This synthetic conception is operationalized in his call to

The high road to ideology is paved by the assimilation of factual statements to value statements.

Both natural-law theologians and positivists, for quite different reasons, deny this distinction between fact and value. McHarg (1970), who falls much closer to the latter than to the former camp, discovers an intrinsic value-system in nature itself. The currency and the inventory are matter in its cycles—the oceans and the hydrologic cycle, life forms, and their roles. He borrows the concept of fitness of the environment from biological evolution. Just as anatomical features adapt to fit the environment, so human artifacts fit if they are adaptive for the environment. Fitness becomes a synoptic requirement of evolutionary success. His ultimate criterion of value is the test of survival. Health and disease are proximate signals of survival potential. The promotion of health becomes the measure of the ethical. This ethic would replace our inherited value-system which, says McHarg, has so grossly misled us.

Crisis Mentality Introduced

Expanding the term "ecology" to include ideological meanings has practical consequences. It contributes to a crisis-mentality and to extreme attitudes. Issues tend to be seen totalistically and in terms of ultimates. It also contributes to the development of a devil theory and to politicizing the fact-defining procedures. Politicization is an attempt to act on the issue of control in man / nature relations. Ideological concerns about ecology also become religious concerns. In that case, solutions to ecological problems tend to include specific religious postures. These postures either reject control by man or regulate its character.

The cries of crisis in the ecological discussion are not limited to publicists. Scientists announce that by 1978 there will be insufficient oxygen in the seas to support fish. Pollution of the oceans will, by then, have destroyed the phytoplankton, the principal source of oxygen. Lake Erie is judged a dead lake. Processes of eutrophication have proceeded beyond the point of no return. Population theorists calculate that at the present rate of world-population increase there will be no standing room in a few hundred years. Long before standing room disappears we will be visited, as Malthus said, by vice and misery. These cries of crisis are, of course, dramatic ways of stating the portentousness of unchecked current trends. Although these are

---

unify physical environmental studies, social science, psychology, and urban and regional planning. Without examining the conceptual obstacles to meshing these disparate schemas, he calls for a new kind of synthesizing discipline. The sound is that of the utopias of the ideologists. The word "whole," like its cognate "holy," induces a therapeutic image.

significant signals, paradigms of emerging dangers, they are not yet death knells. An immediate danger is that cries of crisis may produce impulsive action sterile in its effect. The pressure for action may truncate the analysis needed to understand ecological facts.

In part, the sense of crisis grows out of the ideological tendency to conceive ecological change in terms of ultimates, even in terms of religious ultimates. For instance, Sears (1970), contemplating current ecological problems, says that the possibility of an apocalyptic end of civilization can not be dismissed as a morbid fancy. Slobodkin (1970) parries such diagnoses, calling them practical but nonoperational. If, as has been argued, the ecological crisis is rooted in a religiously based alienation of man from nature, then a mass conversion to the principles of St. Francis, a spirit more sensitive to the common creatureliness of man and beast, might be indicated. While this might fend off ecological crisis, the steps to encourage conversion and the chances of its success are not immediately apparent.

References to ultimates are paralled by references to totalism, an equally ideological element and contributor to the crisis-mentality. Cooley and Wandesford-Smith (1970), for instance, say that no amount of science and technology can escape the ecological fact that every living thing is related to the total environment. The terms "related" and "total" need specification. Everything in the universe is related to everything else, but, obviously, the morality tale about the loss of a kingdom for the loss of a nail is better suited as character-education than as a guide for environmental planning. Scientists and planners must differentiate between proximate and ultimate causes, between differing intensities and differing saliencies of relations. A good theory and a good environmental policy would specify those items related in some appreciable degree and in some strategic way. This is particularly important when choices must be made among lesser evils and among greater goods.* The tendency for ideological terms to be totalistic or to refer to ultimates grows out of their synthetic expansiveness.

Another sign of the shift from scientific to ideological language is the slippage from well-bounded denoting terms to vaguely-bounded connoting terms. For example, Asmussen and Bouchard (1970) discuss the Wild and Scenic Rivers Act of 1968 in terms of a dramatic legislative confrontation

---

* The notion of total, if ecology is not to be synonymous with metaphysics, must refer to a restricted system. The total of a theoretically closed system consists of a set of defined terms and their referent phenomena. Psychological, sociological, chemical, and biological terms occur in as many different theoretical systems. They cannot be treated as members of a single system. Ecological systems, material and energy balances, may be considered closed with respect to a particular process—such as the oxygen cycle as it acts within given areal bounds. The flora and fauna in geographic areas naturally bounded by high mountains or bodies of water may sometimes be considered as a relatively isolated total system. The total biosphere is, of course, a closed system—barring some meteoroid dust and impact of radiant energy. However, trying to consider the total biosphere in ecological planning is subject to Slobodkin's charge of working with nonoperational concepts.

between the needs of the public for recreation and the sanctity of private real estate. Perhaps a clear definition is available for the drama in a legislative confrontation, and perhaps the "sanctity of private real estate" refers to attitudes of some actors in that drama. However, the term "needs of the public" is as vague as any general evaluative notion. It may serve as a call to action. The scientific concept of need has had a troublesome history in psychology. A "need" is offered to explain why someone does something. At the same time, the evidence for the existence of the need is that one does that very thing. Sometimes as many needs are named as things people do— that is, needs are defined in terms of the objects to which they attach. Generic needs may be specified as attributes of the organism.

In the political science literature, the term "need" imputes a goal. Asmussen and Bouchard (1970) use this term to legitimate a right of certain members of the community to use rivers and their shores for recreation against the right of others to treat them as private property. The balancing of individual and collective rights is a focal area for socio-environmental study. Advocacy of a particular balance of rights is a commitment to a conception of social control, a problem in the ideology of ecology.

Man Himself can Become the Enemy

Ideological discourse enhances commitment to some positive purpose. This positive purpose is, however, sometimes paired with negative goals or situations to be corrected. These situations may be personified and a person or organization identified as the culprit. A devil is named and introduced into the debate. The profit motive, which in calmer moments is an economic or psychological concept, may become a blemish, a sign of the exploiter, in the ecology debate. Reporting a television series on ecology, Rienow and Rienow (1970) call upon the reader to place the cause of mankind above that of commercial profit and condemn those interests who defend profit as bringing the end to all of us. Leo Marx (1970) accuses the Puritans of New England of paving the way for the exploitation of nature. In their eyes, the New World landscape was Satan's territory, fit chiefly for conquest. The Puritans have become the culprits.

Man, in general, can become the enemy. The ecological movement may even become misanthropic. Pollard (1970) says that the earth's integrity is independent of man. Overpopulation is, in Pollard's view, one way in which we may destroy the earth. No species has a right to destroy her. We need, Pollard says, to develop a healthy and holy fear of doing so. Reversing the Biblical injunction, Pollard says that once the earth has been filled by man he should stop being fruitful and should cease further multiplication.

Action in support of ecological goals and action against the ecological "devil" precipitate the environment into politics. The politicization of the

term, acting as if by a type of Gresham's law, drives out scientific meanings
and rational planning, replacing them by symbols for action and resolutions
based on human consensus. A consensus is not necessarily rational because
it is influenced by a broad system of social power-relations which may over-
ride the technical requirements for the management of resources.

Ecology as an Issue

Caldwell (1970) examines ecology as a political "issue." An issue is an
ideological term with connotations overshadowing its denotations. A concept
such as environmental quality, writes Caldwell (1970), gains political
strength when it becomes clearer and more widely diffused as a generalizing
concept of environmental development. The synthesizing character of the
ideological term displaces the analytic character of the scientific term. Recognizing the metamorphosis, Caldwell classes the concept of "good environment" with other conceptual foci of public policy such as freedom, prosperity, and security. Thus, the concept which began in the realm of science
comes to connote a judgment of the good life.

Environment, as an issue, a matter of politics, becomes a focus of the
organization of power in the society. Groups disperse and organize with
respect to it. A political movement organized around an ecological issue
would be different from one organized around, for instance, class interests.
Industrial society's cleavage as conceptualized by Marx is intra-industrial.
Exploited industrial workers recognize their common situation. Owners recognize their common interests. Power is organized along class lines.

When power forms around an environmental issue such as pollution, the
industrial producers, both owners and workers, may find themselves allied.
Public interests may be their antagonists.* An environmental issue may
isolate a particular industry within a community, or society may divide on
the very question of industrialization, articulating the issue, as Malthus did,
around the relation of man to resources, instead of around the struggles
among men. The New Left, Weisberg (1970) observes, has developed little
interest in the politics of ecology. This different structuring of power may,
in part, account for their lack of interest.

The concept of "issue" focuses attention on manifest rather than latent
concerns. Some of the public consciously identify it as their "real" concern
and political leaders accept this definition. Were the issue a real expression
of the social tensions which attach to it, governmental response to the issue

* Potter (1970) illustrates a case in which electrical engineers, employees of a
power industry, refused to testify on behalf of opponents of a power plant. Here,
as with other environmental problems, management and labor perceive an identity of
interests. Those attached economically to an industry may be reluctant to attack it as
a source of pollution. The public, for its part, may feel it has no "need" for the
industry which is intruding on its health and aesthetic sensitivities.

would dissipate tensions. If, however, an issue is a relatively arbitrary symbol expressing some more hidden, underlying source of tension, the issue might be dissolved only to release the tensions to attach themselves to a new cause. Issues may emerge and disappear without objective change in the situation on which they focus.

An issue offers a "handle" in a political analysis. From specification of an issue it leads to identification of groups oriented to the issue. Keeping an issue in focus, the political observer may chart the coming and going of supporting and opposing groups. The power of these groups, and the amount of pressure they can exert on an environmental issue, need not derive from their grouping around that environmental attribute but may rest in other aspects of their social position. The problem of air pollution, for instance, emerged during the 1930s in connection with smoke from fossil fuels. On a government level, it drew the attention of the Bureau of Mines. During the 1960s, following the Donora disaster, the relation of air and water pollution to respiratory disease became obvious. Air pollution, as a health problem, became a responsibility of the Department of Health, Education and Welfare. The history of professional participation in air-pollution control links mining engineers to health professionals with a parallel change in constituencies and in the manifest reasons for their adherence to the issue. The objective problem changed little.

Religion as an Issue in Ecology

Ideology may also assume a religious form directing action to cultural, especially value, change. Here again the focus is on control—not the factual analysis but the value judgment about the propriety of man's management of a physical nature. The relation of man and nature is a traditional topic of theological cosmology. Some contemporary writers on ecology, in asserting a disruption in this relation, an alienation of man from nature, have diagnosed the cause as the humanistic or anthropocentric orientations of Western religions. Judaism, Christianity, and Islam postulate a special place in creation for man. Leo Marx (1970) identifies a self-aggrandizing way of life, as reflected in recent Western literature, as a root of our ecological crisis. The philosophical source of this dangerous behavior, says Marx, is an arrogant conception of man, and above all of human consciousness, as wholly unique, as an entity distinct from and potentially independent of the rest of nature. McHarg (1970) calls it simple-minded anthropocentrism. Rienow and Rienow (1970) say in their popular work that, as a species, man imagines himself separate from the animals in the woods and unrelated to the fish in the rivers. When he arrogantly dedicates himself to the idea that he, above all, is God-ordained to tame and overexploit nature, he becomes man against his environment.

The special place of man in creation is associated with a special place for God. Judaism, Christianity, and Islam are committed to a transcendent God, outside of the natural processes which are His creation. Certain Eastern religions such as Buddhism and Hinduism, in contrast, relate to spiritual power which is immanent in nature. In this ecological discussion the idea of transcendence loses its older meaning of synthesizing or drawing together that over which it rules. Rather, it is taken to mean separate and at a distance. McHarg (1970) charges, quite directly, that our ecological plight has been produced by the Judaeo-Christian humanist view. Often cited is the text of Genesis 1:28 in which man is given "dominion over the fish of the sea, and over the fowl of the air, and over every living thing that creepeth upon the earth." Of course, this citation could be set against the seemingly contrary sentiment occurring a few verses later in which man is placed in the Garden of Eden and directed to protect it (Genesis 2:15). The spirit of the Psalmist writing "the earth is the Lord's and the fullness thereof" (Psalms 24:1) hardly recommends the exploitation of nature. In all events, an intimate liaison between current behavior and any particular citation in Holy Writ would be surprising.

A principal difference between the religions of the immanent and those of the transcendent God is that the former relate man and nature directly and substantively. The latter relate them through law—symbols which direct behavior. The notion of "dominion" is translated into laws which govern the relation of the rulers to the ruled.

Freudenstein (1970) in dealing with the posture of Judaism on ecology cites Deuteronomy 20:19–20 which enjoins the Israelite invaders of Canaan not to destroy trees by swinging an axe against them. This citation became the foundation for the Talmudic legal codification forbidding wanton destruction of nature. Freudenstein argues that since the basic text expressed respect for trees in time of war, therefore *a fortiori* respect for nature is enjoined under less extraordinary conditions.* The notion of man's dominion over nature is prelude to specifying man's rights in nature and the limits of his dominion.

Drawing upon Talmudic material, Freudenstein illustrates one type of

---

* Though the concept of a transcendent God, and its corollary of human exceptionalism, does not imply antagonism between the differentiated parts of creation, Jewish and Christian theological postures have not been consistent in all times. It would be surprising if a single tradition reigned over four thousand years and a hemisphere of culture. Thomas Merton (1970) points to Judaeo-Christian ambivalence toward nature as reflected in the Manichaean hostility toward created nature. In Manichaeism the wilderness became the domain of moral wickedness because it favored spontaneity and therefore sin. Merton called for an awareness of man's true place as a dependent member of the biotic community. Nature was viewed as an adversary in the ancient literatures of Greece and Rome as well as in the legends of the Norsemen, Germanic tribes, and in Beowulf (Pollard, 1970). The powers of nature fought one another as well as man.

regulating norm.† The standards limiting destruction of nature, he notes, are relative rather than absolute. The Biblical stance opposed purposeless destruction but not destruction related to economic gain.

Drawing upon the concept of incarnation, as in the Eucharist, Bonifazi (1970) suggests that a transignification of nature occurred in the religions of a transcendent God. The earth was declared holy and nature was given a new meaning. The religions of God immanent in nature treat nature as inherently enchanted. As a result of the disenchantment of nature, its technical use became possible. That is, disenchantment is a prerequisite for the relation of law referred to by Freudenstein.‡

This religio-ideological turn of the ecological literature recapitulates an ancient religious conflict. Hebrew religion was forged in conflict with religions of nature. Its presumption of a transcendent God was developed in contrast to the nature gods of Babylonia worshipped under Asherah, a tree. The idols which Abram destroyed belonged to his father's moon-worship, and the Temple brought down by Samson was dedicated to a Philistine deity in the form of a fish. Christianity, in Europe, developed in contrast to the nature-religions of the Teutons, of Thor and his thunderbolts, and encountered the Druids worshipping under sacred oaks.

The current attack on Jewish and Christian ecological traditions are, in a sense, a renewed defense of these ancient nature-religions and their immanent God. This is not the place either to defend a religious tradition in which man is a unique creation, a religion of a transcendent God, or to draw the implications for life of religions in which man is considered continuous with the other species. The important point here is that ecology has become ideology when the religious issue enters. In this situation that special understanding available through science in the cognitive mode is more difficult to attain.

THE ALIENATIVE CHARACTER
OF ECOLOGICAL SCIENCE

The pejorative connotation of alienation seems to demand the elimination of distance between self and object, between man and nature, between man and man. Yet, if that distance is eliminated so that ecology becomes pri-

---

† Bonifazi (1970), going back to Biblical mentality, reminds us that for the Hebrews the ordered world of interrelating creatures and things was not held together by "natural laws" but sustained by the "breath of God." In Greek philosophical terms, it was a relation of *nomos* rather than *physis,* a relation of symbolic rules rather than a simple deterministic connection.

‡ Pollard (1970), in a passage which seems to blend the religion of transcendence with the religion of immanence, proposes that man actively woo the earth, exercising dominion in love. With a reawakened sense of the sacredness and holiness of the earth and her creatures, a new theology of nature could emerge.

marily a form of action rather than a form of contemplation, the very basis upon which viable action may be taken, the scientific ecological knowledge, will elude us. In the end, we seem to face the ultimate dilemma of choosing either biological extinction or the rejection of our Western religious commitments.

The issue of control has persisted throughout the discussion. Marx labeled as alienation the shift of control over the product of labor from the producer to the capitalist. More recent theorists of alienation say that any control exerted when subject and object are separated is alienating because it places them in an instrumental relation. The ideologists of ecology, pursuing this theme, associate selfish and gluttonous control of the environment with the current crisis. The notion of control merits a few more words.

The term "control" has been used almost generically to refer to technical, social, and cultural control by man over nature. In a technical sense, man's control means that his act can change the state of a natural system. Man builds an irrigation canal permitting water to flow over arid land and, as a consequence, triggers natural, but desired, botanical processes. In a social sense, control refers to allocation of rights in nature. Control is extended through the social processes influencing the distribution of these rights. In a cultural sense, control refers to knowledge about technical processes and about social rights. This is instrumental knowledge concerning the possible consequences of acts. Social and cultural control are logically prior to technical control. Man does not build an irrigation canal unless, culturally, he perceives the possibility of doing so and unless he knows the relation of irrigation to plant-growth. He may not build the canal unless he has the socially granted right to do so.

The social control of nature is determined within a political, legal, religious, or economic framework. The knowledge which informs technical control is, in part, developed by science. This knowledge also sets the possibilities for social control. Scientific knowledge is alienative in its form. It is alienative rather than alienating because science provides one condition, but not a sufficient condition, for alienation. The alienative character of science, and of technology as well, derives from its treatment of nature as an object, free of the influence of the observing self; from its use of a theoretical framework to interpret observations, attending only to limited features of the object; and from its treatment of the object as a means rather than as an end in itself. Arendt (1954) compares this with Archimedes' search for a point upon which to stand and from which he presumed he could move the earth. This point must necessarily be outside the earth. Science requires, Arendt says, the renunciation of the anthropocentric and the geocentric world views and a radical elimination of all anthropomorphic elements and principles as they arise either from the world given to the five human senses or from the categories inherent in the human mind.

The sense in which science "requires" needs clarification. If the requirement affects ways of living, then the renunciation of the anthropocentric world view would place science in conflict with Western religion. This actually was the experience of nineteenth- and early-twentieth-century Christianity. However, the "warfare of science and theology" seems now long past as the notion of science as a system of symbols rather than as a system of action is understood. Of course, positivists who may derive values from science do not recognize this distinction.

The ability of man to control nature and the very act of controlling involves alienation, the separation of the controller from the controlled—though in some measure the act of enslaving binds the master too. Must man act as ecological dominant in order to have the knowledge he needs to survive? Arendt sees a danger to him in his alienated posture. Were one to take the point of view, she says, of Einstein's "observer freely poised in space," then even the activities of men would appear as no more than "overt behavior." We could then study these activities with the same methods we use to study the behavior of rats. Should science reach this point, Arendt continues, the stature of man would not simply be lowered, but would have been destroyed.

Arendt's concern is less with alienation from nature as such than with alienation of man from man. Writers on alienation assert the undesirability of focussing on the activities of men as "overt behavior," of treating them as objects. This is not the place to dispute that moral judgment, though it may be allowed that in some cases it is more human to limit a relationship than to allow it to effervesce in some oceanic way. However, the central question is whether such fundamental alienation is a necessary consequence of science.

The matrices of science are not realities but are heuristics. They are tentative premises and forms of reasoning which appear helpful in providing an understanding of some manifest activities. In treating nature or human activities as objects and in limiting our vision to analytic elements abstracted from those objects, the scientist is engaged in a game of "as if." Whether the man who plays this game is in serious danger of carrying it with him into his life as lived remains to be established. That scientists and engineers are more alienated than, say, teachers and preachers is not obvious.

If the symbolic matrix of science is confused with reality, if the abstract concepts are reified into concrete beings, then, of course, the play at alienation has the potential for becoming vivid, true-life alienation. The cultural symbols of control become the socio-political symbols of action.

Social reification is an empirical possibility. It may occur for reasons of pathology or as simple vulgarization of the scientific concepts. When the specific roles in which people act become their whole selves, then as Marx said the commodity- or exchange-value of man becomes the measure of man. This is a pathological confusion of the part for the whole. To argue against the scientific mode because of the possibility of pathological distortion is like arguing against theater and its players because schizophrenics may confuse characters.

Alienation as described by Marx is an objective structural condition. The concept may be reified through vulgarization by not recognizing both its objectivity and its structural character. Reference to the sense or the feeling of alienation, subjective apprehensions, are vulgarizations of the concept— or, at the very least, are borrowings of the term for another usage. Josephson and Josephson (1962), for instance, define alienation as an individual feeling or state of dissociation from self, from others and from the world at large.

According to Marx, when work becomes external to the worker and not part of his nature, he does not fulfill his self in his work. He then has the feeling of misery and does not develop freely his mental and physical energy (Bottomore, 1963). The feeling of misery may be one consequence when objective alienation is experienced on the individual level. It is not the basic process itself. Objective alienation may have no subjective correlate when the psychological defenses anesthetize the person or, in Marxian terms, when there is false consciousness. Contrariwise, a feeling of loneliness may arise with no basis in contemporary fact. This distortion of the original objective focus of the concept is associated with the second form of vulgarization—neglecting the fact that alienation is a social structural condition. The assumption that it is subjective is especially pernicious in the man–environment area.

Individual attitudinal hostility toward nature is a minor component in human disruptiveness of nature. The recommendation that the alienation of man from nature can be resolved by a change in individual attitudes neglects a basic insight of alienation theory. The individual motive is dissociated from the social consequence. A destructive consequence may emerge from the most salutary of motives. The man–nature disjunction, the real alienation, is a disjunction at the system or collective level. The individual driver of an automobile adds little pollution to the atmosphere. Culpability accrues to the aggregate of drivers within a particular limited area. The fact that large oil-tankers ply the seas with danger of spillage must be traced to the social organization in which oil is used.

The crucial social mechanism by which man is alienated from nature is not the play at alienation as it is carried on in science and technology. The real sense in which man becomes alienated is in terms of social-political control, an inequity in the distribution of rights in nature among men.

Social rules which guarantee an equitable distribution of rights in nature are a safeguard against the degredation of nature. The decision whether an environment is degraded or over-exploited is a social decision. It rests upon whether the environment will support life or is deleterious to its inhabitants.

The desired attributes of the environment are expressed as environmental standards. These statements refer to permissible noise-levels in a factory, permissible densities of chemicals in industrial effluents, or the amount of land required for home-construction. An environmental standard, though expressed in terms of some physical characteristics, rests on a conception of the social value of the environment. No law of nature insists that stream oxygen be at a particular level or that a lake support some level of organic life. It is only the love for man which we attribute to God which encourages us to believe that He would fret were He again to rule a world of methane-producing swamps.

The essential issue is that when a stream is polluted its use is thereby denied to some other person or group. The possibility of such denial rests on the inability of the person or group to exercise rights in the stream. If that other person can exercise property-rights in the water, he can demand that the polluter refrain from co-opting the water as his private sewer. When mutual rights are thus protected then stream quality either does not deteriorate or no one cares if it does. No biological or physical change in the natural environment would be noted as exploitation of the environment were it not perceived as having some deleterious effect on people. These are proper matters for ideology. The extent of real alienation depends upon the way in which these matters are resolved.

A factual understanding of both social relations and natural processes is a prerequisite for attaining the social aims of ideologically directed action. Real alienation is a failure of social relations. The play at alienation in the development of knowledge is a needed prophylactic against real alienation.

To learn about the environment and to plan environmental amelioration requires a willingness to separate self and object. When the self becomes involved in the object *ab initio*, a direction for action imposes itself too early in the search for knowledge—perhaps, truncating that search and, in true alienative style, denying the action the knowledge it needs. Science recedes and is replaced by ideology.

REFERENCES

Amussen, D. G., & Bouchard, T. P. Wild and scenic rivers: Private right and public goods. In R. A. Cooley & J. Wandesford-Smith (Eds.) *Congress and the environment*. Seattle: University of Washington Press, 1970. Pp. 162–174.

Arendt, H. *Between past and future*. New York: Viking, 1954.

Arendt, H. *The human condition*. Chicago: University of Chicago Press, 1958.

Bonifazi, C. Biblical roots of an ecological conscience. In M. Hamilton (Ed.) *This little planet*. New York: Scribner's, 1970. Pp. 203–233.

Bottomore, T. B. (Ed. & trans.) *Karl Marx: Early writings*. New York: McGraw-Hill, 1963.

Caldwell, L. K. *Environment: A challenge for modern society*. Garden City, N.Y.: Natural History Press, 1970.

Cooley, R. A., & Wandesford-Smith, J. (Eds.) *Congress and the environment.* Seattle: University of Washington Press, 1970.

Freudenstein, E. G. Ecology and the Jewish tradition. *Judaism,* 1970, *19,* 406–414.

Hare, F. K. How should we treat environment? *Science,* 1970, *167,* 352–355 (January 23, 1970).

Josephson, E., & Josephson, M. Introduction. In E. Josephson & M. Josephson (Eds.) *Man alone: Alienation in modern society.* New York: Dell, 1962. Pp. 9–53.

Lichtheim, G. Alienation. In D. L. Sills (Ed.) *International Encyclopedia of the Social Sciences* (17 vols.) New York: Macmillan, 1968. Vol. 1, pp. 264–268.

MacIntyre, A. C. *Marxism and Christianity.* New York: Schocken, 1968.

Marx, L. American institutions and ecological ideals. *Science,* 1970, *170,* 945–952 (November 27, 1970).

McHarg, I. L. Values, process and form. In R. Disch (Ed.) *Ecological conscience: Values for survival.* Englewood Cliffs, N.J.: Prentice-Hall, 1970. Pp. 21–36.

Merton, T. The wild places. In R. Disch (Ed.) *Ecological conscience: Values for survival.* Englewood Cliffs, N.J.: Prentice-Hall, 1970. Pp. 37–43.

Pollard, W. G. God and his creation. In M. Hamilton (Ed.) *This little planet.* New York: Scribner's, 1970. Pp. 43–78.

Potter, F. M., Jr. Everybody wants to save the environment. In R. Disch (Ed.) *Ecological conscience: Values for survival.* Englewood Cliffs, N.J.: Prentice-Hall, 1970. Pp. 130–140.

Rienow, R., & Rienow, L. T. *Man against his environment.* Baltimore: Ballantine, 1970.

Sears, P. B. The injured earth. In M. Hamilton (Ed.) *This little planet.* New York: Scribner's, 1970. Pp. 11–42.

Shephard, P. Ecology and man—a viewpoint. In R. Disch (Ed.) *Ecological conscience: Values for survival.* Englewood Cliffs, N.J.: Prentice-Hall, 1970. Pp. 56–66.

Slobodkin, L. B. Aspects of the future of ecology. In R. Disch (Ed.) *Ecological conscience: Values for survival.* Englewood Cliffs, N.J.: Prentice-Hall, 1970. Pp. 71–90.

Weisberg, B. The politics of ecology. In R. Disch (Ed.) *Ecological conscience: Values for survival.* Englewood Cliffs, N.J.: Prentice-Hall, 1970. Pp. 154–160.

White, L., Jr. *Machina ex deo: Essays in the dynamism of western culture.* Cambridge, Mass.: MIT Press, 1968.

Alienation in
Psychological Perspective

JOSEPH G. KEEGAN, S.J.

Father Joseph G. Keegan, S.J., who is an associate professor of psychology at Fordham University, received his A.B. degree from Woodstock College in 1929 and his M.A. (1943) and Ph.D. (1949) degrees from Yale University. He was chairman of the psychology department at Fordham University from 1949 to 1958, and director of the Counseling Center from 1961 to 1966. He is a member of many professional organizations, including the British Psychological Society, the American Psychological Association, and the American Catholic Psychological Association, of which he was president from 1961 to 1962. Father Keegan has been intimately associated with the entire series of Pastoral Psychology Institutes, having been a member of the Organizing Committee for each Institute.

The technological revolution of the current age would be seen by many as the most fantastic and far-reaching manifestation of unexpected change and challenge. The actual production and the use of stupendous charges of energy, the automation and computerization of processes and projects hitherto regarded as insurmountably time-consuming and difficult, the conquest of space and exploration of remote planets—these are but a few of the marvels which justify the designation of the age as technocratic. There are those, however, among them Aldous Huxley, who see all other

51

revolutions as dwarfed by comparison with the psychological revolution which is rapidly approaching. In such a context the encroaching conflict would be that, as technocracy enlarges, human freedom is seen as more seriously threatened.

What are the current manifestations of this psychological revolution? What are its roots? Must it run its dire predictable course—to produce a race of men outclassed and subdued by the threat of the machine, no longer capable of offering resistance to forces outside and inside themselves? Or is there the possibility of preserving human rationality and human freedom vis-à-vis the mechanized and electronic controls which modern *homo faber* has already fashioned and will fashion in the future? It is in the context of trying to answer questions such as these that the psychologist might focus on alienation as a major human phenomenon present with us now and threatening to enlarge its scope in the predictable future.

THE CONCEPT OF ALIENATION

Of course a psychological appraisal of alienation is not the whole story. But it would be a necessary step preliminary to any analysis of its sources, and the latter in turn a prerequisite to the exploration of appropriate remedies. Hence we start with an effort at the description and portrayal of man's current alienated condition. Though the same word, alienation, is employed, the current context is by no means synonymous with the older, more classical use of the term to designate persons who have lost the use of their senses or of their minds and who consequently were said to be separated from reality. For one thing the modern connotation would refer to a wider range of persons, even various groups of people who though sensing and perceiving are nevertheless "turned off," estranged.

Having entertained and supported a plethora of movements and projects bearing the label "progress" and hopefulness, the modern American has to a considerable extent been psychologically numbed by his many disappointments. In a sense he has seen and perceived and been confused by too much reality—the reality of unfulfilled expectations or the reality of the unsolicited side-effects of expected achievement. He has largely come to regard his important hopes and expectations, his vision of a better world, his design for constructive fraternity and altruistic togetherness, as a grandiose illusion. In this century he has witnessed two major wars to end all wars, has experienced a world-wide economic depression, has seen the dislocations he attributes to economic expansion, and continues to fear more of the same—expanding poverty for the many as well as increased affluence for the few and a creeping paralysis in the institutions he trusted to correct the flaws in the system. The litany of symptoms could be interminable.

alienated individual who has forsaken others to embrace a loner's existence. But there is, after all, a certain unity in that each of these seemingly diverse reactions represents the abandonment of self-determination or true individuality and autonomy. The former is active but hardly the regulator of selfhood; the latter has lost all meaning for action.

This underlying theme of self-surrender and loss of personal identity might be assumed to be the challenge to which an increasing number of humanistic psychologists have recently been responding. Among psychologists the emergence of a stress on self-actualizing people is evident in the works of Rollo May (1953), Carl Rogers (1961), Erik Erikson (1959), and Abraham Maslow (1970), to name but a few. Related perhaps to their professional interest in psychotherapy, they have come close to the individual client as an individual so as to be impressed with his basic potentialities for self-realization. They see the chasm between what he thinks of himself and his true capacity for self-realization and meaningfulness. At any rate they share an optimistic belief in man's inner capacity to surmount and control environmental conditions so as to emerge as an autonomous person. If the person is alienated, the sense of self has been reduced to the vanishing point and it is difficult to actualize potentialities when they are rated as null.

PSYCHOLOGICAL ROOTS OF ALIENATION

No doubt it would have occurred to us that, even in its relatively brief experience as a science interested in personality and in social phenomena, psychology should be able to come up with reasonable models—models adapted to other areas of personality research and, we hope, capable of yielding some clarity about the dynamics of alienation. However, it should be clear from what has been thus far presented that there is at best only partial agreement among behavioral scientists concerning the precise definition of alienation and its adequate differentiation from other related states. In addition, the picture usually presented portrays a situation in which the individual's responses appear to be related in some general way to his inability to accept or even to live with the demands and pressures of society. In this setting perhaps the psychologist may count upon some forbearance if he seeks deeper understanding in terms of hypotheses similar to those which have contributed a measure of clarity in respect of other psychosocial relationships.

Psychoanalytic thinking would doubtless have something to offer in this connection, especially in reference to our unconscious responses or the mechanisms of defense evoked by various developmental crises. As Frederick Weiss (1962) points out, even though Freud did not formally mention alienation, several writers experienced in analytic therapy have clearly sensed the equivalent of alienation in persons whose early relationships were characterized either by lack of physical and emotional closeness or by unrelieved symbiotic attachment to parents. The ensuing defense is to protect the ego from basic anxiety. In this sense the alienated person has been buffeted by opposing currents; he would avoid, for instance, the pain of severe conflict between his dependency needs and his ineffectual urge to be free.

> By remaining alienated from himself and detached from others, the patient avoids the anxiety connected with emotional involvement in conflict. But he pays for this with a steadily increasing restriction of his life, his feelings, and his wants; he pays with a loss of his self [Weiss, 1962, p. 468].

Looking for answers, the psychologist might be prone to re-examine some of the attempted psychological analyses of transactional processes, such as those involved in frustration and its sequelae, a topic which has elicited a fair amount of research within several schools of psychological thought. Another source of hypotheses might be the psychological theorizing and research which have attempted to unravel the dynamics of conflict. Our treatment of these will be necessarily brief.

With particular reference to frustration theory there are those who claim to see therein a model or paradigm for the analysis of alienation and its dynamics. But to accept this is probably to have recourse to a highly over-simplified solution. For one thing it seems to narrow its focus on some extreme manifestations of social unrest such as riots in the inner city, wild-cat strikes, or fears of violence on the part of the Black Panthers. By the same token such a view fails to take into account that reactions akin to aggression are by no means the universally consistent accompaniment of alienation. As a matter of fact what we can probably best learn from the experience of psychologists with frustration theory and their attempts to exploit it in controlled situations is the exercise of patience and a healthy reluctance about accepting any formula resembling a one-to-one relation-ship between a postulated antecedent variable such as frustration and its consequent, aggression. Even brief experience revealed to the proponents of that theory the necessity of recognizing several alternative modes of response, albeit aggression, direct and vicarious, remained as a possibility.

It seems to have been an incautious acceptance of frustration theory which led some students of alienation to see in dissatisfaction with work or work-alienation the kingpin among all forms of alienation. But Melvin Seeman (1959) who has conducted a fair amount of empirical research on the topic of alienation found in several settings, in both Europe and the United States, a lack of significant correlation between work alienation and several indexes such as frustration might lead us to expect. For instance, among samples of manually employed as well as among white-collar blacks, out-group hostility as well as in-group solidarity were unrelated to work-alienation. In fact Seeman's data indicate a much more substantial correlation of his measures of social discontent and ethnic prejudice with a facet of alienation he designates as powerlessness.

Although supporting empirical data are scant, a re-examination of the varied manifestations of alienation—Seeman's (1959) powerlessness, meaninglessness, normlessness, personal or self-estrangement, and social isolation—would also suggest the relevance of some form of conflict-theory. It would not be our intention to risk the implication that the human person possesses in actuality a multiplicity of selves. However, in most of the conflicts we sustain we become at least vaguely conscious that aspects of the self are not very much in harmony. This is most clearly apprehended in what would be called internal–internal conflict. The person is polarized from within. An example of such a psychologically damaging conflict would be the person who is unable to master a habit such as smoking or drug use, despite clear-cut and repeated medical indications that he is inflicting serious damage upon himself. Any observer could tell him that he is locked in a self-defeating process and the keen observer might also note the debilitating symptoms of his guilt feelings.

Self-defeating behavior associated with intense conflict may also emerge in situations which can be designated as external–internal. In these situations the external component would come from the environment or from societal pressures. Such would be the conflicting pressures on the marginal man, for instance, or for some individuals role-pressures which most persons are able to sustain without obvious collapse. Role-conflict is certainly one facet of life concerning which societal structure itself can be "alienating."

Without departing far from the concept of role-conflict it is not too difficult to imagine kindred cleavages within the totality of personality—cleavages which disrupt and hamper personality integration. The core consideration is not simply low self-esteem or negative feelings of self-regard. The rift is deeper. After all, many people accept their limitations, both physical and psychological, and function meaningfully, perhaps on the basis of a reappraisal of their positive traits. Rather, what is damaging and debilitating would be the conflict situation arising in the perception of an intolerable cleavage or a severe dissonance between overt action and the appraisal of one's underlying self. When a person's behavior fails to match his major ways of conceiving of himself, another mode of representing the situation would be to focus on the conflict between the actual and the ideal self. There is an existential rift at the core of personality and the person is psychologically thwarted or even paralyzed at the prospect. In this setting, self-identity may be said to be diminished to the vanishing point. Needless to say, the psychologist would be deeply interested if he could unravel the dynamics involved in this ultimate conflict. Seeman (1959) has made an attempt to obtain comparative data on some of the personality traits which might serve to differentiate between alienated and nonalienated persons, but generally we lack an empirical basis from which to derive firm conclusions.

Recently a brand of psychology has taken on new life which gives promise of being an antidote or a corrective at least for American psychology's relative neglect of the inner psyche, the self, or ego. It would be seen as a liberalizing movement stressing humanistic elements and is generally referred to as Existential Psychology. Its emphasis on the liberating role of the self makes for relevance in the context of our discussion of alienation. The French Resistance movement during World War II fostered the growth, or rather the rebirth, of a liberation of the spirit and the emergence of an influential advance in existentialist thinking. For an assortment of artists, writers, university students, and journalists, existentialism came to mean many things. In the realm of psychology this resurgence chiefly resurrected the thinking of Martin Heidegger and Karl Jaspers. The central thought would be that man is being-in-the-world, not a thing or just a body interacting with other things. Conversely the world has its existence because there is a being to disclose it.

Though initially a European movement, existentialism has had a distinct role to play in recent American developments—Rollo May (1953) and Adrian Van Kaam (1966), for instance. As Van Kaam would put it, phenomenology became the chosen method of analyzing psychological experience—"a method in psychology [which] seeks to disclose and elucidate the phenomena of behavior as they manifest themselves in their perceived immediacy" (Van Kamm, 1966, p. 15). Another distinctive feature would be its emphasis on motivation rather than on causality in the ordinary sense of determination. Incidentally, phenomenology had already been emphasized in Gestalt psychology. But it remained for the existentialist approach to stress its explicit use in an in-depth exploration of personality. We might, then, propose a tentative definition of existential psychology: an empirical science of human existence which employs the method of phenomenological analysis.

A comparable movement in psychology and psychiatry, Viktor Frankl's Logotherapy, was forged in the fire of anguish and suffering—a declaration of the will to live in the face of apparent hopelessness. Paramount was to struggle to stay alive, to maintain one's being.

A man's character became involved to the point that he was caught in a mental turmoil which threatened all the values he held and threw them into doubt. Under the influence of a world which no longer recognized the value of human life and human dignity, which had robbed man of his will and had made him an object to be exterminated (having planned, however, to make full use of him first—to the last ounce of his physical resources)—under this influence the personal ego finally suffered a loss of values. If the man in the concentration camp did not struggle against this in a last effort to save his self-respect, he lost the feeling of being an individual, a being with a mind, with inner freedom and personal value [Frankl, 1962, p. 49].

Despite Søren Kierkegaard's preoccupation with anxiety and "sickness unto death," existentialism is not wanting in optimism, particularly if one reads Frankl who makes a major point of the necessity of carrying hope to the very jaws of death. It is helpful to remember that the existentialist theme of freedom also implies responsibility, and therefore guilt: "I am completely responsible for my existence." "To refuse to become all that I am capable of becoming is to lock myself in darkness."

REFERENCES

Camus, A. *The Stranger.* New York: Knopf, 1946.

Erikson, E. H. Identity and the life cycle. *Psychological Issues,* 1959, *1,* No. 1 (Monograph 1).

Frankl, V. E. *Man's search for meaning: An introduction to logotherapy* (trans. by I. Lasch). Boston: Beacon, 1962.

Fromm, E. *The sane society.* New York: Holt, Rinehart and Winston, 1955.

Keniston, K. *The uncommitted: Alienated youth in American society.* New York: Harcourt, Brace, 1965.

Maslow, A. H. *Motivation and personality.* (2nd ed.) New York: Harper & Row, 1970.

May, R. *Man's search for himself.* New York: Norton, 1953.

Merton, R. K. *Social theory and social structure: Toward the codification of theory and research.* New York: Free Press, 1957.

Mills, C. W. *White collar: The American middle classes.* New York: Oxford University Press, 1951.

Rogers, C. *On becoming a person.* Boston: Houghton Mifflin, 1961.

Seeman, M. On the meaning of alienation. *American Sociological Review,* 1959, *24,* 783–791.

Van Kaam, A. L. *Existential foundations of psychology.* Pittsburgh: Duquesne University Press, 1966.

Weiss, F. A. Self-alienation: Dynamics and therapy. In E. Josephson & M. Josephson (Eds.) *Man alone: Alienation in modern society.* New York: Dell, 1962. Pp. 463–479.

Alienation in Psychiatric Perspective

WILLIAM W. MEISSNER, S.J.

Father William W. Meissner, S.J. received his A.B., M.A., and Ph.L. degrees from St. Louis University, his S.T.L. from Woodstock College, and his M.D. from Harvard University. In addition to an increasing number of articles, his published works include four books: Annotated bibliography in religion and psychology *(1961),* Group dynamics in the religious life *(1965),* Foundations for a psychology of grace *(1966), and* The assault on authority *(1971). He has been a Research Fellow in Psychiatry at both the Massachusetts General Hospital and the Massachusetts Mental Health Center. Father Meissner is a member of the Boston Psychoanalytic Society, and currently is an instructor in psychiatry at the Harvard Medical School.*

The problem of alienation has broad implications for modern psychiatry. The concept of alienation has in the past more properly been the property of sociology—particularly in relation to the concept of anomie, as we shall see. Alienation in psychiatry has until recently been more or less circumscribed in its connotation. In a restrictive psychiatric sense, alienation refers to a variant of depersonalization in which the loss of reality sense takes the form of a feeling of estrangement, isolation, distance, and loneliness. However, with the shift in psychiatric thinking from a more strictly intrapsychic to a more interpsychic perspective, the concept of alienation has been broadened to express pathological manifestations which relate to the interface between man and his fellow-men—between man and society.

One of the major emphases in this development of the notion of alienation has come from existential analytic thinking. Existential thought has emphasized the modern experience of man's alienation from the world of his being. Particularly Nietzsche and Kierkegaard pointed out man's sense of loss of meaningful relatedness to the world of his experience. Existential analysts have continued to stress the loneliness and estrangement of modern man, whose "being-in-the-world" is precarious and fragile. The "world" of which the existentialists speak is the world of meaningful relationships within which the individual defines and locates his personal sense of inner worth and relevance (May, Angel, & Ellenberger, 1958). In the existential sense, alienation implies not merely a disturbance of meaningful relationships with other human beings, but a more basic disturbance of relatedness with both the inanimate structures which constitute one's environment and the historical structures which provide the substance and continuity of one's experience of self.

The problems of loneliness, estrangement, and isolation have been increasingly the focus of psychiatric concern over the last several years. Psychoanalytic thinking has undergone a slow evolution which serves to shift the emphasis in its formulations from forms of psychopathology rooted in the disturbance of instinctual life to forms of psychopathology which have more to do with the impairment of object relations. There is considerably more attention paid these days to character defects of a narcissistic, depressive, or schizoid variety. There is a definite shift from the type of instinctual pathology Freud found in his "hysterical" patients to the type of characterological problems met with in analytic patients today. In a significant proportion of the patients seen these days, certain schizoid features are apparent—detachment, poor capacity for object relations, isolated and withdrawn affect, intellectualizing defenses, etc.

It is of interest historically that the shift in psychiatric interest toward alienation was stimulated by some of the so-called Neofreudians who tried to bring into focus some of the social and cultural aspects of the individual's life-involvement. I am thinking particularly of Horney and Fromm. For many years, their thinking was regarded as more or less deviationist— particularly in that they seemed to be abandoning the more orthodox analytic emphasis on instinctual life and inner conflicts as the basis for the understanding and treatment of neuroses. The charge may have been justified in that the Neofreudian influence—seen from a contemporary vantage-point—seems to have overstated its case and to have undercut important considerations in the treatment of neurotic patients. But the point of historical interest is that, as a result of the emergence and development of analytic ego-psychology in the last few years, the relationship between man's intrapsychic life and the familial, social, and cultural contexts in which he develops and functions has undergone a profound reconsideration. In this more extended understanding of man's psychic development and structure, it has become possible to rethink Neofreudian contributions and to integrate them meaningfully into the main body of analytic understanding. This is a work of theoretical development which is still in progress—and will be for some time to come.

Horney related the problem of alienation to the disparity between the idealized self and the real self. Because of his neurotic failure to measure up to the ideal, the neurotic hates himself—hates his own limitations and inadequacies. This self-hate expresses itself in relentless demands on oneself, repeated self-accusations, self-devaluation, forms of self-torment, and self-destructive behavior. In its extreme forms such alienation can take the form of amnesias and states of loss of reality sense and depersonalization. But more pervasively, alienation can take the form of a feeling of numbness and remoteness. The individual tends to become more impersonal in all his dealings, he loses the capacity to feel or to be able to recognize and acknowledge his true feelings. He loses a sense of responsibility for himself and for the direction of his life and activity. His continual sense of disappointment with himself and with his interaction with his environment leads to a gradual disowning of his real self and a retreat into an ineffectual style of life (Horney, 1950).

One of the serious questions which confronts us is the extent to which this pattern of life-experience is emerging as a cultural type. The line between psychopathology and cultural adaptation becomes thin and highly permeable. Alienation in its many guises and "formes frustres" may well have permeated our society to such an extent that it can no longer be regarded as deviant or as pathological in that sense. Riesman (1950) made the argument in his *The lonely crowd* that the isolated, lonely, and alienated character-type is endemic to our society and that the trends in that direction have been increasing with time. Camus' stranger is the contemporary alienated man who wanders through his world a stranger to those he seeks to know or pretends to love—he wanders in a continual state of homelessness and diffuseness, without any sense of connection, as if a stranger in a foreign land unable to communicate with his fellows and doomed to wander in quiet despair and lonely frustration (Camus, 1946).

The concern with alienation, therefore, carries psychiatric concern to the interface between intrapsychic dynamics and the social and cultural processes which surround the individual, and inevitably influence his development and capacity to function. Alienation thus becomes a sort of middle ground on which psychiatric concern mingles with and to some extent overlaps with the concern of more social approaches to human behavior. The concept of alienation can thus be seen to carry an implicit reference to the social context which continually influences the individual and with which he is in constant interaction. Alienation is an alienation from something which is around and outside the individual. One of the most valuable insights of modern social science is not that patterns of deviant behavior are merely the product of disordered intrapsychic processes or impediments of development—although these play an unquestioned and critical role—but that the organization of social structures and social processes within which the individual functions has a determinate influence on the patterns of individual adaptation.

Merton (1957) has cast this process in terms of the interplay of culturally defined goals and institutionalized norms. Cultural goals consist of the goals, objectives, and aims which are held out to all members of a society as legitimate objectives for which they can and should strive. These are integrated in varying degrees according to a hierarchical system of values embedded in the culture and its institutions. The institutionalized norms operate to define, regulate, and control the acceptable or available modes of striving for these goals. These two cultural elements vary independently of each other and may receive different degrees of emphasis in any given social structure. They may operate differentially in different strata or segments of society. At some levels of social organization, the culturally defined goals may be considerably more available than in other segments— although the goals are held out to each segment of the society as equally valid and desirable. Thus where culturally defined goals function without the institutionalized means for their attainment, they set up a situation of continual frustration and cultural estrangement.

In the analysis of adaptation to these cultural elements, Merton (1957) has provided a typology which describes the ways in which individuals can respond to them. These patterns may vary in different social contexts or in reference to different culturally determined goals. Individuals can *conform* by accepting both the cultural goals and the existing institutionalized means. Such a pattern insures the stability and continuity of the social structure and represents the pattern of modal behavior oriented to the basic values of the society. A second pattern of adaptation is *innovation*— the individual has assimilated the cultural emphasis on the goal, but has not equivalently internalized the institutional norms governing the means for its attainment. Individuals may thus make use of institutionally proscribed but nonetheless effective means for attaining the desired goals. Merton uses the example of sharp business practices or organized crime as deviant means for attaining the culturally acceptable goals of financial success. In this modality the failure to accept or abide by institutionalized means offering the promise of financial success and a relative unavailability of such means creates pressures which tend to reinforce deviant patterns of behavior. The combination of cultural emphasis and the limitations of social structure creates the pressure toward deviation.

The third modality is *ritualism*. This pattern involves the scaling-down of cultural objectives to meet the relative capacity one enjoys within the available institutionalized means. This response is more characteristic of the middle-class orientation which emphasizes adherence to institutionalized norms much more than do lower-class attitudes. Anxiety is avoided by retreating from competitive struggle for achievement and rigidly adhering to established social mores.

The fourth pattern is that of *retreatism*. This modality involves the rejection of both cultural goals and institutionalized means. These people are in the society but not of it. They are the social dropouts—the vagabonds, tramps, hippies, drunks, and drug addicts.

The last modality of adapting to these social pressures is that of *rebellion*. These individuals not only reject the existing social structure and its values, but actively seek to overthrow it and to replace it with an entirely new social structure in which cultural standards would be significantly modified and the emphasis placed on merit, effort, and reward in social processes. The rebellious individual is caught up in diffuse feelings of hate, envy, and rage. He has a continual sense of impotent hostility—an inner anger which cannot be adequately expressed or relieved. The rebel regards the norms and standards of contemporary society as arbitrary and meaningless. As such they might as well be done away with—especially insofar as they provide him and other underprivileged groups with which he aligns himself with significant impediments to achieving important goals (not necessarily those endorsed by the surrounding society).

These modalities of adaptation are patterns of response to anomie in the social structure. The concept of anomie as originally proposed by Durkheim had more to do with a relative lack of social norms. The subjective aspect of this concept has been extended to include a state of mind which is marked by a sense of purposelessness and isolation. Corresponding to this psychological dimension of anomie is a social dimension which refers to a breakdown in cultural organizations. As Merton puts it,

> Anomie is then conceived as a breakdown in the cultural structure, occurring particularly when there is an acute disjunction between the cultural norms and goals and the socially structured capacities of members of the group to act in accord with them. In this conception, cultural values may help to produce behavior which is at odds with the mandates of the values themselves.
>
> On this view, the social structure strains the cultural values, making action in accord with them readily possible for those occupying certain

statuses within the society and difficult or impossible for others. The social structure acts as a barrier or as an open door to the acting out of cultural mandates. When the cultural and the social structure are malintegrated, the first calling for behavior and attitudes which the second precludes, there is a strain toward the breakdown of the norms, toward normlessness [Merton, 1957, pp. 162–163].

The problem of alienation is closely related to the problem of anomie—they are two faces of the same problem. Social anomie produces and is reflected in a psychological anomie on the individual level. The latter is what we have been describing as alienation.

The interrelation between social anomie and psychological alienation is complex. The cultural disparity involved in anomie has its psychological counterpart in the disorganization and inner conflicts of values within the individual. The basic question we have to face in understanding this problem is how intrapsychic and social processes influence each other in the complex process of value-formation and value-change. Merton has suggested that the organization of our contemporary culture with its emphasis on material wealth and competitiveness creates a certain strain toward anomie. The shift of cultural emphasis from the satisfactions involved in competitive effort to an almost exclusive concern with the outcome—in terms of measurable criteria of wealth and power—tends to create a stress on the regulatory structures and an attenuation of institutional controls. Cultural and personal values are undermined and calculations of personal advantage and risks of punishment become the main regulatory resource. We can note that this social strain toward anomie can be paralleled by a failure of internalization processes and a regression from internalized sources of inner regulation to a more primitive and externalized reliance on external rewards and punishments, on directives and prohibitions of external authorities. The social strain toward anomie is paralleled by an inner strain toward extremes of conformity or rebellion.

THE ALIENATION SYNDROME

I would like to try to focus the remainder of this paper on a specific constellation of features which has become increasingly clear in the literature and in recent clinical experience, and which I will call "the alienation syndrome." The syndrome I have in mind is reflected in the patterns of retreatism and rebellion described in Merton's analysis of anomie. The alienation syndrome has become an increasingly prominent phenomenon on the social horizon. Among psychiatrists who work in clinical settings which draw upon the college population, there is a consensus that this constellation of features is increasingly evident. The prominence of the general phenomenon has been underlined by Kenneth Keniston's (1965) analysis in *The uncommitted*.

The Syndrome Among the Young

The syndrome has been described primarily within the adolescent and post-adolescent group, but I think it has wider application than that. The elements of the syndrome include a basic sense of loneliness—the feeling that one somehow does not belong, is not a part of things, not in the mainstream of life and interests which surround one. There is a sense of estrangement and a chronic sense of frustration. The alienated person carries with him a continual sense of opposition between his own wishes and desires and the wishes and desires of those around him—with the additional feeling that his wishes, desires, and ambitions are actively being denied by others. He lives in a chronic state of disappointment—others are continually letting him down, disappointing his expectations, frustrating his designs, pressuring him to conform to their wishes and desires. His disappointment and chronic frustration produce an inner state of continual and unrelenting anger which serves to isolate him further and to put him in a condition of estrangement. Occasionally the anger will erupt in destructive outbursts which leave him even less satisfied and further disappointed.

An important element in the syndrome is the alienated person's sense of continuing frustration. He carries within him a chronic despair—a sense of hopelessness and helplessness which he sees as unremitting. When this sense of hopelessness dominates the picture, alienation tends to take the drop-out, give-up form of retreatism. The individual may resort to any number of pathological forms of behavior to alleviate his sense of inner frustration—including alcohol, drugs, or other forms of escape. Much of what we have seen over the years in the skid-row phenomenon and much of what we are seeing on the contemporary drug scene has this quality of frustrated retreatism. When the sense of frustrated rage dominates the picture, however, we are much more likely to see its manifestations in rebellious behavior of one kind or other. The sense of helplessness and the sense of smoldering rage can easily coexist in the same individual—so that the helpless victim may find himself striking out in impotent rage from time to time.

The loneliness which is characteristic of the alienation syndrome is a deep loneliness. It is not the same as the sort of acute and temporary loneliness that is produced by the loss of significant objects. Rather it is a deep-seated loneliness which the individual carries with him as a part of his inner conviction about himself and the world. It is akin to the experience of existential dread which Kierkegaard placed at the center of the existential concern—the loneliness of self-assertion, self-determination, and the assumption of the ultimate responsibility for the exercise of freedom and choice. As we shall see, that inner dread has a more clinically relevant context; but patients will go to extremes in their efforts to escape from this inner anxiety. The list includes alcoholism, drug addiction, hypochondriasis, compulsive behaviors, masturbation, suicidal gestures, etc. Often such deviant forms of behavior are attempts to get significant others concerned and involved; but the failure of the significant other to respond in a manner which satisfies the individual's expectations leads to further frustration and rage and disappointment.

Value Divergence is Central to the Alienation Syndrome

A central element is the rejection of or conflict over social values. The syndrome, as we have already noted, lies at the interface between the person and social processes. This feature raises a problem in differential diagnosis. Psychiatrists have tended to see the clinical manifestations of the alienation syndrome more in terms of the parameters of inner psychic dysfunction and less in terms of the social parameters. Thus the syndrome is usually described in terms of some form of character pathology, or in terms of its narcissistic aspects, or in terms of its depressive aspects. It is quite accurate to say that these individuals are indeed depressed, that they show many of the manifestations of narcissistic entitlement, and that they suffer from a variety of character defects. But a critical aspect of their clinical picture is the sense of estrangement from the cultural and social milieu in which they live. This estrangement relates specifically to the rejection of values which the society embodies and implicitly requires that they accept. Their rejection of these values may leave them in a relatively valueless vacuum—or they may actively foster divergent values which they oppose to the prevailing values of the culture around them. Or there may arise an inner conflict between partially accepted values of the general culture and partially accepted values of a divergent nature.

Thus a depressive syndrome may include feelings of loneliness and isolation, but it is more likely to embrace feelings of guilt over the failure to live up to certain values and standards which are generally accepted. The rejection of cultural values is not part of a depressive syndrome. Similarly, narcissistic personalities may hold themselves aloof and above the norms acceptable for other people; they may entertain an inner sense of entitlement which results in disappointed expectations and a sense of frustration, but the narcissistic investment does not necessarily involve a rejection of cultural values as such. Often narcissistic individuals find their narcissistic gratification precisely in their ability to gain the recognition and acknowledgment from others by fulfilling cultural expectations. The alienation syndrome adds specifically to these other well-known clinical pictures the aspect of value-conflict and a tendency to reject the accepted cultural-value system of their own society.

The rebellious expression of the syndrome is characterized by the formulation or acceptance of a divergent set of values. Often this takes place in conjunction with a group of likeminded individuals who can share the same set of deviant values. (It should be noted that the term "deviant" in this context does not have the connotation of better or worse, but simply emphasizes that the values of the subgroup stand somehow in opposition to those of the general culture.) Such value-oriented subgroupings are alienated from the larger social group, but may be quite unified within themselves. This allows the alienated individual to achieve a compensatory sense of belonging. This compensatory aspect of group formation is a significant part of the motivation behind adolescent gangs and the youth movement in general. The value deviance can be focussed and expressed in almost any aspect of behavior—clothing, hairstyles, sexual mores, language, expression of values, attitudes, beliefs, etc.

Rejection of Pre-existing Values

The important dimension of this value-divergence is not so much the formation of new and constructive and meaningful values; the emphasis in the syndrome falls on the rejection and, in the rebellious extreme, on the overthrow of pre-existing values. Divergent alienated groups seize on any ideology or any formulation of divergent attitudes to express their rejection. Often, in the service of frustrated and impotent rage, the objective seems to be to find the most extreme form of articulation of values which might fly in the face of the prevailing social values. Thus, rebellious groups spout the most extreme socialist and communist rhetoric—the thoughts of Chairman Mao are preferred in many quarters. There is also a need to question and challenge and confront social institutions and practices on all levels.

An interesting expression of this ideological challenging of established institutions is in the form of a short dictionary of educational terms which was republished in *The New York Times Magazine* (Amis & Conquest, 1971). It expresses this rejecting and value-divergent attitude quite well. I offer a small selection of definitions:

> *alphabet:* A set of arbitrary signs which children are still often compelled to learn by rote; usually taught, moreover, in an arbitrary order. For the (equally arbitrary) methods long prescribed in joining these signs, see *spelling.*
>
> *arbitrary:* Prescribed by bourgeois tradition and consensus, as: "The arbitrary divisions between subjects," "The arbitrary exclusion of illiterates from university entrance," etc.

examination: An irrelevant, external test purporting to check a student's knowledge by a set of written questions often repugnant to his personality and failing to take into account the distractions inevitable in a concerned life. [The "concerned life," incidentally, is the commitment to the propagation of left-wing ideology.]

grammar: Supposed rules covering the structure of a language, especially English. The teaching of grammar inhibits creativity.

spelling: A bourgeois pseudo-accomplishment designed to inhibit creativity, self-expression, etc.

standards: Irrelevant academic concept designed to exclude or penalize students distinguished for either concern or creativity or both.

teach: Impose irrelevant facts and bourgeois indoctrination upon.

If such formulations are amusing when taken out of context, they become less amusing when reinserted into their living context. I have heard quite similar sentiments and ideologically dictated reinterpretations of social processes from the mouths of my own alienated patients. I am not concerned here with educational ideology, or with social ideology for that matter. I wish only to underline the aspect of rejection of values which lies at the heart of this syndrome.

One of the basic questions I wish to raise in this discussion is concerned with the formation of divergent values. The capacity to reformulate and revitalize values is essential to the continuing flexibility, strength, and vitality of any social system. The formation of divergent or deviant values can have a constructive impact on the social system, or it can have a decidedly destructive impact. Thus there is an inherent ambiguity about alienation. Is it an expression of psychopathology, or does it carry the potential for growth and the revitalization of social values? Are the elements of the alienation syndrome, as I have described them, a form of pathological failure to mature or the product of inner conflicts—or are they a necessary byproduct of a dialectic of deviance and revolt which the reformulation of social values requires? It is not so easy to disentangle these elements. They may be closely intertwined, and one has to examine each individual case carefully in order to gain some approach to resolution. The extremes of rebellious alienation are rarely met. Rarely does one see the naked wish to overthrow and destroy—without an accompanying ideology and a wish to replace what is rejected by something better. In the rest of this paper we shall have this ambiguity in the forefront of our concern.

PROTEST AND THE USES OF VIOLENCE

The problem and the paradox of alienation are acutely focused in the use of social protest and frankly revolutionary violence. Revolution and the uses of violence in the service of revolution is obviously nothing new, but it has taken on new social implications in our own time. The threat of violence has become a familiar refrain from all sorts of disaffected and dissatisfied subcultural groups. We hear it from student revolutionaries and radicals, from black radicals and militants, and even from Women's Lib extremists.

The first important consideration is that we live in a culture which sanctions violence as a means of conflict-resolution. We approve of some forms of violence and disapprove of others. Even on the level of the cowboy flick, or the standard television cops-and-crooks episodes, we disapprove of the brutality and violence of the bad guys, but we approve of the violence of the good guys. Our best heroes are those who are the toughest and who are capable of the greatest violence. The principle applies from the level of comicbook superheroes to the likes of Shane or Joe Mannix. Of course, we rationalize the violence of our heroes—they are violent only in the service of justice and the protection of the weak and innocent. As a nation, we use a similar rationale for our participation in the paroxysms of violence and destruction which are the staples of war. The violence of the enemy is evil and without justice, while our own violence is found to be just and good. The psychology of legitimate violence requires our being able to attribute to the bad guys or the enemy evil intentions and motives. Because they are violent, we are forced to be violent also—and because their violence is evil, our violence must be good. The inevitable conclusion is that if I can find a justification, if I can convince myself that what I oppose is unjust or evil, I am thereby justified in using violence to destroy it. This is precisely the rhetoric and the rationale of the use of violence among student radicals and black militants.

Protest and Dissent

We must be clear about the role of protest and dissent in social processes. The process of dissent, protest, challenge, and innovation is an essential part of human progress at all levels. It is an essential aspect of individual human psychological development, it is inherent in many forms of intellectual and scientific progress, it is a necessary channel by which social structures correct intrinsic defects and adapt to changing conditions of social life. The principle of dissent is an essential part of the democratic process politically. The democratic principle is not only based on the right of the minority to have a point of view different from that of the majority; it includes both the freedom and the political necessity that the minority make an effort to persuade the majority to accept its point of view. There are two important elements necessary to preserve this basic aspect of the democratic process. There must be the willingness and the courage on the part of those who dissent to express their view and to persuade others to accept it. It is also necessary, however, that the majority make it possible for the minority to express its view and that they safeguard the means by which effective dissent can be expressed. Both the minority and the majority have an interest in the expression and effective channeling of dissent.

The protest of students is particularly interesting in this regard. The protest of student radicals runs deep. It is a protest about and a rebellion against some important and basic values which form the essential fabric of our society. However destructive and pathological the means by which students chose to express this divergence, we miss the essential dimension if we ignore that the core issue in their dissent is a matter of values. Youth is not merely objecting to a style of life or a pattern of living in adult society; it is protesting and rebelling against the system of values which govern and guide that adult society. This raises a severe problem in that adults and administrators at all levels, from the family to the larger units of social organization in educational and governmental institutions, can often see their way to discussion and debate over matters of fact, but they are usually unable to see or find their way to debate matters of value. As a result, confrontations turn out to be unsatisfactory on both sides because the real issues are never joined.

The Use of Violence

If protest and dissent have a place in social process, what about violence? The student radical is committed to violence. The rhetoric of radical students proclaims that social injustice is too deeply rooted to permit the reform of our social institutions. They view social institutions as based on the exploitation of the many in the interest of a few. They see such institutions as unjust and evil, as controlled by a concern for nothing but power and money, and as an evil to be destroyed. They see no possibility for reform or change from within. The only effective means for getting rid of such evil and oppressive institutions and the values which govern them is violent overthrow and destruction. They see violent confrontation and destruction by bombings or burnings as necessary for the advancement of the cause they are promoting.

Student demands are often presented in such a way as to provoke confrontation and to elicit rejection. Administrators are often frightened of the threat of violence, and thus yield to student demands through fear. Sometimes they react in repressive and controlling ways. Capitulation through fear or control by force are both ways of avoiding dealing with students as real individuals. Either tactic creates a sense of distance and indifference to them as persons which strikes a deep chord of resentment and rage in many of these young people. Recently a psychiatrist who has had considerable experience in dealing with the complaints of student radicals observed that a significant part of the problem in campus disorders and student revolt stemmed from the fact that university administrators and leaders remained relatively inaccessible and remote from students. Adult leaders remain distant, unavailable, and apparently indifferent to student concerns and feelings. The result is that young people feel that they do not count, that any worth or significance they might have as human beings is being ignored and undermined. They respond with rage and resentment (Nicholi, 1970).

Utopian Idealism

Behind this current of discontent and dissatisfaction there lies a strong ideologically colored commitment to a form of utopian idealism. Erikson (1964) has taught us that ideological commitment is a necessary ingredient in the growth of youth to maturity. But ideology can be put in the service either of inner growth and the confirmation of cultural integration or of infantile needs and the dynamisms of alienation (Meissner, 1970). Social idealism has served as an inspiration and a guiding dream for human social and political aspirations for centuries. But utopian ideals can represent the prolongation of infantile narcissism and wishes. It can come to embody infantile wishes to have unconditional love, protection, care, and freedom from those powerful sources which represent the omnipotent parents. It may also represent the opposite and equally unrealizable wish to obtain such omnipotence for oneself.

For many of today's more fanatical youth, the utopian wish must be responded to and fulfilled immediately—without delay, planning, consideration, reflection, or questioning. They have no patience for the slow process of cultural change, they cannot wait for the plodding deliberation and interaction of positions and interests which constitute the political process, they demonstrate little capacity for toleration of delay and postponement of gratification of their wishes and demands. There is a sense of urgency and immediacy to their often petulant demands. Their rejection of social values and the intensity of their rage lead them to believe that the solution to their frustration lies in the destruction of whatever opposes their demands. The supposition is that if one destroys what one believes to be evil, good will automatically spring up in its place. In the impulsivity of their inner needs and the impetuousness of their demands, they ignore and bypass the essential nature of social and cultural processes (Greenacre, 1970).

The frustration and denial of such pressing inner demands and the deeper narcissistic expectations which so often lie beneath them lead to a sense of inner disappointment and rage. We have seen how the sense of powerlessness, worthlessness, meaninglessness, and social and self-estrangement can easily lead to the expression of frustrated rage. There is increasing evidence to suggest that much of the violent confrontation, which seems so frequent these days, is produced by a relatively small group of alienated individuals who are acting out their infantile needs and wishes in immature ways—lashing out with destructive rage without any constructive plan or purpose. There is no doubt that deeply unconscious, irrational, and infantile wishes are frequently rationalized under the guise of social idealism, and that the frustration of such wishes lies at the heart of the pressure for violent social reorganization. But the analysis of inner psychodynamics does not explain away or substitute for social change. The infantile needs and behavior of a few radicals does not obliterate the need for social change —nor do the conditions in our society which make such change desirable or necessary.

INTERACTION BETWEEN CULTURAL PROCESSES
AND INTERNAL PSYCHODYNAMICS

The interaction between cultural processes and the organization of psychodynamics is complex. The complexity makes it difficult for us to understand how it is that in a nation in which material prosperity is relatively high and in which repressive attitudes and the harsh restriction or discipline of youth has markedly receded, we are faced with growing alienation and rejection of adult social values on the part of so many of our young people. One aspect of the problem was suggested by the Lowenfelds recently:

> The discontent with our civilization has obviously grown in the last four decades. Freud attributed this discontent to the inevitable suppression of drives and hoped that a greater freedom of drives and a greater satisfaction of human needs through technical development might facilitate reconciliation of man with civilization. Yet the liberation has apparently not led to acceptance of civilization; rather in many layers of society, particularly the affluent ones, it has led to an intensification of restlessness and discontent.
>
> Drive liberation, the consequence of the exercise by the older generation of less pressure on the younger generation, has not diminished the conflict between the generations, but heightened it. Sexual liberation and the easier opportunity of sexual gratification for today's youth have not produced a lessening of aggression [Lowenfeld & Lowenfeld, 1970, p. 592].

As Freud had originally proposed in his discussion of the superego, the more externally-directed aggression is inhibited, the more is the aggression internalized and channeled against the self by way of the superego. Conversely, the failure in superego formation may result in an increased tendency to externalization and legitimation of destructive impulses. We are forced to acknowledge that the internal system of drive regulation and direction embodied in the superego is an essential aspect of inner psychic growth and the capacity for adaptive integration with the culture.

Failure in Superego Development

Superego development is subject to multiple vicissitudes in the course of a child's growth to maturity—but one of the staples of positive superego integration is the availability of a stable parental object which offers the child firm, constant, reasonable, and strongly-but-lovingly-reinforced restriction and disciplined frustration of wishes and impulses. If the parental object is lacking in constancy and consistency, or if discipline is defective in the direction either of excessive harshness and repressiveness or of excessive permissiveness and liberality, the internal formation and integration of the child's superego will be defective. The child's need to define himself as a unique individual and to separate himself effectively from his parents requires a firm and unyielding parental object against which he can struggle and from which he can separate. Every clinician and every good parent knows that the rebelliousness of the adolescent may be an unconscious appeal for firm and restraining discipline. The growth-inducing response is to provide a discipline which is effective, appropriate for the situation, and rationally determined. Not to discipline, to leave the young person at the mercy of his inner impulses, to ignore or abandon him, or to respond in permissiveness or out of the fear of confronting his destructive wishes and impulses—these responses are devastating to the child. They are forms of abandonment which both disappoints and deprives the child of what he needs to grow and become the adult he wishes to be. In this light, adult permissiveness and the failure to guide and direct the energies of youth is destructive in its own right.

The behavior of many parents in relation to their children is an appalling aspect of this problem. The history of many alienated young people is one of continually and repeatedly trying to provoke control from the parents—particularly the father—in order to prevent the expression of destructive or self-destructive impulses. The response of the parents can be better described as retreat and abandonment than permissiveness. Such parents characteristically are unable to see their children objectively as unique individuals and are afraid to confront the child's feelings—particularly the hostile and destructive feelings. The child tends to see this inability or reluctance on the part of the parents as a withdrawal or an abandonment. The problem is that the child's feelings and impulses are most intensely stirred when he most needs the support and responsiveness of the parent —and that is precisely the time when the parent best demonstrates his incapacity and reluctance to give the child what he needs. This avoidance of conflict and pattern of parental withdrawal is often rationalized under the guise of closeness or the illusion of good communication. The conflicts avoided and the feelings not directly expressed are regarded as though they did not exist.

A Case History of Alienation

A patient of mine demonstrates nicely the many aspects of the alienation syndrome. His early life-experience was dominated by a highly ambivalent and somewhat symbiotic attachment to his mother. Her mothering took the form of excessive demands on him for performance in the service of her own narcissistic needs, along with rather inconstant but severe punishments for his failure to meet her demands. That highly ambivalent relationship was complemented by his nonrelationship with his father who was a cold, undemonstrative, distant, and relatively uninvolved man. The father spent little time with this boy, never really got to know him, and kept himself quite aloof. Whenever there was any difficulty between the boy and his mother the father would withdraw. The father also worked as a traveling salesman for a time and would spend long periods away from home. The boy saw this as an abandonment in which his father left him to the mercy of his mother's whims. The boy was left exposed to both his aggressive impulses and the sexual provocation of his somewhat seductive—and at the same time punitive—mother.

The story goes on to display the distancing and indifference between this boy and his parents—especially the father. For most of his adolescent years he was boarded in preparatory schools, with little contact from the parents who were living in a foreign country as a part of the father's business. This young man was a college student when he came into therapy. He was a student radical, a leader of one of the radical segments of Students for a Democratic Society (SDS) in his university, and extremely active in student politics. He spouted a highly developed rhetoric which was leftist, idealistic, and suffused with intense feeling. The burden of his diatribes against the national administration, against government at all levels, against the university administration, was that they were motivated by selfish interest in money and profits. They did not care a whit about human needs and the burdens imposed on underprivileged people by the system. Again and again I heard his complaints and rage at authority figures for their indifference, callousness, and lack of concern. He would spend whole hours raging against certain administrators for their lack of consideration and concern for individuals. He expressed his feelings of impotent rage: no matter how violent or destructive one became, one could not change the inevitable operation of a system which used people for its own ends and did not care in the least about how it hurt or crushed people.

It did not take long for both of us to realize that the diatribe was a displacement of his rage against his parents—particularly his father—to the broader range of authority and administrative structures. He was enraged really that his father showed no concern for or interest in him, that his parents' decisions to put him in boarding schools and to abandon him were made with no consideration for his wishes and needs. Further, he saw his parents as the victims of an inexorable capitalistic system which forced them to live abroad and to abandon him out of economic necessity. His rage was thus directed at the whole economic and political system which made such things necessary. The same sense of frustrated hopes and expectations which caused him such rage at his parents was extended into his experience in his student political activity. He was motivated by the constant hope that he could do something effective to change things; the failure to achieve that change and the continuing unresponsiveness of the adult world to his inner needs and demands left him in a situation of continual disappointment and rage.

I will not elaborate the parallels between this boy's relations with his parents and the establishment—they are considerable. But I would like to focus on the therapeutic problem which he and I came to face. We could see that much of his resentment derived from infantile levels and had to do with his rage at his parents. That rage was intense and bitter. But he was too politically informed and astute to ignore some of the real social problems and shortcomings of government and university structure and administration. We could not simply agree that his problem was only one of his own displaced rage against his parents. There were indeed political and social realities which he confronted and which he found lacking and imperfect. The therapeutic task would have been vastly simplified if we had been able to conclude that there was nothing wrong with the social structures, and that the problem was exclusively intrapsychic. The task was to help him disentangle what derived from infantile residues and what was real and reasonable outside himself. Even though difficult, that was at least a possible and meaningful therapeutic task. However, we continually ran up against situations which he found intolerable and infuriating, in which it seemed as though the administrators in his school or the national administration were acting as real replacements for the parents of his infantile projections. Again and again situations arose in which administrators failed to listen to student complaints, acted without student participation or without any sign of regard for student wishes or interests, acted harshly or repressively, etc. The Kent State episode was particularly difficult for this boy who was so conflicted and had to struggle with such pain and anguish to integrate his own destructive rage. His worst fantasies of the destructiveness and lack of concern in the society around him were materialized in the killing of those students. He saw himself in their shoes—the helpless

continuing growth and adaptation in human culture and social existence. In dealing with alienated patients, psychiatrists cannot concern themselves with the resolution of inner conflict to the detriment or undermining of individuality and positive difference. It is in the unique individuality and difference of each human being that his resource for meaningful social contribution lies. However, only to the extent that the individual becomes authentically free—free from the enmeshment in inner conflicts, from infantile impediments and struggles with the projected demons from his own intrapsychic world—can he utilize and constructively direct that inner potentiality.

The therapeutic task, therefore, on both an individual and a social level, is to oppose and eliminate what is infantile and destructive—but at the same time to respect and respond to the ideal. If we destroy the ideal and the faith and the hope which engender it, we destroy something precious in itself and crucial to our own betterment and survival. The crucial question which confronts our society and our culture at the present hour is whether we can eliminate, reject, control, or cure the residues of infantile rage and resentment without at the same time undermining and destroying the ideals, values, faith, and hope which are the lifeblood of society.

REFERENCES

Anis, K., & Conquest, R. A short educational dictionary. *New York Times Magazine,* January 10, 1971.

Bychowski, G. The archaic object and alienation. *International Journal of Psychoanalysis,* 1967, *48,* 384–393.

Camus, A. *The stranger.* New York: Knopf, 1946.

Erikson, E. H. *Insight and responsibility.* New York: Norton, 1964.

Greenacre, P. Youth, growth and violence. *Psychoanalytic Study of the Child,* 1970, *25,* 340–359.

Horney, K. *Neurosis and human growth.* New York: Norton, 1950.

Keniston, K. *The uncommitted: Alienated youth in American society.* New York: Harcourt, Brace, 1965.

Lowenfeld, H., & Lowenfeld, Y. Permissive society and the superego: Some current thoughts about Freud's cultural concepts. *Psychoanalytic Quarterly,* 1970, *39,* 590–608.

May, R., Angel, E., & Ellenberger, H. F. (Eds.) *Existence: A new dimension in psychiatry and psychology.* New York: Simon & Schuster, 1958.

Meissner, W. W. (s.j.) Erikson's truth: The search for ethical identity. *Theological Studies,* 1970, *31,* 310–319.

Merton, R. K. *Social theory and social structure: Toward the codification of theory and research.* New York: Free Press, 1957.

Nicholi, A. M. Campus disorders: A problem of adult leadership. *American Journal of Psychiatry,* 1970, *127,* 424–429.

Riesman, D. *The lonely crowd.* New Haven: Yale University Press, 1950.

III
POLITICAL AND
SOCIAL ALIENATION

Dimensions of
Political Alienation

H. MARK ROELOFS

H. Mark Roelofs, who is professor, department of politics, New York University, received a B.A. degree from Amherst College in 1947, after which he studied in England, receiving a second B.A. degree from Balliol College, Oxford, in 1949 and a B.Litt. degree from Oxford University in 1950. Prior to coming to New York University, Professor Roelofs taught at Colgate University from 1950 to 1952, and at Cornell University from 1952 to 1958. During the fall semester of 1954 he had a Fellowship from the Fund for the Republic, and another in the spring semester of 1958 from the Rockefeller Foundation. Since 1965 he has been the Director of the Metropolitan Leadership Program in the Liberal Arts at New York University, an experimental "college within the College" program, funded by the Danforth Foundation and other sources. Professor Roelofs is the author of two books: The tension of citizenship *(1957) and* The language of modern politics *(1967)*

Political alienation, especially in America, is but one aspect of our general alienated condition. I will have to refer constantly to this larger problem and, in the end, will have to show how our special focus is linked to alienation in general.

The method of the paper will be to work almost exclusively at defining terms. To do that task well, in the present context, will be no mean accomplishment. Alienation, in all its forms, is a notoriously complicated business. Moreover, to define a term is to shape a concept so as to grasp at experience —that is, to define a term is to make it possible for a question to be asked; and, in any line of inquiry, to determine with precision the *right* question is always the first, and often the most difficult, step.

The paper will proceed first by attempting a definition of alienation as a general concept referring to a range of problems which have been mainly characteristic of and significant for advanced industrial societies of the Western European sort during the past fifty to one hundred years. Political alienation will be derived from this general concept, and be itself then subdivided into three subtypes of increasing severity—particular, systemic, and absolute. The field of reference for these subtypes will be primarily the American political experience.

GENERAL CONCEPT OF ALIENATION

There are philosophers, especially those existentialists stressing the paradox and ambiguity of human action as derived from Hegelian perceptions of nature's dialectical inconclusiveness, who see man's alienation as rooted in his simply being alive. In this light, the abolition of alienation can be brought about only by death; death, for this reason, may be more or less eagerly sought. Regardless of this view of the matter, there is, at least, another emphasis in Hegel, the acknowledged founder of modern concerns about alienation. Alienation in this other emphasis is still rooted fundamentally in Hegel's large notion that life proceeds through thrusts, contradictions, tensions, leaps, and resolutions, but this is seen now as descriptive explicitly of the history of civilization. Alienation, therefore, is now not only essentially a social condition; it is also, by being social, malleable. The alienated man is one who, resistingly, has been crushed into his condition. More important, overcoming alienation is a triumph of life. Alienation is, in fact, any condition falling short of life's transcendent goal, the achievement of concrete freedom which, according to Hegel, consists in this:

> that personal individuality and its particular interests not only achieve their complete development and gain explicit recognition for their right (as they do in the sphere of the family and civil society) but, for one thing, they also pass over of their own accord into the interest of the universal, and, for another thing, they know and will the universal; they even recognize it as their own substantive mind; they take it as their end and aim and are active in its pursuit [Knox, 1942, p. 160].

It is an assumption of this paper that our contemporary concerns for the degrees of political alienation prevalent in America today go back ultimately to this Hegelian conception that alienation is in some sense an unpardonable blockage of life's possibilities, and to the equally Hegelian hope that life's possibilities finally consist in highly complex notions of a fulfilling union in society between particular self and universalized other.

Marx, prophet of the charge that alienation diseases capitalistic societies to the core, based his thinking on this same positive idealism about life's possibilities. For him, man was essentially active, a producer confronting nature, but also always in potential an artist who would through the object of his creativity knowingly fulfill his own particular capacity in the context of his social needs and resources. Capitalism's systemization of mutual selfishness negates all that. Men work, grotesquely, not for themselves but for other men's money, and mostly in tasks so routinized that the object of labor bears only a minimal and stagnant relationship to the laborer's artistic potential.

> What constitutes the alienation of labour? First, that the work is *external* to the worker, that it is not part of his nature; and that, consequently, he does not fulfil himself in his work but denies himself, has a feeling of misery rather than well-being, does not develop freely his mental and physical energies but is physically exhausted and mentally debased. The worker, therefore, feels himself at home only during his leisure time, whereas at work he feels homeless. His work is . . . not the satisfaction of a need, but only a *means* for satisfying other needs [Bottomore, 1963, pp. 124–125].

From these quotations—the Hegelian expressing an extreme positive and the Marxian an extreme negative of a shared idealism—the major features of the contemporary alienation-concept can be extrapolated. The most obvious of these, that alienation represents a failure of ideal achievement, barely discerns the concept's surface. Profoundly, the concept postulates a separation between particular, individual man as an actual existant and, on the other hand, an objectively real but idealized possible man, what Marx called man's *species-being*. Whether this division of human experience makes Hegel and Marx as in some way essentialists is a hard question. What is beyond dispute is that for them, and for all of us who travel in their tradition by using this most notable of their concepts, man in his actual, daily existence, and by his efforts there, projects beyond the measure of his mundane accomplishments a vision of what he might be, which commands the same degree of historical power as any of his actual achievements.

The second major feature of the Hegelian–Marxian alienation-concept is that our failure to achieve our human possibilities is not an individual affair. We are all crushed, for we are all victims of the structure of our particular social and historical situations. The fault lies not in ourselves but in our societies.

POLITICAL ALIENATION

Alienation's final major feature springs directly from its second. Because of alienation's social causation, our individual emotional response to it consists of feelings not of guilt and remorse but of anxiety and despair. We are caught in history's jaws and compelled by forces we cannot control to act out lives of self-debasement.

Political alienation is a particular application of this vision of man's forced self-estrangement. Comparably, there are problems of economic alienation, educational alienation, cultural alienation, and so forth. Political alienation is an especially acute problem in democracies because, there, bringing every citizen into the political process is a broad social goal and the estrangement of the citizen from the political process must be seen as a particularly sharp affront to suppositions about man's being a political animal. Democratic political alienation therefore represents both an institutional failure and a sundering of each citizen from one of the highest visions of his own possibilities, that of himself as an active, intelligent participant in the most self-conscious domain of communal life. When this loss of selfhood is strongly felt, as it apparently is in the United States, the result must be more than moods of anxiety and despair. These moods will spill back into prolonged periods of privatistic apathy, or forwards into outbursts of public, but individually meaningless, acts of violence—that is, in either event, into patterns of social disintegration.

In this light, the subtypes of political alienation can be distinguished sharply. It will be seen that each of them exhibits, in a particular way, the major features of alienation generally. Each will posit a distinction between an actual self and an ideal self from which it is estranged, each will see this estrangement as a consequent not of personal fault but of social conditions, and each will show itself as yielding, therefore, feelings of impotence rather than guilt.

Particular Alienation

Particular alienation can be defined as that condition in which an individual or class of individuals feels locked out of a particular aspect of the established social and political system, and for no good reason. Examples of this kind of alienation in America today spring to mind: blacks, educated middle-class women, Jews and other ethnic groups, even intellectuals and similar persons if they become known to have strong and critical views of their country. These examples underline the fact that the affected individuals have a clear vision, in each case, of that social self which they might otherwise be. The black wants to own a home, send his children to school, vote, and obtain employment on the same terms his white neighbor now enjoys. The woman believes she is barred from a professional position in which, all too obviously, a man now sits. The social critic believes himself a more sincere and far-seeing patriot than precisely those super-patriots who suspect him of treason. And he believes he should be heard, in the system and by it.

As clear as the roles from which the particularly alienated are excluded are the reasons for the exclusions. They are deeply and broadly social. America is a racist society, permeated by male chauvinism, and dominated by a provincialism which rejects outright all serious efforts at self-criticism. Against such forces the individual alone is powerless. He—or she—must organize and campaign; then, over a long term, educate the nation into new patterns of social consciousness. In the interim, rage is the only outlet for the individual.

Systemic Alienation

Serious and painful as particular alienation is, systemic alienation is worse. Its conditions are more profound and are ineradicable. Moreover, being both broader and deeper, systemic alienation for the people suffering from it is far more difficult to comprehend. In this condition, the individual's disillusioning experiences have proceeded so far that he moves qualitatively from being unhappy about this or that particular aspect of the sociopolitical system in which he finds himself to wanting to give up on it totally. He is or has been in, at least partially; now he wants out—altogether.

It is easy to trace the development of this dimension of political alienation in terms of the same examples used above with particular alienation. The black, as can be seen, albeit variously and to differing extremes (in the careers of Malcolm X, Martin Luther King, and James Baldwin, for example), comes to perceive that the racism which discriminates against him is not only a prejudice of society but is also constituent to it. Blacks, in America, exist to make white men white, to make them what they are. The educated woman, through "consciousness-rising" sessions and reflection, will learn in time that her condition is rooted in a broad range of attitudes and institutions permeating every aspect of sex and sex-related activities in our society. In a phrase, the liberation of women will require also the liberation of men.

More narrowly and politically, the social critic, agonizing over this nation's involvement in Vietnam, for an instance, and ingesting all that has been revealed, especially recently in the *New York Times,* about the process through which that involvement developed,* must conclude more than that the disaster there was the result of bad policy-choices. Analysis, in fact, must even point to conclusions more ominous than that the process was marked at every critical stage by duplicity and myopia. The ultimate conclusion which must be reached is that throughout the process, within tolerable limits of human performance, the people concerned, from the president on down, by and large did their duty according to their particular positions in the political system as these might be illuminated by a fair reading of the values and policy-drives of the American political tradition. Arthur Schlesinger, Jr., remarked several years ago that our involvement in Southeast Asia was the consequence of what he called "a politics of inadvertence." Nothing since revealed disturbs that basic judgment. But its implications are dreadful. If that is how we got into Vietnam, how will we get out? More to the point, what does all this say about the character of our political system? Is debacle, both military and moral, an inevitable product of the system's normal operation?

The systemically alienated are compelled to give up on the established political environment in which they find themselves because, once the system as such has been indicted, there can no longer be any thought that within it there may be somewhere a perspective to which one can talk reasonably and from which one might hope for a sympathetic, understanding response. Political life, in the sense both of the democratic ideal of "government by discussion" and of personal fulfillment through participation in communal self-rule, is precluded. The idealized self from which the alienated individual is now cut off is, no doubt, vaguer and more generalized than is the case with instances of particular alienation. But as an ideal, it is no less real and is certainly endowed with a more transcendent significance. And the denial of its reasonable possibility must bring on, for expectations both individual and social, an overwhelming collapse of hope. There is nothing for it now save revolution, the only conceivable way out for the systemically alienated.

Absolute Alienation

But the prospects for revolution in America are dim to the point of being unthinkable. With that thought our argument goes beyond systemic alienation and arrives at the category of absolute alienation. To introduce it as a possible attribute of American political experience, this example will be presented.

* This is a reference to the Pentagon Study of U.S. Involvement in Vietnam, publication of which started in the *New York Times* the week prior to the Institute.—Ed.

In 1965, a production was staged in London of Bertolt Brecht's *Mother Courage* (Brecht, 1961). The presentation was forceful, and the play's theme, drawn clearly from a Marxist understanding of history, was well stressed. Mother Courage, a bourgeois-minded camp-follower helping to supply the armies fighting the endless wars of her time, was shown in situation after situation as a woman compelled by forces she knew nothing of to abort every effort at emotional self-expression and to reduce every joy and tragedy of her life to a miserable transaction in petty cash. If the production itself had not made this theme clear, the program notes, written by Eric Bentley, would have. Bentley was in fact at pains to contrast the London production to an earlier New York staging, one which had been recorded in the press there as a critical failure despite its having had a star-studded cast led by Anne Bancroft. The New York producers, Bentley argued, and the New York critics as well, fundamentally misinterpreted Brecht's theme. They saw the play as a study in individual courage, a work celebrating one woman's heroism in the face of events. Despite flawing ambiguities in the central character's presentation, the Americans did feel that the play came to a fitting climax in the final scene in which Mother Courage, having lost friends, family, and fortune, nevertheless picked up the tongue of her store wagon and, with the perseverance of Job, soldiered on into the darkening stage. Bentley noted that Tennessee Williams was so moved by this bit of theater that he had said that he wished he had written it himself.

Bentley's conclusion was that the Americans had misread Brecht's play and forced upon it this "Oh! Pioneers!"-type interpretation simply because they were adverse to seeing the Marxist theme in it. William Appleman Williams (1964), in *The great evasion*, would carry the argument further. Americans must evade Marx because to confront him would be to admit him into our midst as a singularly well-qualified critic of our capitalistic civilization. But the argument can be pressed further still. It may be that we cannot admit Marx—or any other similarly sensitive thinker about the broad nature of historical and social change which might accompany a genuine American revolution—because we do not see him at all. We may hear, off stage as it were, his critical thunderbolts but we cannot comprehend any of the basic terms in which they are advanced. Dominated by the thought-parameters of our national, limited, and petrified Liberal tradition, our range of political concepts is so narrow that we have no capacity to do anything except to translate Marx, everything that Marxist thought has touched, and, as a matter of course, all our own social problems and aspirations, into terms standard and comprehensible to ourselves. And these terms know nothing about the problems of social class, structure, and power which Marx wished to discuss. Our national political thought-patterns remain with the Declaration of Independence, from which we have not moved because in it are none of the large, social concepts necessary to any engineering of social change.

As a result, the American black man, the American woman, the American social critic, not to mention America's disoriented youth in whom some place so much confidence for transforming the nation—all see their problems in terms of clichés about individual rights and the need to purify and preserve the principles of free government. At bottom, it is more important to note that these people are Americans, than that they are individually black, female, critical, or young. For all of them, regardless of their objective situations and the systemic alienation thereby engendered, revolution, except in the self-conserving, one-dimensional terms in which we fought our own, is an unthinkable thought. If it is said that revolution, in the sense of a radical, social, and political restructuring of our established values and institutions, is for Americans the only way out, then it must also be said that revolution in that sense is beyond our communal intellectual reach. Our alienation from what we might otherwise become, an America purposefully on the way toward radical self-regeneration, must, therefore, be called absolute. We are condemned to think not as men might but as Americans do.

SUMMARY

The passage from particular alienation through systemic alienation and on to an alienation called absolute, because in it men are denied even the possibility of thinking themselves out of their problems, has been shown in this paper to be a logical development and, for the American environment, perhaps also a natural one. But it should be pointed out that this final dimension of political self-estrangement returns us to the concept of alienation generally. The ideal of concrete freedom, once again, is that in it men would be enabled, in thinking and willing and gaining explicit right and recognition for their individual interests, to think and will and give explicit right and recognition to the needs of all men. That is, in the first analysis, a political ideal. But Americans are denied access to it not through political failure. Theirs is ultimately an intellectual incapacity. They are therefore to be seen as ultimately estranged from the ideal of manhood itself.

That is a harsh judgment and the bias of the paper is obviously in its favor. But the declared purpose of the paper remains controlling, to construct in series the categories of political alienation. In their construction, very considerable foreknowledge of what their possession would enable us to grasp and measure was employed. The paper has been, it is hoped, illustrated profusely. But the accurate application of the dimensions of political alienation to the American political experience has not been in any way systematically attempted here, either analytically or empirically. So far, only a few tools have been set out.

REFERENCES

Bottomore, T. B. (Ed. & trans.) *Karl Marx: Early writings.* New York: McGraw-Hill, 1963.
Brecht, B. *Seven plays* (Ed. E. Bentley). New York: Grove Press, 1961.
Knox, T. M. (trans.) *Hegel's philosophy of right.* New York: Oxford University Press, 1942.
Williams, W. A. *The great evasion.* Chicago: Quadrangle Books, 1964.

Alienation among Minority Groups

MADELINE H. ENGEL

Madeline Helena Engel received her A.B. degree from Barnard College in 1961. She then came to Fordham University for graduate work in sociology, receiving her M.A. degree in 1963 and her Ph.D. in 1966. Dr. Engel is currently assistant professor of sociology in Lehman College, City University of New York, and a research assistant in the Institute of Social Research at Fordham University. She is also assistant editor of International Migration Review. *In 1971 she was the author of one book,* Inequality in America, *and co-editor (with S. M. Tomasi) of* The Italian experience in the United States. *Dr. Engel is a member of the American Sociological Association, the Eastern Sociological Association, and the American Criminological Association. In private life she is Mrs. Thomas P. Moran.*

> Burn, baby, burn!
>> Kill the Pigs!
>>> Power to the People!

These three phrases, now common in the streets and mass media of the United States, reflect one type of response to alienation among minorities. It is the most extreme, to some the most frightening, and to others the most

94

hopeful form. Moreover, it is the form which interests us in the present discussion.

ALIENATION: A THEORETICAL ANALYSIS OF ITS ROOTS*

If we look at the work of Marx, Weber, or Durkheim, we see that European sociologists have long been interested in alienation (Naegele, 1957; Bell, 1959).

For the most part, however, American-trained social scientists tended to ignore the concept, seeming to think that it belonged exclusively to the realm of the psychologist, whose theoretical framework allowed him to analyze best the lonely, cowering figure in the corridor of the mental hospital, the staggering derelict on the Bowery, or other alienated individuals.

It was not until the problems of workers were brought to our attention by the trade-union movement that we began to conceive of alienation as something which characterized groups, as well as individuals. It was not until this time, therefore, that American sociologists became noticeably interested in the phenomenon of alienation and its roots (Bonjean, 1968; Morgan, 1921; Ross, 1918; Tanner, 1908; Tead, 1917; Dubin, 1956).

Although the influence of classical theorists is still evident, particularly in the writings of Merton or C. Wright Mills, today's theorists have greatly modified and elaborated earlier conceptualizations of alienation (Mills, 1956). In so doing, they have focused attention upon four different types or forms of the phenomenon, each stemming from a slightly different root and each producing a different response on the part of affected individuals or groups (Dean, 1961; Nettler, 1957; Pappenheim, 1959). To be specific, theorists now speak of meaninglessness, normlessness, isolation, and powerlessness as the varieties of alienation common in our society (Seeman, 1959). Of these, only isolation and powerlessness are relevant to an analysis of minority groups and their current reactions to the American scene.

In speaking of isolation, we mean that modern man feels divorced from nature, God, his community, and the major social institutions which at one time constituted the basis for his social relationships and feeling of belonging in the society (Josephson & Josephson, 1962). We would emphasize that modern man not only *feels* isolated but *is* isolated. In other words, the isolation is a realistic factor and not merely the product of a fruitful, even paranoic imagination.

In the first place, man is now separated or isolated from nature. He does not enjoy a sense of relationship with, let us say, wildlife. In fact, while

---

* The theoretical orientation for this paper has drawn heavily from Josephson & Josephson (1962) and Seeman (1959) for its view of alienation; and from Marden & Meyer (1962) and Engel (1971) for the perspective on minorities.

thinking that he has scientifically mastered his environment, he has actually all but declared war on it, as is evident from the current ecological crisis. Rising incidents of air and water pollution, deforestation, and the destruction of species of fish, animals, birds, and plants amply document this point.

In the second place, modern man senses his separation from the deity. In our highly secularized society, fewer and fewer people attend religious services. Furthermore, such attendance, if it serves any function, is for many people a way of keeping up with the Joneses or meeting suitable potential mates and business contacts (Herberg, 1955).

Next, man is now often devoid of communal ties, especially in areas where integrated, high-rise apartment complexes have replaced small, homogeneous neighborhoods (Nisbet, 1953; Stein, 1960). In these areas, for example, branches of supermarket chain stores have replaced the familiar corner butcher, candy-store owner, or grocer specializing in spumoni, chitterlings, tamales, or gefilte fish, and ready to greet his customer by name, as a friend.

Lastly, men in our society have lost their ties to the major institutions which were once significant in their lives. Some years ago, the family, for instance, changed from a large, extended kinship group to a small, relatively isolated conjugal unit, consisting of husband, wife, and children. Today that small unit is threatened by a divorce and desertion rate that affects one out of every three or four marriages, by a generation gap which renders dialogue between parents and children all but impossible, and by a technology which allows people to live longer, retire earlier, and find themselves outcasts abandoned to old-age "homes" by their families. If religion and the family no longer function effectively to provide people with necessary linkages into the social system, then they must look to the other major institutions—namely, the economy, education, and politics.

Let us consider the economy first. Men leave their homes daily to go to work, returning only after eight hours on the job and one or two more spent in commuting to and from it. They see little of their children, who spend the day in school or with their mothers, unless, as is becoming more common, the mother works too. On the job, men and women alike find themselves using the company's tools to perform one small task in the manufacture of an end-product which they may never even see, in which they sense no pride, accomplishment, or vested interest. Just as local storeowners gave way to supermarkets, craftsmen yielded to automation and the assembly line, and individual professionals blended into law firms, medical groups, and huge universities to which hundreds or thousands of clients, patients, or students are no more than a sea of faces. What is worse, many people (5 per cent of the whites and 10 per cent of the non-whites) are unemployed, and millions more are underemployed. These people at the bottom of the heap are even more isolated from the institutional complex and mainstream of the society than are the workers and consumers previously described.

So much for the economy as man's linkage with the social system. But what about the educational institutions with which he is in contact? Our schools are fast becoming crowded, large-scale bureaucracies which function to adjust children to the *status quo*, to assimilate them rather than to educate them or to teach them *how* to think. High suicide rates, riots, boycotts, cries of irrelevancy and non-negotiable demands by students tell us that the educational institutions of our nation have failed—failed to win the conformity of their charges, to relate to them or become a meaningful element in their lives. Our increasing drop-out rate, so significant in fostering "social dynamite"—youths out of school and out of work—is another sign of the failure of schools to relate to the young or involve them in the fabric of society (Conant, 1961).

This leaves only politics as a major social institution which could integrate people into American society. To the extent that people feel unable to influence the slate, platform, voting, or candidates of a given party, they feel isolated. To the extent that they also feel that the federal government is "taking over," they feel not only isolated and alone but powerless to change their position. There are few bosses or ward machines to negotiate the system for them, to act as liaison with it for them, to get them jobs, to mourn with them, or to rejoice with them. The elite, the "Establishment," has taken over—or so many people think (Levin, 1960; Mills, 1956; Thompson, 1960; Dean, 1960; Horton, 1962; McDill, 1963).

The question of power mentioned in the preceding paragraph merits special attention. Power is displayed in many ways, as is powerlessness. One is in the political realm where voting or not voting affects your ability to make the government respond to your needs. Power is also evident in the economy, where a boycott can force a given store to lower its prices or serve minority-group customers. Similarly, it is obvious in the threat of a riot or a labor strike.

The power of a group refers to "its ability to cope with and manipulate its environment; to form workable links with other groups; to manage and own the institutions which affect its everyday life; and, finally, to control the decision-making processes that govern the lives of its members" (Engel, 1971, p. 29). This means that the power of a group determines its ability to deal with other groups and major bureaucracies, such as schools, courts, departments of welfare, and police departments. Powerless groups are at a disadvantage because "they cannot control their own lives; powerless groups are treated as if they were inferior because they have no way of correcting the situations" (Engel, 1971, p. 29). Most groups are aware of the importance of power and perceive their relationship with or isolation from the larger society in terms of it.

The power of a group, as we have already noted, lies in its ability to influence the people and situations which confront it. This power stems from the group's recognition of its common prideful identity and a set of common needs incorporated into the structure of an organization which can give purpose and direction to its individual members. If a group has no sense of identity, no pride in its identity, or no organizational base from which to operate, it will feel and will be powerless. It will continue to be treated as if it were not the equal of the powerful, and, therefore, will continue to feel alienated from the powerful who soon become equated with the Establishment.

In our society, men must face automation, bureaucratization, depersonalization, almost dehumanization—John Smith has now become # 196–43–0290. But what is worse, some men must face these things without the support, the sense of belonging and power that comes from social ties. Thus, they are like detached cogs in a machine, peripheral to its inner workings. Many of them begin to feel like robots, whose lives are being fed into a computer; they feel segregated, unsatisfied, powerless in the face of mounting challenges.

Obviously, not all men are alienated or, more important, severely alienated. Minority groups are more frequently and more severely locked out of institutions than are other people, and their communities are more frequently and more severely devastated—for example, by urban renewal. Therefore, they are more likely than others to feel isolated and powerless. Hence, by definition, they are more likely to be alienated than are other people. Consequently, they are more likely to withdraw from society or threaten its existence, as they have no stake in conformity to norms, a life-style, and a value system, which they feel does not belong to them. In a sense, many minority-group members feel that they have nothing to lose and everything to gain by changing and attacking the system from which they are alienated.

DEFINITION OF MINORITY GROUPS

Most people think of a small group when they hear the word "minority." However, in a sociological framework, the blacks in South Africa are the minority, so size is an inadequate definition of such a group. In general, minority groups have characteristics which are disparaged, while dominant-group members have those which enjoy high prestige. Members of the dominant group hold high political offices and economic statuses, live in the nicest areas, and enjoy social advantages, including the best education available, the most luxurious material possessions, and preferred treatment before public bodies. Whatever the dominant group says, does, or thinks, society accepts as right, proper, and normal. This group, then, sets the standards for the society as a whole. Any deviation from the dominant group in terms of physical appearance, behavior, or ideology is criticized. The dominant group, which in our society is a segment of the WASP (white, Anglo-Saxon, Protestant) group, acts to preserve its privileged position and to keep other groups less prestigious and less powerful.

The basis for the inequities which eventually contribute to the alienation of some isolated, powerless minority groups is visibility, in either the physical or cultural realm. Most people think of their own physical attributes as the best and consider all other physical attributes inferior. The traits most highly prized in our society are those of the Nordic Caucasian. Where differences from these are perceived, we speak of biological visibility. While the man in the street may speak of physical differences—for example, in skin color, eye color, eye shape, facial feature, hair color, or texture— as differences in "race," the scientist does not. Social scientists prefer to avoid the technical label altogether or to use it only in a limited way—namely, to refer to distinguishable, aboriginal groups which have maintained a biological integrity and avoided contact with all other groups. Scientifically, a race is distinguished by its genetic composition and blood type; characteristics clearly not visible to the human eye. In everyday parlance, a race refers to what is actually a *social* category consisting of people who share a particular skin color. Objectively, it is impossible to establish the physical or intellectual superiority of one race over another. However, this does not prevent Americans from thinking, talking, and acting as if people whom they label as Negroes were inferior.

While physical difference has been the basis for the greatest degree of alienation in this society, cultural visibility has also been used as the basis for defining a group as a minority and subjecting it to unfair treatment. Often, the language, dress, behavior, or entire life-style of a group has resulted in its isolation and powerlessness. Traditionally, a culturally visible group has been taken to mean an ethnic group or the descendants of immigrants. Today, the term also subsumes groups which, because of their social class, age, religion, or sex, exhibit a life-style at variance with that of the dominant group. Hence, the poor, the young, the aged, the Jews, the Catholics, and the women of this country constitute minority groups. Most subgroups within each minority adhere to a life-style which shares some ways of thinking, feeling, and acting with the dominant group but, simultaneously, exhibits enough variance with the WASP way to be classified as different. These groups have life-styles which have developed parallel to those of the larger society within which they constitute subcultures. Other segments within minorities adhere to life-styles purposely and consciously designed to be different from, in fact the reverse of, WASP ways. These segments, small in size and few in number, are contracultural groups whose alienation is usually extreme and whose views have, of late, attracted a great deal of attention in the mass media.

Once a group is perceived as visibly different, the dominant group acts to preserve its own position and integrity. To do so, it uses the variety of coercive and legal measures available to it, as well as a set of customs. For example, Southern whites had long prevented Negroes from voting by threatening them and forcing them to pay poll taxes or repeat the Constitution *verbatim* from memory. Customs were such in the South that Negroes tended to defer to whites, and, therefore, they rarely challenged the system by appearing at polling places anyway. In general, the strategies by which the dominant group keeps itself dominant are structural moves, chiefly involving segregation, discrimination, and power. The dominant group insures its own position by forcing minorities to live in dilapidated houses and work in low-paying, low-status jobs. They can do this because they have power, while the minority does not. Power here means precisely what it meant in our discussion of alienation. Hence, both alienation and minority status can be defined in terms of powerlessness. However, the two statuses come together only when the minority group, as a group, *senses* its powerlessness. As long as the group's members act as disparate, isolated individuals, or as long as it is unaware of its inability to cope with situations and to govern its own members' lives, the group is a minority, but not an alienated one.

Related to the structural devices available to the dominant group are psychological mechanisms which also help to perpetuate its position. The most important of the psychological mechanisms is prejudice, an attitude directed against all members of minority groups. Prejudice, the tendency to pre-judge, stems from fear of people, lack of or limited contact with them, and consequent ignorance about their ways. Prejudice is enhanced by stereotypes which single out traits differentiating a group from the dominant group. These traits are then used as the basis for the complete characterization of the group and, therefore, as the excuse for differential, unequal treatment. In general, stereotypes are built on the characteristics deemed virtuous in the dominant group. The stereotyped minority is depicted as having too much or too little of the trait which in moderation is prized by the WASPs. For example, in typical stereotypes Negroes are seen as lazy and shiftless (insufficiently hardworking) and Jews and the Japanese are seen as overly ambitious (too hardworking). It is interesting that when members of the dominant group come into contact with a minority-group member who does not fit their stereotype they immediately conclude that the individual is unique; they do not alter their stereotypes. The stereotype is further reinforced if the minority-group member agrees that he is *not* typical of his group. This often serves his own interest, even though it continues to hurt his group's image.

Prejudice is characteristic of poorly educated people, because it is correlated with ignorance about different peoples' ways of life. However, it also stems in part from the need of some people to feel superior, to have a good self-image. In these cases, prejudice is characteristic of those with peculiar personality needs, who choose the nearest, most defenseless group as their scapegoat. Personality plays still another role in prejudice when the person involved has what is termed an authoritarian personality.

Individual idiosyncrasies aside, prejudice also arises and spreads in times of panic. Anxiety and unrest make people susceptible to propaganda and mob-psychology. They then develop attitudes which they would not have had in quieter moments. Growing panic in white communities today comes from the riots, high crime-rates, and the unstable economy which characterize our cities. It has created open prejudice among many who were not overtly prejudiced before the panic.

Mention of the riots leads us to note the last mechanism by which the dominant group's and the minority group's positions are maintained—the vicious circle. Discrimination or white racism was a major cause of the riots (Kerner, 1968). The riots fostered increased prejudice which, in turn, enhanced discrimination and retaliation against minorities. Once established, relations between so-called unequal groups tend to be perpetuated by a series of interconnected institutions which keep the minority disadvantaged.

While the dominant group is using every device in its power wittingly and unwittingly to maintain the *status quo,* the minority has available to it a number of alternative patterns of adaptation. Most minorities choose to accommodate themselves to the ways of the larger society. They assimilate or acculturate. That is, they take on the values of the dominant society and try to live in accordance with them. This is the assumed, preferred pattern of adaptation in our society, despite the lip-service we give to the idea of cultural pluralism. Groups which opt to assimilate are usually not alienated, because they feel that they have the potential to become a part of the system and they feel a stake in its existence and perpetuation. Individual members of these groups may become alienated when they feel that their situation is one of hopeless isolation and powerlessness. However, as long as they remain disparate individuals and do not become part of a social movement, they are more amenable to psychological and psychiatric analyses than sociological ones. Sociologists are more concerned with the minorities or segments of minority groups which openly challenge the system, because they feel that they are not a part of it and because it has alienated them. It must be noted that these groups are small in size and number, but of great significance. They are likely to be militants who are vociferous and, at times, violent. They represent an ideological, moral, and political threat to the society because their life-style is that of a counter-culture rather than a subculture and they have no stake in the *status quo*. In their eyes massive social change can only better, certainly not worsen, their position. They seek that change, perhaps calling it a revolution, attained by means of "liberation." They want to set up a social system which would afford them power and prestige, which would give them a sense of belonging, which would afford the current minority group dominance and the present dominant group subservience. Our general ideas about alienation, dominant–minority group relations and their preservation will now be illustrated; later we will discuss their implications.

THE NEGROES AND THE BLACKS

We all acknowledge the minority status of Negroes in the United States and the fact that they are still, despite recent strides under new, federally imposed legislation, discriminated against in economic, political, educational, and social spheres. While it is true that closed unions, disenfranchised populations, Ivy League college quotas, and private clubs are disappearing, prejudice against non-whites seems to be increasing. Since the mid-1960s, public opinion has swung more and more against ghetto residents who, unlike the young people involved in sit-ins and freedom rides in earlier years, enjoy the support of neither the press nor the public.

Along with discrimination and prejudice, power defines a minority group. Despite the election and appointment of a number of non-whites to positions of significance in politics, business, and education, the Negro community is still unable to control, manipulate, or, at times, even influence the bureaucracies whose functioning affects its members' everyday lives. Aside from isolated efforts at community control, non-whites do not own or manage the corporations, schools, courts, departments of welfare, or police precincts whose administrators and staff reflect the culture of "the Man" and act to protect *his* interests.

Still, most non-white groups are not alienated; they continue to believe in the American dream, thinking they can make it in the system, if they just try a little harder to look and act like the whites. Many still use hair-straighteners and skin-lighteners, thinking these will help their efforts. Most continue to assimilate the ways of the white world, hoping that by doing so they will become acceptable and will be able to achieve a higher socio-economic status. The vast majority of Negroes are not alienated. However, a relatively small group has arisen within the Negro population as a distinct entity with a life-style all its own. This group, the Blacks, is alienated. It recognizes the power imbalance in our social system and has decided to do something about it, whatever the costs. While we have no precise statistics on the number of Blacks in the country today, we do know that, as compared with Negroes, they tend to be younger, northern-born, ghetto-raised, and relatively well educated (that is, they have attended and perhaps completed high school or college) (Kerner, 1968).

Negroes, comprising an older, more passive, traditionally reared, and southern-born group, are often as shocked as whites by the attitudes and actions of the Blacks. However, with each passing day, more and more Negroes are becoming adherents of the Black subgroup whose way of life reflects a unique subculture, one containing many ideological and behavioral countercultural elements.

In terms of ideology, Negroes were, and some still are, attuned to the ways of the late Martin Luther King, Jr. Blacks reject King and passive resistance in favor of Stokely Carmichael, H. Rap Brown, Eldridge Cleaver, Huey Newton, Bobby Seale, Angela Davis, and threats, if not actual use, of violence to achieve their ends. Negroes sought to be absorbed into the existing system, to open its opportunities to their people; Blacks seek to overthrow the existing system and create a new one which would better suit their interests.

The Black movement, perhaps initially better termed an attempted revolution, can only be understood in its sociohistorical context. This necessitates going back to the time of slavery, when white owners destroyed the family stability and culture characteristic of the Africans involuntarily brought to our shores. Family members were sold to different owners; slaves could not legally marry; Negro women were sexually exploited. The Negroes who had the highest status were house servants rather than field hands. Although both statuses tended to become permanent social positions rather than temporary economic conditions, the two groups differed in characteristics. House servants were more likely to be light-skinned, perhaps mulatto, and they personified the shuffling, happy Uncle Tom, Sambo, or Aunt Jemima of the stereotypes now used by Blacks as epithets directed against Negroes who seek to accommodate themselves to "the Man."

During Reconstruction, the Negroes were given liberty but not equality. Their lives remained hazardous and they became even more peripheral or marginal to the society than they had been during slavery. The Negro man, especially in the South, was perceived as a threat, an economic and sexual competitor of the white man, who spared no effort or expense to "keep him in his place." Negro women posed no threat to the whites or their social system. Therefore, they found it easier to get jobs and support themselves and their children, with the result that they soon became accustomed to playing the dominant role in the already weakened, poor Negro family (Frazier, 1939).

If life in the rural areas of the South was bad, conditions in its cities were not going to be much better for Negroes. America was rapidly undergoing urbanization, a phenomenon which in and of itself produces disorganization. For all groups, the indices of family disruption—divorce, separation, desertion, broken homes, illegitimacy—were higher in urban areas than in rural ones. But for the Negro, the contrast was even greater than for the white (Moynihan, 1965). Thus, Negroes who migrated to the cities were likely to be bewildered, confused, and disappointed.

The vast majority (75 per cent) of the Negro population stayed in the South and faced the conditions we have just described, but by 1915 the war gave impetus to a migration to the North in search of employment (Marden & Meyer, 1962). Although there is no doubt that during the World War I years the economic status of Negroes improved, their living conditions worsened for this was the time of the growth of ghettos in northern cities. A second migration occurred in 1940, this time attributable to World War II and the consequent demand for labor in northern and eastern industrial plants. Poverty, ignorance, and color again forced the Negroes into slums which, with each passing year, had become still more deteriorated ghettos. Moreover, practically all institutional life had disappeared within the ghettos, leaving their residents isolated from the larger society and powerless to change their position within it. The absence of effective, large-scale organizations with any but spiritual goals meant that the powerlessness would be perpetuated.

In the late 1950s, a civil-rights movement began to gain momentum, under the auspices of northern-based, bi-racial organizations, including the National Association for the Advancement of Colored People (NAACP), the Congress of Racial Equality (CORE), and the Student Non-violent Coordinating Committee (SNCC). Negroes were making progress, but there were signs that it was too little, too late.

Many important things have happened since 1961, most of which have involved violence. In 1962, legislation was passed to ban discrimination in federally subsidized housing. In 1963 Negroes and whites clashed in the Birmingham march; Medgar Evers, field secretary for the NAACP, was shot; civil-rights supporters marched on Washington; and a Negro church in Birmingham was bombed, resulting in the death of four children.

Violence continued in 1964. Three white civil-rights workers disappeared and several months later their murdered bodies were found in Mississippi. The summer, like that of 1963, was a time of repeated, sporadic riots. Congress finally reacted by passing the 1964 Civil Rights Act, probably more in response to the killings of the three white workers than the gross injustices and injuries sustained by Negroes. In 1965, Malcolm X, a leader of the Afro-oriented Black Muslims, was assassinated by someone within his own organization, showing there were growing power-struggles within the Negro movement itself.

The federal government's answer to increasing racial strife was partly cased in terms of plans for the Great Society, which were to have as little success as the administration's earlier War on Poverty. Meanwhile, the nation witnessed more deaths in connection with the civil-rights movement. Whites became indignant and incensed when a white, northern minister was killed, and many, including church leaders, began to take a more active role in demonstrating for Negro rights. Finally, the ghettos across the country exploded in a series of riots, whose acts of arson, looting, and shooting left scars on almost every major city.

The disastrous Watts riot and others like it were signs of the white man's failure to solve the racial problems he had been instrumental in creating over the last three centuries. They were also signs that he and Dr. King would play less and less of a role in efforts to affect the position of non-whites in this society. The nation went on, horrified by the headlines, but unwilling to do anything constructive about the powerlessness and isolation of the Negroes (Bullough, 1968; Coleman, 1965; Ransford, 1969; Seeman, 1964; Gordon, 1965).

Whites felt secure within the confines of their ethnic enclaves, failing to recognize the extent of despair, poverty, violence, and alienation in the ghettos. They failed to respond because neither their consciences nor their sense of economic, psychological, and physical security was threatened. They naïvely thought that Watts was merely the end of a movement when, in fact, it was also the beginning of a new one—the Black Revolution (Kerner, 1968).

The Black Revolution can be traced at least as far back as June, 1966, when James Meredith was shot, an incident which helped trigger another series of riots. Things worsened the next year when riots were almost everyday occurrences. Militants became spokesmen for tens of thousands of young ghetto residents and a separatist Black group split from the larger Negro community.

The Kerner Commission had no sooner released its findings regarding the riots than white racism reached an all-time high. Martin Luther King, Jr., was assassinated, and another set of riots occurred which in the summer alone, following the Poor People's March on Washington, affected 126 cities. Black militance in the ghettos and on the campuses took on a more violent tone, as seen in the early days of the Black Panthers.

By 1970, massive riots and demonstrations were accompanied by sporadic bombings of selected public buildings and businesses. We also observed new patterns of violence, prime among which was sniper shooting, especially that directed at the police, who are taken by certain Blacks as symbols of white racism, repression, and power.

Whites no longer ignore Black alienation. Instead, they have entered a period of panicked backlash, seeking to cordon off the ghetto, physically, economically, socially, and psychologically, thereby further alienating its residents and making more Negroes become Blacks.

Blacks and their move for power can be the beginning of organization, self-respect, and a prideful identity for them. It can be the beginning of their attempt to gain access to the rewards offered by this society by getting Blacks elected to office, by patronizing Black businesses, and by endorsing the idea that "Black is beautiful," as is the Afro haircut and the dashiki. In its more extreme forms, however, Black Power can mean, and has meant, militancy and violence, often by fringe groups who enjoy little support from the masses. In this case, it can mark the start of a long, bloody, and bitter conflict. In the long run, the greatest physical and economic harm will come to the Blacks themselves, because the police, national guard, and armed forces are controlled by whites. "Law and order" and "crime in the streets" slogans can turn into new ways to keep the Blacks disadvantaged.

The Kerner Commission suggested that we are facing the prospect of a polarization which would leave us with two societies—one black, and one white (Kerner, 1968). White prejudice is clear in voting patterns and new stereotypes which depict Blacks as promiscuous, violent criminals, and drug-addicts. Meanwhile, Blacks are becoming more alienated and more organized. Their chosen targets, besides the police, are Negroes who favor integration, whites in general for their role in rendering Blacks powerless, and Jews in particular, because they symbolize "the Man's" presence in the ghetto as landlord, shopkeeper, employer, school teacher, and social worker.

Powerlessness has been a root of Black alienation; the search for power has been one of its outgrowths. The results of that search cannot yet be predicted. Blacks may find power and wield it to become an integral part of this society; they may attain it and use it to divorce themselves further from the larger society, much like the Amish, Hassidim, and other separatists; they may attain it and use it against those who had put them down; they may not attain it and may go on, increasingly alienated, producing individuals and splinter groups bent on killing a cop a week, bombing a monument a month, or kidnapping a prominent white a season. In the long run, this last choice is unlikely, but for now it outweighs all others, at least in terms of the attention paid to it by the white community, the radical left, and other Third World groups.

If ever there was a time when the alienation of minorities and its roots in the sense of powerlessness and isolation were clear, it is now. The Blacks' efforts at changing their minority status and ending their alienation are cast exclusively in terms of power and the expansion of Black organizations and institutions. Whites would do well also to acknowledge that "power is the name of the game," to quote Meyer Cahane's recent statement.

THE PUERTO RICANS

Besides the Negroes and the Blacks, the most frequently discussed minorities in this country are ethnic groups, immigrants and their descendants

who came to the United States in search of economic advance, political
refuge, or religious freedom. A significant literature has developed in the
social sciences regarding the process by which these groups adopt American
ways and become absorbed into the social system (Glazer & Moynihan,
1963; Gordon, 1964). This literature, usually referred to as assimilation
theory, was originally cast in terms of Anglo-conformity or the rapid
Americanization of immigrants. It emphasized their conversion into people
who, to the greatest extent possible, looked, sounded, and acted like Anglo-
Saxons. Empirical evidence did not support the theory. In fact, data suggested that the more rapid Americanization was forced upon people, the
slower they assimilated to American ways. This early version of the theory
of assimilation was soon abandoned in favor of a conceptual scheme called
the melting-pot theory, which posited that people of many different nation-
alities would come together and melt, fuse, or blend into a common end-
product to which they all contributed equally. Religious and racial ties
were so long-lasting that this did not happen either. Catholics continued
to marry Catholics, Jews married Jews, whites married whites, and so on.
For a while the melting-pot notion gave way to one which envisioned three
or four pots in which all Catholics would blend into one type, all Jews
into a second, Protestants into a third, and Negroes into a fourth (Kennedy, 1944). Finally, those interested in the cultural transformation of
newcomers settled upon a theory which emphasized cultural pluralism or
the perpetuation of the ethnic group, often with its own enclave, and a
life-style which could persist as a permanent subcultural variation of WASP
ways.

Recently, several sociologists have suggested that the adjustment of immigrants to the United States might be better understood in added terms of
power, rather than from the analysis of culture alone (Fitzpatrick, 1968).
It is within this framework that we would like to discuss the adjustment of
Puerto Ricans to New York, as a case illustration of the alienation currently
found within ethnic groups.

Before doing this, however, let us be clear about the ways in which
Puerto Ricans constitute a unique group, unlike the Italians, Irish, Poles,
Russians, or other ethnic people in this country. Firstly, they are actually
commuters, internal migrants a mere three-and-a-half hours away from
their island home. Secondly, despite differences in terms of their culture,
they are citizens of the United States. Thirdly, they are the "first group of
newcomers who bring with them a cultural practice of widespread inter-
mingling and intermarriage of people of different color" (Fitzpatrick, 1968,
p. 9). Finally, they come to the mainland, especially New York City, at a
time when the movements for civil rights and Black power are at their
height and when automation is eliminating thousands of the jobs which
were once channels for immigrant advancement.

Central to the adjustment and assimilation of an ethnic group is the question of identity, which is less strong among Puerto Ricans than it was among earlier groups. This is attributable to the facts that the island's political status is peculiar and ambiguous, its people have undergone culture shock in the face of recent, rapid urbanization and industrialization, and its church is foreign-run. Thus, politics, culture, and religion, rather than uniting the group as they did for previous newcomers, actually split the Puerto Ricans into subgroups. Moreover, when they arrive in New York their identity crisis is complicated by the problem of color. The Puerto Ricans, while conscious of color, neither discriminate nor make prejudicial judgments based on it the way we do on the mainland (Fitzpatrick, 1959). Furthermore, neither the parish, which is now territorially rather than nationally organized, nor the apartment house, which is now likely to be integrated by law, provides a source of identity for Puerto Ricans as it did for earlier ethnic groups. Without a sense of identity and community, a group is likely to feel isolated and powerless. It would be logical, therefore, to hypothesize that Puerto Ricans in New York are a minority which is alienated, perhaps severely, by the mainland's social system.

That the Puerto Ricans are a minority needs no documentation. They are culturally and physically visible; they are discriminated against, especially if they are dark-skinned; a variety of epithets indicative of prejudiced attitudes is directed against them daily. Despite their position or status, most Puerto Ricans do not seem to be alienated. Perhaps this is because their sense of community and their identity *are* developing, not around culture as for other groups, but around organizational and power issues. "It is possible that their militancy around their interests in anti-poverty programs, education, public welfare, housing, etc., may enable them to develop a sense of identity and community solidarity which, thus far, they have found difficult to achieve" (Fitzpatrick, 1968, p. 17). At any rate, Puerto Ricans have been able to form an amazing number of social, economic, political, and religious organizations (Senior, 1968).

Moreover, they are assimilating into the larger society as quickly as other ethnic groups, as is apparent in their educational attainment, income, and occupational mobility (Kantrowitz, 1968), the rate at which they intermarry with other groups (Fitzpatrick, 1966), and their election and appointment to political office (Senior, 1968). For those who do not or cannot assimilate, as well as for those who feel no sense of belonging or power in this system, it is always possible for $57.00 and a three-and-a-half-hour airplane ride to return to the island. The proximity of their original home and their speed of assimilation have, in many cases, contributed to the existence of fewer adjustment problems and a lower incidence of alienation than might otherwise have been the case.

For some within the Puerto Rican community, however, progress is too slow. They do not yet feel that they are functional parts of the mainland system, or, in other instances, they do not wish to become a part of this system and would prefer to see another created in its place. Those alienated by the system sense the isolation of Puerto Ricans within it or their powerlessness in the face of coping with it. Some of these people choose to return to San Juan; others stay on the mainland and attempt to launch a social movement to correct what they perceive to be problematic about their collective feelings and position. It is this latter group which interests us, but who are its members? Again, as in the case of Blacks, statistics are hard to come by, but we do know that the alienated Puerto Ricans who remain on the mainland and attempt to affect social change, to get their own "piece of the action," tend to be young and dark-skinned. The fact that dark-skinned Puerto Ricans have a harder time adjusting to the mainland is reflected in their disproportionate number of drug-addicts (Berle, 1958), and their sometimes ambiguous position even within the confines of their own homes and families (Thomas, 1967, p. 31).

One of the best indicators of growing alienation on the part of a small segment of the Puerto Rican community has been the development of the Young Lords and their increasing popularity, especially among young, second-generation Puerto Ricans. Their militant demonstrations, seizure of a church in Spanish Harlem, and free-lunch program have made them heroes in the eyes of many Puerto Rican youths. The Young Lords are discontented with society in its present form and seek to change it to their advantage. In a word, they want power—power to manipulate the system, rather than let it grind on, working to their disadvantage. Fashioning themselves somewhat after Black Power groups, who have become models for virtually every other militant minority in the society, their cry is now for Puerto Rican power.

An increasing number of theoreticians acknowledge the relevance of power for an understanding of the Puerto Ricans and other ethnoracial minorities. People whom these theoreticians thought to be biologically inferior in the 1920s, psychologically depraved or mentally retarded in the 1940s, culturally deprived in the 1950s and 1960s, are now recognized to be merely powerless. Much of the theoretical recognition of power is derived from empirical evidence stemming from minority-group movements, like those seeking Black power, Puerto Rican power, and, more recently, Italian power and Jewish power (witness the rise of the Italian Anti-Defamation League and the Jewish Defense League). However, what most practitioners and theorists still fail to realize, or perhaps are merely reluctant to state, is that the powerlessness and isolation which characterize our minorities and the alienated segments of our population are major sociopolitical issues not amenable to traditional lines of analysis. Blacks and Puerto Ricans are not talking about prejudice and discrimination. For them, the issue is power; personality tests, psychoanalysis, and lengthy discussions of culture are no longer relevant. In fact, they will only add to the alienation of the groups under discussion.

If alienation stems from powerlessness and isolation, and minority status is, in part, also defined by powerlessness, then it is fairly easy to see the connection between the two concepts even in groups which are ethno-racially similar to the dominant WASP community.

Moreover, the chief implication of our line of analysis has been that most minority groups pose no threat or challenge to the social system; their existence is entirely compatible with American ideology, which has long focused on the idea of a melting pot, but has given at least lip-service to the ideal of cultural pluralism. However, alienated minority-groups present a different case. They currently pose a dilemma for our society in that they are a product of the ideological inconsistency of claiming that all men are equal and then denying full equality to a variety of groups. If their numbers continue to rise, they will also present a marked political, cultural, and psychological challenge. In terms of politics, their goal may well become revolutionary or, at least, disruptive; culturally they may opt for life-styles more countercultural than subcultural in tone, thereby threatening seriously to affect our mores, customs, and laws; psychologically, if their political and cultural efforts are defeated, they may become more estranged and disillusioned, with the result that some of their members may develop a variety of mental illnesses.

The problem of alienated minorities has a number of possible solutions. One is the removal of the alienated by means of deportation or annihilation. A second is the extensive resocialization of the American people so that they no longer believe that all men are equal or that they should strive to be. A third possible solution is to recognize the sociopolitical realities of the system. This option would allow, perhaps encourage, minority groups to develop a prideful identity and the organizational base necessary for them to function as effective, integral parts of American society. It would mean that society would have to undergo massive changes as it sought to absorb the peripheral and powerless groups which are now locked out or have willingly dropped out of its institutions. The first two solutions demand a change in American ideology which has always pictured this as a nation of immigrants and other minorities to whom it willingly gave refuge and equality. The third demands that Americans behave as if they actually were committed to the ideology to which they now give lip-service.

While society searches for a solution to the problem of alienated minorities, their numbers are likely to continue to increase. Similarly, they are likely to continue to band together to confront the Establishment and its adherents. Without some kind of change, this portends increased violence, culture conflict, psychic frustration, and maladjustment. Alienation among minorities has only recently been recognized. Given the present state of our knowledge, it is impossible to predict the course that alienated minorities will take especially in their efforts to gain power. Thus, it is impossible to predict the results of their actions. Practical, specific solutions to the problems posed by the process of alienation can evolve in time only by means of ongoing dialogue between minority and dominant-group members. This paper is offered as one small step toward an understanding of the process so that alienation will be dealt with in a manner which will be the most functional and least disruptive for all concerned.

REFERENCES

Bell, D. The "rediscovery" of alienation: Some notes on the quest for the historical Marx. *Journal of Philosophy*, 1959, *56*, 83–89.

Berle, B. *Eighty Puerto Rican families in New York City*. New York: Columbia University Press, 1958.

Bonjean, C. M. Mass, class and the industrial community: A comparative analysis of managers, businessmen and workers. *American Journal of Sociology*, 1968, *72*, 149–162.

Bullough, B. Alienation in the ghetto. *American Journal of Sociology*, 1968, *72*, 469–478.

Coleman, J. S. Alienation and social learning in a reformatory. *American Journal of Sociology*, 1965, *70*, 76–78.

Conant, J. *Slums and suburbs*. New York: McGraw-Hill, 1961.

Dean, D. Alienation and political apathy. *Social Forces*, 1960, *38*, 185–189.

Dean, D. Meaning and measurement of alienation. *American Sociological Review*, 1961, *26*, 753–758.

Dubin, R. Industrial workers' worlds. *Social Problems*, 1956, *3*, 61–68.

Engel, M. H. *Inequality in America*. New York: Crowell, 1971.

Fitzpatrick, J. P. (s.j.) Attitudes of Puerto Ricans toward color. *American Catholic Sociological Review*, 1959, *20*, 219–233.

Fitzpatrick, J. P. (s.j.) Intermarriage of Puerto Ricans in New York City. *American Journal of Sociology*, 1966, *71*, 395–406.

Fitzpatrick, J. P. (s.j.) Puerto Ricans in perspective. *International Migration Review*, 1968, *2*, 7–20.

Frazier, E. F. *The Negro family in the United States*. Chicago: University of Chicago Press, 1939.

Glazer, N., & Moynihan, D. P. *Beyond the melting pot*. Cambridge: MIT & Harvard University Presses, 1963.

Gordon, D. N. A note on Negro alienation. *American Journal of Sociology*, 1965, *70*, 477–480.

Gordon, M. *Assimilation in American life*. New York: Oxford University Press, 1964.

Herberg, W. *Protestant, Catholic, Jew*. New York: Doubleday, 1955.

Horton, J. E. Powerlessness and political negativism. *American Journal of Sociology*, 1962, *67*, 485–493.

Kantrowitz, N. Social mobility of Puerto Ricans. *International Migration Review*, 1968, *2*, 53–70.

Kennedy, R. J. Single or triple melting pot? Intermarriage trends in New Haven, 1870–1940. *American Journal of Sociology*, 1944, *49*, 341–349.

Kerner Commission. *Report of the National Advisory Commission on Civil Disorders*. New York: Bantam, 1968.

Josephson, E., & Josephson, M. (Eds.) *Man alone: Alienation in modern society.* New York: Dell, 1962.

Levin, M. *The alienated voter.* New York: Holt, Rinehart & Winston, 1960.

Macisco, J. Assimilation of Puerto Ricans on the mainland. *International Migration Review*, 1968, *2*, 21–39.

Marden, C., & Meyer, G. *Minorities in American society.* (2nd ed.) New York: American Book, 1962.

McDill, E. L., & Thompson, W. E. Status, anomie, political alienation and political participation. *American Journal of Sociology*, 1963, *68*, 205–213.

Mills, C. W. *The power elite.* New York: Oxford University Press, 1956.

Morgan, J. J. B. Why men strike. *American Journal of Sociology*, 1921, *26*, 207–211.

Moynihan, D. P. *The Negro family.* Washington, D.C.: Government Printing Office, 1965.

Naegele, K. Attachment and alienation: Complementarity of aspects of the work of Durkheim and Simmel. *American Journal of Sociology*, 1957, *63*, 580–589.

Nettler, G. A measure of alienation. *American Sociological Review*, 1957, *22*, 670–677.

Nisbet, R. *The quest for community.* New York: Oxford University Press, 1953.

Pappenheim, F. *The alienation of modern man.* New York: Monthly Review Press, 1959.

Ransford, H. E. Isolation, powerlessness and violence: A study of attitudes and participation in the Watts riot. *American Journal of Sociology*, 1969, *73*, 581–591.

Ross, E. A. Adult recreation as a social problem. *American Journal of Sociology*, 1918, *23*, 516–528.

Seeman, M. On the meaning of alienation. *American Sociological Review*, 1959, *24*, 783–791.

Seeman, M. Alienation and social learning in a reformatory. *American Journal of Sociology*, 1964, *69*, 270–284.

Senior, C. The Puerto Ricans in New York: A progress note. *International Migration Review*, 1968, *2*, 73–80.

Stein, M. *The eclipse of community.* Princeton: Princeton University Press, 1960.

Tanner, A. E. Glimpses into the mind of a waitress. *American Journal of Sociology*, 1908, *13*, 48–55.

Tead, O. Trade unions and efficiency. *American Journal of Sociology*, 1917, *22*, 130–137.

Thomas, P. *Down these mean streets.* New York: Signet, 1967.

Thompson, W., & Horton, J. Political alienation as a force in political action. *Social Forces*, 1960, *38*, 190–195.

Alienation in the
Developing Countries

JOSEPH B. SCHUYLER, S.J.

Father Joseph B. Schuyler, S.J., received an M.A. degree from St. Louis University in 1945, and a Ph.D. from Fordham University in 1956. After completing his own studies, he taught sociology at Fordham University for several years. In 1963 Father Schuyler went to Nigeria, where he is currently associate professor of sociology and chairman of the sociology department at the University of Lagos. In 1950, in collaboration with C. S. Mihanovich, he wrote Current social problems, *and in 1960 on his own* Northern parish. *Since going to Africa, Father Schuyler has been a frequent contributor to socio-religious studies on Tropical Africa, particularly on Nigeria. He is a member of the American Sociological Association, the Nigerian Economic Society, the International African Institute, and the African Studies Association.*

"Do you not agree that Christianity, in coming to Africa, has only succeeded in alienating us?" The question came from a sociology student in one of my seminars.

Fred Welbourn, a lecturer for many years in Uganda, recounts a similar plaint with more sensitivity:

One of the undergraduates of my hall of residence was an Ismaili, born and educated in East Africa—but brought up to believe that he and all his

113

possessions belonged unreservedly to a divine Aga Khan living across the seas. On the one hand his family upbringing pointed him away from Africa, made him feel that he could never be more than a stranger and a pilgrim, owing his ultimate allegiance elsewhere. On the other hand—because he had grown up in Africa, been burnt by African sun, drenched by African rains, because he had come to love the maize and the rice and the snows of Kilimanjaro—he knew that he belonged to Africa and that she would never let him go. He lived (still, I think, lives) in this conflict of loyalties and said, quite openly, "I do not know who I am."

There was also an African lecturer. . . . He said, in effect, "I am an African. The political hopes, the political faith of African nationalism are mine. I feel with a large part of me that Christianity is the spiritual edge of colonialism. Yet I have been brought up to be a Christian. In a sense, all my adolescent experience and my adult interests have made me into a black European. The scholarly values, by which I live, are international. They are found far more in the west, which I reject with the political part of me, than in the Africa which I love as my motherland. I think there's such a thing as the African Personality; but I still have to find it. I do not know who I am" [Welbourn, 1964, pp. 1–2].

Evidently Africa is aware of the identity/alienation crisis. The so-called Third World—developing Africa, Asia, and Latin America—knows of the alienation of intellectuals and industrial workers, and of students groping for answers to anomie. What are the dimensions and manifestations of this alienation in developing countries?

Many a time in Nigeria I have been visited by former students who are incarnations of frustration. Graduates, proud parents, well-dressed, their anguish derives from failure—self-defined failure. Mere secondary-school teachers, they despise their jobs and pine for a desk job in the civil service or with some commercial firm. These jobs are not numerous enough, so they are "reduced" to teaching. Though their degrees and salaries place them in the top one per cent of all African society, they are almost physically sick and almost literally die daily deaths, as they think of the amenities and prospects for higher status which mere teaching does not provide. Whether we consider these relatively-high-positioned people, or the primary-school dropouts heading for city employment, or the low-paid marginal worker resenting the elevated status of his more fortunate fellow-citizen, we find many types of the alienated in developing countries.

DIVERSITY OF PEOPLES AND CULTURES
IN THE DEVELOPING COUNTRIES

In view of the great variety of peoples and cultures which constitute the Third World, generalizing about personality-types and life-situations is more than ordinarily hazardous. The expectations' explosion has transformed them. Gunnar Myrdal's mammoth *Asian drama* pleads inability to cope adequately with his subject (sub-title: *An inquiry into the poverty of nations*) because of its tremendous scope and diversity (Myrdal, 1968, p. xiii). But if we use alienation to mean both personal maladjustment and a societal structure which precludes widespread personal fulfillment, it can serve as an umbrella to cover the whole roster of personal and social ills. I know that this is not a completely satisfactory definition, but then the term is ambiguous. Maybe, for our purpose, this is a blessing.

Can one speak of the "African Personality" which is particularly subject to its own kind of alienation?; or of "Asian values"? Perhaps, but not very helpfully. They can be seen to stand for something positive—certain combinations of personality influences, and certain societal responses to environmental and historical contexts. More realistically, President Leopold Senghor's *Negritude* and Aimé Cesaire's "African Personality" (Jahn, 1968, pp. 239–276) are reactions to a history of white domination and poetic attempts to restore the black African's consciousness of dignity.

"Oriental values" likewise expresses a defensive or aggressive reaction to an experience of Western dominance and white men's assumption of superiority. Both expressions, generating more problems than they can possibly solve, are scientifically worthless (Myrdal, 1968, pp. 94–101). Jawaharlal Nehru, cited by Myrdal, says shrewdly:

> Many western writers have encouraged the notion that Indians are other-worldly. I suppose the poor and unfortunate in every country become to some extent other-worldly, unless they become revolutionaries, for this world is evidently not meant for them. So also subject peoples. . . . I won't put it that way, that Indians are "more spiritual." I would say that a static society talks more about so-called spirituality [Myrdal, 1968, p. 100].

ECONOMIC FACTORS

Despite the mass migrations to unprepared cities, nearly two-thirds of the world's population, and a far greater proportion of the Third World's people, are still rural. A high proportion of these latter, despite the revolutions of communications and expectations, are still little influenced by modernization and the call to civilization's blessings. Their problems are often those of hunger, poverty, illness, and the struggle for survival (Myrdal, 1968, pp. 529–579; Roullet, 1963; Mertens, 1963). But without the impassioned knowledge that their lot could be better, they are not the victims of alienation in the subjective sense. Poverty itself is not alienating, but only when accompanied by conviction of its wrongness. One could say (with or without Marx) that a world, a community of peoples, which maintains a social system of such division between haves and have-nots is objectively alienated whether anyone realizes it or not. This raises the question of aid to the underdeveloped—the illiterate, the hungry, those with a life expectancy of 30 years, with an infant-mortality expectancy of over 50 per cent, with an annual per capita income of less than $50.00.

But the painfully alienated are those who want more and cannot have it. Many of those about whom we have just been talking do not know enough to want outside goods and services, and others know enough not to want them. For example, not all people agree that going to school is necessarily good. They find that children who go to school drop out after the most rudimentary training, swell the ranks of unemployed children in the cities, and let their parents' farms go unharvested (Callaway, 1965).* Many are unimpressed, or rather impressed unfavorably, by civilization's religions, politics, industrial pressures, and crowded cities. But there are multiple millions who leave the land each year, move to the cities, take up unaccustomed ways, and enter into the struggle for the better life (Breese, 1969; Mabogunje, 1968).† Often they find one which is worse, but remain with the hope that jobs will materialize, that their children will find non-existent places in insufficient secondary schools, that they too might possess the anticipated fruits of independence. The great personal agony is wanting a job with all it implies and not finding one, thus being useless; the great social deficiency is stimulation of new pressing needs with no provision to satisfy them.

CULTURAL FACTORS

According to Doob, "the most conspicuous psychological fact about Africa is the simultaneous and continuous exposure of Africans to traditional and Western forms of culture" (Doob, 1960, p. 466). Many townsmen have their real homes in the villages, where traditional authorities, rituals, festivities, sanctions, and lifeways retain their loyalties. Many other townsmen seek, more or less successfully, to break the hold of their family ties and traditions (Watson, 1970; Mayer, 1965).

Their successful kinsmen have been Europeanized: is Europe the road to success? Cannot one be truly African and truly developed? Despite a great

* Latest Nigerian data show the extremity of the problem. Some 250,000 youngsters complete their primary schooling each year, and another 400,000 drop out before completion. There are currently only 70,000 places open in secondary schools, and only 30,000 paying jobs in the labor market at the appropriate level. The whole of Nigeria has only some 500,000 employees receiving salary or wages. Despite the abundant supply of cheap labor, industry is not sufficiently expanded to make use of it.

† The Breese volume pays particular attention to all the underdeveloped areas—Africa, Asia, and Latin America—as this brief paper cannot do. The Mabogunje study uses Lagos to exemplify "parasitic urbanism," i.e., the phenomenon of cities which cannot support themselves, whose economic opportunities are not enough for the population. The tragic irony here is that the more jobs created and the more housing supplied, the more unemployed and shelterless or overcrowded people there will be. For, every new job and every new house will attract 100 new applicants.

number of apparently dedicated Christians and Muslims, it is still truly questionable whether the God of Christianity and Islam is indeed the God of many nominally Christian and Muslim Africans; or conversely, whether the High God of the various tribes retains his place (Mbiti, 1969, pp. 229–260; Idowu, 1962, pp. 202–215). Many prominent church-goers have been found knee-deep in political chicanery, their hands deep in the till of bribery and payoffs; the tribal gods would never have allowed this.

Schools produce certificates which win money-paying jobs, but they do not teach Africans how to be Africans. What can it mean to be African in a continent of multiple races, a thousand tribes, as many languages, and different environments, religions, and social classes? How can one be a national when one's tribe remains the most important reality in one's life? Tribes were joined into political entities, then joined to fight for independence, then reverted to rivalry over the treasures of independence.

Independence promised freedom and prosperity. But freedom has not grown, only the masters are different—formerly colonial, now native; prosperity is still the lot of the chosen few. René Dumont entitles one of the chapters of his *False start in Africa* "Independence Is Not Always 'Decolonization,'" describing the new "elite" as "a modern version of Louis XVI's court," and showing how the "life's work of a peasant equals one and one-half months' work (?) of a deputy" or legislator (Dumont, 1969, pp. 78ff.).

SOCIAL FACTORS

The family used to be the core of life (Colson, 1970). A man's prestige came from the number of his wives and children working his farms. Now one wife should be enough, children should be limited, and besides both go off to get money-paying jobs and independence for themselves (Gutkind, 1970). It used to be that families arranged their children's marriages, more or less successfully (Omari, 1965). Now youth has freedom, but the taste is not all that sweet. Families still exercise a veto, and marriage is not what it used to be. Rather than a functional unity in which affection proceeds perhaps in due course, it now tends to be idealized as a marriage of equals in an affectionate companionship. But the definition of both man and woman has been changing, as well as of their respective roles (LeVine, 1970; Aldous, 1965; Jahoda, 1965). Does a university woman still serve her husband? Is a man not to be served? Adjustment is difficult, broken families are numerous. One unpublished survey found 43 per cent of 6,000 Lagos marriages broken or evidently unhappy.*

* I do not wish to imply universal patterns of family structures. In some societies women are quite independent; some marriage systems place no emphasis on affection and companionship; family-arranged marriages are still dominant in perhaps the largest portion of developing countries' populations. The problem, alienative and anomic, comes from moving into unaccustomed life-situations for which there has been no preparation. This is the point of the Simpson (1970) study.

The new elite are not sure of their place (Smythe & Smythe, 1960). They have often studied abroad, and moved into the offices of their colonial predecessors: why should they not have all the compensations and emoluments of their American and European contemporaries? Yet their advantage in income over their less-well-educated countrymen is already in the neighborhood of 10 to 1, whereas the Eur-American graduate or administrator more ordinarily has an advantage of 2 to 1 or 3 to 2 over manual workers. They have claimed or inherited the gigantic task of making new countries grow to prosperity for all. They want to be free of foreign influence, but see that it is at least temporarily impossible. The job is too difficult; system, resources, and personnel are not yet nearly adequate. The anonymous security of the inherited civil service is available.† Meanwhile their underprivileged countrymen resent the patent inequality and demand relief and opportunity. Many Africans and Asians learned their new religion in mission churches and schools. They then went on to universities abroad without preparation to retain or integrate their religion with their intellectual growth, and returned without any systematic religion. Hesitant to respond to nativist challenges, having outgrown the faith of their teachers, they do not know quite where they are or what they believe.‡

Others have joined the flourishing independent churches in dissatisfaction with the established missionary churches (Sundkler, 1961; Turner, 1967; Peel, 1968).

CONCLUSION

In speaking of alienation we are speaking of a problem, of a kind of deformity. Unfortunately we have no consensus on the criterion of due conformity, unless perhaps the satisfaction of something like Etzioni's (1968) "basic human needs," so the cure for the malady cannot be confidently prescribed. Doob (1960, pp. 471–472) makes the point that, although the conflictive pressures on Africans constitutes "a bleak state of affairs" with no foreseeable outcome, their impact on modern Africans is not so devastating. To be depressed one should understand the dynamics and outcome of the conflict, and very few persons—whether in the developing or developed countries—can do this.

Personal adjustments are the order of the day, whether they lead unknowingly to bliss or to chaos. There is evident experience of both. The farmer boy drawn to the city does not know that his first paycheck and

† The civil-servant class in the newly developing societies has been likened to the bourgeoisie in Marxian class-struggle theory. There is basis for the comparison.

‡ Many Africans are comfortably and strongly attached to their Christian or Muslim faith. Whereas there seems to be a great number of marginal affiliates, the reasoned sturdiness of many defenders of their faith—against both the old traditionalism and the new secularism—is a quite edifying phenomenon. For views appreciative and critical of African Christianity, see Schuyler (1968).

housekeys may unlock the Pandora's box not always accurately called civilization. The titles of two of Nigeria's most famous novels (Achebe, 1958, 1960) reflect the tensions of cultural confrontations: *Things fall apart* and *No longer at ease*. In the first, the hero hangs himself in frustration as the white man's world deranges his own; in the second, the hero sinks into anomic degeneracy, again in the context of conflicting values, of the old order yielding to the new.

Humanity's job remains: to find what is good for man and to help him to see it, and to build the kind of society which will enable him to achieve it. Meanwhile, for many, alienation must be commonplace, and anomie is normal.

REFERENCES

Achebe, C. *Things fall apart*. London: Heinemann, 1958.

Achebe, C. *No longer at ease*. London: Heinemann, 1960.

Aldous, J. Urbanization, the extended family, and kinship ties in West Africa. In P. L. Van den Berghe (Ed.) *Africa: Social problems of change and conflict*. San Francisco: Chandler, 1965, Pp. 128–142.

Breese, G. (Ed.) *The city in newly developing countries*. Englewood Cliffs, N.J.: Prentice-Hall, 1969.

Callaway, A. Unemployment among African school leavers. In L. G. Cowan, J. O'Connell, & D. G. Scanlon (Eds.) *Education and nation building in Africa*. New York: Praeger, 1965. Pp. 235–256.

Colson, E. Family change in contemporary Africa. In J. Middleton (Ed.) *Black Africa: Its peoples and their cultures today*. New York: Macmillan, 1970. Pp. 152–158.

Doob, L. W. The psychological pressure upon modern Africans. *Journal of Human Relations*, 1960, *8*, 465–472.

Dumont, R. *False start in Africa* (trans. by P. N. Ott). (2nd ed.) New York: Praeger, 1969.

Etzioni, A. Basic human needs, alienation and inauthenticity. *American Sociological Review*, 1968, *33*, 870–885.

Gutkind, P. C. W. African urban family life and the urban system. In J. Middleton (Ed.) *Black Africa: Its peoples and their cultures today*. New York: Macmillan, 1970. Pp. 181–187.

Idowu, E. B. *Olodumare: God in Yoruba belief*. London: Longmans, 1962.

Jahn, J. *Neo-African literature: A history of black writing*. New York: Grove, 1968.

Jahoda, G. Love, marriage and social change: Letters to the advice column of a West African newspaper. In P. L. Van den Berghe (Ed.) *Africa: Social problems of change and conflict*. San Francisco: Chandler, 1965. Pp. 143–158.

LeVine, R. A. Sex roles and academic change in Africa. In J. Middleton (Ed.) *Black Africa: Its peoples and their cultures today*. 1970. Pp. 174–180.

Mabogunje, A. L. *Urbanization in Nigeria*. London: University of London Press, 1968.

Mayer, P. Migrancy and the study of Africans in towns. In P. L. Van den Berghe (Ed.) *Africa: Social problems of change and conflict*. San Francisco: Chandler, 1965. Pp. 305–324.

Mbiti, J. S. *African religions and philosophy*. London: Heinemann, 1969.
Merten, C. (s.J.) Demographic expansion and world poverty. In A. McCormack
    (Ed.) *Christian responsibility and world poverty*. Westminster, Md.: Newman,
    1963.
Myrdal, G. *Asian drama: An inquiry into the poverty of nations*. (3 vols.) New
    York: Pantheon, 1968.
Omari, T. P. Role expectations in the courtship situation in Ghana. In P. L. Van
    den Berghe (Ed.) *Africa: Social problems of change and conflict*. San Fran-
    cisco: Chandler, 1965. Pp. 128–142.
Peel, J. D. Y. *Aladura: A religious movement among the Yoruba*. New York:
    Oxford University Press, 1968.
Roullet, M. O. The extent of world poverty and underdevelopment. In
    A. McCormack (Ed.) *Christian responsibility and world poverty*. Westminster,
    Md.: Newman, 1963.
Schuyler, J. B. (s.J.) Conceptions of Christianity in the context of Tropical
    Africa: Nigerian reactions to its advent. In C. Baeta (Ed.) *Christianity in
    Tropical Africa*. New York: Oxford University Press, 1968. Pp. 200–223.
Simpson, M. E. Social mobility, normlessness and powerlessness in two cultures.
    American Sociological Review, 1970, *35*, 1002–1013.
Smythe, H. H., & Smythe, M. M. *The new Nigerian elite*. Stanford: Stanford
    University Press, 1960.
Sundkler, B. G. M. *Bantu prophets in South Africa*. (2nd ed.) New York:
    Oxford University Press, 1961.
Turner, H. W. *African independent church*. (2 vols.) New York: Oxford Uni-
    versity Press, 1967.
Watson, W. Migrant labor and detribalization. In J. Middleton (Ed.) *Black
    Africa: Its peoples and their cultures today*. New York: Macmillan, 1970.
    Pp. 38–48.
Welbourn, F. B. *A department of religious studies in an African university*.
    Ibadan: University of Ife, 1964.

IV
ALIENATION
OF YOUTH

Alienation as a
Phenomenon of Youth

WILLIAM C. KVARACEUS

*William C. Kvaraceus is professor of education
and sociology, and chairman of the department of
education at Clark University. He also holds an
appointment as research associate in psychology
in the department of psychiatry, Harvard Medical
School. Prior to joining the staff of Clark University, he was at Boston University (1945–
1963), where he headed the department of special education, and at Tufts University (1963–
1968), where he served as professor of education
and director of youth studies in the Lincoln
Filene Center for Citizenship and Public Affairs.
Dr. Kvaraceus has written widely in the fields of
juvenile delinquency, psychological measurements,
and education. His most recent books include*
Anxious youth: Dynamics of delinquency *(1966),
and* If your child is handicapped *(1969). Dr.
Kvaraceus received his formal education in Massachusetts, taking his Bachelor of Arts degree at
Boston College and both his graduate degrees
at Harvard University.*

Working with youth and studying youth produces many reflections—most
of them disturbing and discomforting. There is little agreement on the
normality and deviation of youthful behavior; most adults dislike and
envy youth; many feel awkward in their presence; few can maintain a
serious conversation with them for any length of time; in any dialogue,

short or long, most adults find youth hard to listen to and even harder "to take." The result is that our perceptions of youth are colored ("tainted" is a better word) by our own myopic needs. Let me illustrate from the highest governmental level.

President Nixon (1971) in his address on youth at the University of Nebraska Convocation, January 14, 1971, declared that "There can be no generation gap in America" and yet urged, "Let us forge an alliance between generations." After listing the major problems facing us in this country, he called for a togetherness in sharing and solving these problems and complained that "There has been too much emphasis on the differences between generations."

More recently, Stephen Hess, after chairing two White House Conferences on Children and Youth, left his post with the public reassurance that "There is no unusual generation gap in the United States at this time" (Hess, 1971, p. 29).

Mr. Hess went on to point out how the experience of the White House Conference on Youth strongly supports the "no-gap" theory. They had set up ten adult–youth task forces in August of 1970. These forces dealt for eight months with some of the most controversial and emotion-charged issues in American life—Vietnam, drugs, racism, etc. Yet there was not a single instance in which the groups voted by age, the youth against the adults. There were ideological differences, Mr. Hess concluded, but not generation differences.

We should not forget that for the first time in 1971 a White House Conference on Youth was safely set high in the Rockies—far from Pennsylvania Avenue. Geographic distance, yes; generation differences, maybe. We will need to ask: "What do empirical studies tell us?" But first let us define our terms and basic assumptions.

DEFINITIONS AND ASSUMPTIONS

Considering the full range of adolescent behavior, we have always had difficulty in distinguishing normal turmoil from pathological processes. Anna Freud (1958) has pointed out that (1) Adolescence is by nature an interruption of peaceful growth, and (2) that the upholding of a steady equilibrium during the adolescent process is in itself abnormal. She concludes: "Where adolescence is concerned, it seems easier to describe its pathological manifestations than the normal processes" (Freud, 1958, p. 275).

Recognizing the "normal processes" to be filled with spurts and stops, with ruts and potholes, today's youth face even greater hazards than previously in managing this difficult period. It is hard to be a youth today.

It is true that "youth never had it so good" but, at the same time, "they never had it so bad." We need to be mindful of the rapid multiplication of hurdles and hazards which must be managed by most youth as they try to maintain their shaky equilibrium.

Today's youth must cope with forces unknown in earlier times. With the knowledge-explosion, compulsory schooling, and credit-pressure, there is more and more to learn, which one must learn faster and faster, and there are better and better tests to see if one has learned anything at all. Except for their role as students, youth can find little or no function in today's society; politically and economically they have been held powerless; they have had little or no leverage with which to negotiate with the adult community; they have been held incommunicado; they have been exploited by the mass media to titillate the adult community with stories featuring their deeds and misdeeds and by the business community or the crime syndicate who would sell them down the river for a fast buck; they have been labeled in pejorative terms and have been used as scapegoats by home, school, church, and law. The popular theme of the day should be: "Ain't you glad you're not a youth?"

In studying alienation as one aspect of youth, we will need to consider how much of the process of alienation is a natural phenomenon and how much an artifact. An alienated youth is one who has become estranged from one or more of the social institutions—family, school, church, work, law. Three component dimensions of the alienation process have been identified by Byles (1969). The measure of alienation of youth in a given system—family, school, church, etc.—is a function of

(1) *affiliation*—either the youth is still a member of a family, is in or out of school, has a job or is out of work, etc.
(2) *identification*—the youth tends either to accept or to reject the aims and values of the family, school, etc.
(3) *achievement*—the youth finds his performance as a member of a given system, school, family, etc., as satisfying or unsatisfying.

The converse of alienation is integration, or the feeling of one's self as a part of something. Alienation and integration exist on a continuum. It is always a question of degree. At the same time, youth can be alienated at home or in school but integrated in some other system such as the world of work.

In studying the youth process we will also need to differentiate among youth. Youth is not a monolithic concept. We will need to differentiate between boys and girls, between upper classes and lower classes, between early- and later-adolescent youth, between city, suburban, and rural youth, between ethnic groups, and between activist youth and the more passiveretreatist subgroups. Unfortunately, the need for differentiating among youth is only now making its impact felt in studies of the alienation process.

SOME EARLIER PROFILES OF YOUTH*

As in the past, the American adolescent is, and will continue to be, the delight and despair of the adult community. We have the adolescent constantly under the microscope. Within the past few years there has been a deluge of books on the adolescent—how to know him, how to get along with him, how to defend ourselves from him. In fact, a quick look at the shelves of the psychology and sociology sections of any bookstore specializing in paperback editions will reveal our almost pathological concern with youth. Youth is a phenomenon which sometimes threatens us, frequently exasperates us, often pleases us, and usually baffles us.

The image of the adolescent has undergone an interesting series of changes in a matter of just a few years. Only a short while ago he was represented as a figure of fun: callow, foolish, given to sudden infatuations, wild enthusiasms, and unpredictable mood-swings. His prototype was Penrod, Andy Hardy, and Henry Aldrich. Or he was sometimes seen as a rather harmless poet: sensitive, emotionally troubled, overly sentimental. In either case the figure was seen as lovable, though sometimes exasperating, and not to be taken too seriously. He would get over it—whatever it might be—in time. Douvan and Adelson (1966) of the University of Michigan call this type of adolescent the *Fool*.

More recently, two new images have supplanted the *Fool* figure, and between them they depict the contemporary adolescent. One of these Douvan and Adelson call the *Visionary* or the *Victimized*. He is distinguished by a purity of moral vision which allows him to perceive or to state the moral simplicity of situations which is obscured by adult complications. He is betrayed, exploited, or neglected by adults, too busy with their own affairs; or as an innocent bystander he may be victimized by adult corruption. The prototypes here are Salinger's adolescents Holden Caulfield or Franny Glass. Whereas the *Fool* is essentially unrelated to the adult world, the *Visionary–Victim* is connected with it, but is passive and powerless.

The antitype to the *Victimized* is the *Victimizer*, leather-jacketed, long-haired and disheveled, cruel, sinister, amoral, smoker of pot. This adolescent stands in direct contrast to the *Visionary* or *Victimized*; one is innocent, the other evil; one is powerless, the other omnipotent.

When any one of us looks at, or perhaps looks for, the visible adolescent, the image is formed through the lens of our personal attitudes and values.

---

* I am indebted to Helen J. Kenney for her assistance in the original study of youth values (Kvaraceus, 1968) and for her contribution to this section and the next.

We will see what to us *is* the visible adolescent—that is, the profile which emerges from a systematic and objective study of what adolescence and the adolescent may be all about. A number of professionals working with and studying the adolescent have produced interesting, and sometimes conflicting, data on the youth of today. In what follows, some quoted highlights of recent writings—necessarily selective but, we hope, representative —will be presented to show the range of current knowledge on the very important issues of young people and their place in modern American society.

EDGAR FRIEDENBERG—"The Vanishing Adolescent"

> I believe that adolescence, as a developmental process, is becoming obsolete. The kind of personal integration which results from conflict between a growing human being and his society is no longer the mode of maturity our society cultivates. We expect—indeed, we usually demand —from adults quite a different sort of behavior than that which exemplifies a well-defined and well-established self [Friedenberg, 1959, p. 203].

KENNETH KENISTON—"The Uncommitted Adolescent"
Keniston asks and answers the question:

> Why should a group of talented and privileged young men reject the basic values of their culture? It is these youth—the uncommitted and the alienated—who see only too clearly the failings, failures, and flaws in American society. They yearn passionately for values and commitments that will give their life coherence and meaning; they seek after, albeit unsuccessfully, the implicit goals of integrated and whole men—openness, creativity, and dedication [Keniston, 1965].*

WILLIAM KVARACEUS—"The Non-Functional Adolescent"

> One of the most hazardous occupations in developed and developing countries today is to be a youth. With the steady and conclusive shift from farm and rural culture to organized and technological society, the importance and function of youth have diminished to the point where youth now represent a surplus commodity on a glutted market. Lacking any important role or function, youth face the problems of growing up in exile or, worse, in nihilo [Kvaraceus, 1966, p. 1].

In order to check out these impressions, as well as those of the White House, let us examine some of the major findings in four recent studies of youth as they relate to the alienation process. These studies include:

* This is a paraphrase of Keniston's thought.—Ed.

Kvaraceus (1968, 1971), Center for Research and Development for Higher Education at the University of California (1967), and Byles (1969).

Under the auspices of the New England School Development Council the youth in five communities engaged in a study of their own values, the values of their teachers, and those of their parents (Kvaraceus, 1968). Two instruments were developed (a Value Scale and an Irritation to Deviancy Measure), and data were gathered, including the adults' perceptions of the values espoused by youth, and youths' perceptions of the values held by adults.

An analysis of the responses of the combined five communities points to the following major findings:

1. The outstanding category of disagreement was found in the area of personal appearance. Youth and their parents and teachers are furthest apart on values related to dress, coiffure, makeup, and cleanliness. This is the major battleground of irritation between youth and adults. Yet any major victory here may not be worth the battle. This is the easiest and cheapest route of rebellion and nonconformity for many youth. Other areas in which youth and adults differ significantly include social behavior, morality, academic behavior, rules and regulations, and aggressive behavior.

2. Very few significant disagreements between youth and their teachers and parents were noted on items related to social consciousness and extracurricular activities. Both youth and adults generally agree concerning the acceptability of values related to these two areas. In contrast to the conflicts in dress, hairdo, and makeup, youth and adults were found very closely aligned concerning such behavior as serving as a volunteer in a hospital, burning a draft card, participating in civil-rights demonstrations, and assisting in political campaigns. The question can be raised whether there is too much conformity with the adult world in this area and whether the ideational adolescent rebel really exists. Perhaps it is here that youth should be helped to dissent, to rebel, and to differ in seeking out more effective solutions to new and difficult political, social, and personal problems. The data suggest that youth tag along too closely on the heels of the adults.

While teachers, parents, and youth agreed concerning the desirability of participating in the school band, serving on the student council, writing for the school newspaper, holding a class office, the youngsters were less sanguine concerning extracurricular activities. They felt that ultimately participation in these activities ran a bad second to the need for high academic grades and good test scores, but they agreed about their inherent worth.

3. In the analysis of youth's perceptions of adult value-ratings and adults' perceptions of the values held by youth, it appears that youths are better psychologists than their parents or teachers. Youths anticipate and "size up" with considerable accuracy the way their parents and teachers will react to deviant behavior. In contrast, adults are not nearly so accurate in their perceptions of the values and attitudes actually maintained by youths themselves. In view of the authority role played by parents and teachers, youth, perhaps out of necessity, have learned to anticipate their parents' and teachers' attitudes and values. How could the adolescent survive otherwise?

4. In comparing the degree to which teachers and parents agreed with youths' own acceptance or rejection of deviant behavior, teachers rather consistently stood closer to the students than did their parents. In other words, parental authority proved to be further away from values held by youth than the more sympathetic posture held by school authority. However, a consistent trend for the adults to overestimate youth's tolerance of deviancy was noted. To restate this finding: Both parents and teachers projected a more negative image of youth as being more accepting of deviant behavior than youth's self-reports indicated.

5. The responses of youth on the open-end question of "the person most admired" revealed that hero-models were drawn most frequently from within the immediate family circle. However, political figures also ran high. Significantly, a very restricted range was noted in the fields from which persons most admired were drawn. Very few authors, scientists, humanitarians, artists, and clergymen were mentioned. The predominance of political figures may well reflect the power and prestige of politicians as reflected in frontpage headlines. It may also reflect the overemphasis in schools on the contributions of the politician as against other segments of the community in the modern world. It is significant that the home still prevails as a place of prestigious and admired personalities which may have more potential in the child's growth-process than some of the more pessimistic observers from the family-life-education field may have believed.

6. All youth say that they value education highly. They see it as the only way out. But all youth also report that school is a boring experience and a source of severe pressures. Their heaviest pressures derive from schools and tests. The worst thing that could happen to them, they say, is to fail in school or to fail to get into a college. School people must face the question: Why is it that school remains a boring ritual to be sweated out?

7. Youth attest to popularity within the group; they have the most fun when they are socializing within their primary reference-groups.

8. Youth perceive adults as autocratic and as provoking to rebellion; teachers perceive the parents as autocratic, lax, and inconsistent; parents agree that they tend to be autocratic and lax, but also state that they are trying

to be helpful. Obviously, there is much to be discussed and reconciled among these three forces.

9. The "secret of success," youth report, is to be found in "education and hard work." To this parents and teachers add "ambition." Some students indicate that there is no "secret to success."

10. All groups—youth, teachers, and parents—responded almost unanimously that "most teenagers are OK." But the youngsters also state that youth are overcriticized and misunderstood. It is true that we have youth constantly under the microscope (as in this study), and it may be that there is in adult preoccupation with youth some degree of adult pathology. Nevertheless, it is refreshing to find the strong and positive response in all five communities that most youth are OK. This says something about the communities as well as about the teenagers.

UNITED STATES SURVEY FOR U.N. YOUTH STUDY

As a part of the United Nations Study on the World Social Situation of Youth, eight minuscule samples of homogeneous youth were drawn representing different socio-economic-ethnic populations (Kvaraceus, 1971). These groups were interviewed by college youth using a four-part questionnaire, in an attempt to ascertain the nature and extent of similarities and differences between youth groups drawn from allegedly varying populations. The samples studied consisted of the following groups: urban blacks, lower-class; suburban blacks, upwardly mobile; upper-middle-class school- and college-dropouts; middle-class "straight"; poor Southern white; intellectual-activist college youth; lower-class Portuguese immigrant youth.

In addition to outlining the range of questionnaire responses for the total sample, it was also possible to describe several areas in which the youth-group responses differed markedly from one another.*

Group response-differences appear to vary primarily in terms of the degree of identification of a given group of youth with the adult population. Several groups including the Portuguese and middle-class students, for example, seem to identify more with the traditional adult community than with the culture of youth which normally rejects many of the values of the adult community. In addition, it seems possible to note differences in terms of social class and cultural identification. In other words, more idealistic, liberal, youthful responses come from those who either have rejected the cultural mainstream or are aspiring to change it.

Self-Role and Function: While the total sample is concerned with developing self-concept and identity—or, "getting it all together"—as a measure of success or accomplishment, it is possible to view this process as a means to

---

* I am indebted to Richard Boardman for his assistance in performing an analysis of variance on the interviewed groups.

a series of ends. For example, self-development for the middle-class youth has to do with arriving ultimately at a state of material accomplishment (this is also true for the traditional immigrant group), while the lower-class groups are more concerned with self-development in terms of independence and freedom from oppressive social conditions. For the affluent dropout, the development of self takes on a religious-life-style characteristic, largely apart from the traditional social expectation.

Dealing with adults and the world of problems they represent provides a common experience which all the youth face. However, the expression of this varies by group. For middle-class youth the problem is played out in dealing with adult pressures for achievement and success. For the lower-class youth this struggle involves dealing with the prejudice and bigotry of the adult community. For the social dropout, the behavior of the established adult community is a source of considerable annoyance.

Education and Training: Indeed, preparation for adult life is central to all of the respondents. How one is prepared or prepares himself does differ by group. For the immigrant and the middle-class youth, formal schooling is the primary vehicle for preparation, even though in many cases it is recognized as inadequate. Lower-class youth and some more-liberal upper-class youth feel that preparation is primarily an individual responsibility which goes on in spite of formal schooling in some instances. The youth who has dropped out of the mainstream sees his development as antithetical to the formal system. He develops within his subculture, apart from the mainstream.

Work: Four trends of opinion on work emerge clearly from the responses to the questionnaire. First, there is a group of mainstream, middle-class youth (this includes the traditional immigrants) who look forward to the world of work and expect to gain a sense of accomplishment from it. A second group, again mostly from the middle class but somewhat less traditional, are prepared to tolerate work and a job as a necessary evil in one's adult life, and as a way to provide a means for doing more enjoyable leisure-time activities. A third strain, made up of more marginal social elements such as minority lower-class youth, feel that work provides among other things another occasion in which to experience the prejudice of the adult mainstream. Poor pay and inadequate job-security are expectations of a large percentage of this group. Finally, a fourth group is the social dropout for whom work is play, is freedom, is love.

National and International Involvement: There is agreement on both the range and the intensity of national and international problems among the respondents. Where the difference occurs in this area is in the expression of both optimism for and commitment to solution. Awareness of the United Nations seems to vary according to the involvement and concern of a given group with the mainstream, with lower-class minority groups knowing the least and the middle-class groups knowing more. Opinions on the worth of the U.N., however, are distributed in almost the reverse order. The expression of the importance of the role of youth in dealing with world problems seems to vary with both self-sufficiency and exposure to the range of problems. In this instance, then, it is the more affluent and the more liberal who appear in agreement with the need for the involvement of youth in the solutions to problems facing mankind.

CLASS GAP OR GENERATION GAP?

The U.N. study strongly suggests that differences among youth of diverse backgrounds may tend to be substantial and significant. This conclusion finds support from data gathered on college freshmen in three different campus settings by the Center for Research and Development for Higher Education at the University of California at Berkeley (1967, p. 11).

The data from the Center for Research and Development confirm the existence of a primary gap within the younger generation itself, but not a gap between the younger generation and the older generation. This conclusion also echoes the findings of the New England Values Study (Kvaraceus, 1968).

In a comparison of the attitudes and interests of the young and their parents, close affinity was found among the rich and the poor students and their parents on issues of civil rights, expansion of the Vietnam War, financial aid to underprivileged minorities, and general social-welfare policies. However, substantial differences on these same issues were noted among youth groups representing different class-stratification. Similar consensus was found among the freshmen and their parents in artistic and cultural interests, financial interests, humanitarian ideals, politics, and religion. Again, the disagreements among the youth themselves exceeded by a significant margin any differences noted between parents and their offspring. The significant gap is a class gap and not a generation gap, according to this report. President Nixon and the White House Conference on Youth may be right!

ALIENATION, DEVIANCE, AND SOCIAL CONTROL

In a careful study of "unreached youth" in Metropolitan Toronto, Byles (1969) confirms that alienation, deviance, and social control represent separate but interdependent processes. But they are found to operate differently for boys than for girls. Hence, alienation of youth is not a useful concept. We must think of alienation of girls and alienation of boys.

For boys, Byles reports that conflicts with parents, being labeled with derogatory names by adults, and the feeling of powerlessness appear to contribute to alienation for boys, but not for girls. Even though the girls in Byles's study appeared to be more alienated than the boys, few of the variables, singly or in combination, showed any strong relationship with the index of female alienation. Alienation of girls appeared to increase (1) as they tended to identify with the "head" (hippie) subculture; (2) as they experienced fewer satisfying relationships with adults; (3) as they placed less importance on religion; and (4) as they became more tolerant of deviant behavior. However, the combinations of these four factors did not produce a significant multiple correlation.

The Toronto study also reports that both alienation and deviant behavior tend to increase as social status increases. The most alienated subgroups represent the hippie or "head" culture, most of whom reflect middle- and upper-middle-class origins.

Byles also has a significant comment to make regarding the delinquent and other categories or types of youngsters. He also suspects, as pointed out in the U.N. Youth study, that the differences within categories may be greater than the differences between categories of youth. He states:

> Although the delinquent sub-group is also more alienated than youth generally in the community, it is suggested that the processes operate quite differently: that "hippies" tend to become deviant as a consequence of their alienation from society, but delinquents tend to become alienated as a consequence of their deviance and resulting confinement and isolation from society. However, there are probably more differences among types than there are between types, so that these labels tend more to confuse than to assist understanding. Some youth living in both the North and South communities are as alienated from community institutions as are some hippies and delinquents. Also, alienation from at least one of the above-mentioned institutions is the norm, not the exception, among youth living in these communities [Byles, 1969, p. vi].

SUMMARY

In carrying on further research and study on the alienation processes and in planning programs to prevent or reduce unhealthy alienation, we may find the following observations culled from the prior discussion helpful.

1. Alienation as a phenomenon must be viewed by sex, class status, and primary reference-group. The alienation process varies with different subgroups such as hippies, political activists, and delinquents. Hippies tend to become deviant as a consequence of their alienation, whereas delinquents become alienated as a result of their deviance. The generalized category of youth is not a meaningful concept.

2. The difference between generations appears less than the gap found among youth themselves.

3. Alienation within types or categories of youth appear to be as wide as or wider than that between groups. However, significant differences can be found among some types of youngsters.

4. The greatest difference between youth, on the one hand, and their parents and teachers, on the other, centers on matters of dress, coiffure, and cleanliness. This is an insignificant battleground and does not merit energy-input attributed to holding the line on the part of adults. However, it may prove the cheapest, easiest, and most innocent form of alienation and may be worth fostering.

5. Both parents and teachers project a more negative image of youth as being accepting of deviant behavior and attitudes than youth's self-reports indicate.

6. In view of the family conflict as a source of alienation, particularly for boys, family-life education, family counseling, and family therapy need to be considered in helping to integrate youngsters within the community.

7. Opportunities for increasing the feeling of power in influencing decision-making may have a strong integrating effect on youth, particularly on boys.

8. Since alienated youngsters, particularly girls, have too few meaningful relationships with adults, opportunities must be provided to develop closer and deeper relationships with adults. Opportunity for prolonged dialogue with adults centered on significant issues can break the isolation barriers between the young and the old, male and female.

9. Calling youth derogatory names tends to stimulate the alienation process. Consideration should be given by parents, teachers, and the mass media to ways and means of projecting positive rather than pejorative images of youth. Even the term "adolescent" has a negative ring as one implores: "Don't be an adolescent."

10. A large segment of the youth population tends to tag along on the heels of their parents. The existence of the adolescent rebel is a *rara avis*. Except for such obvious dissenters as the political activists, the "heads" or hippies, the "delinquent," and the drug-users who form a relatively small minority of the total youth-population, alienation among youth is an uncommon phenomenon. When it does occur, as in the groups named, it tends to capture and hold public interest and attention, like any rare event.

REFERENCES

Byles, J. A. *Alienation, deviance and social control: Interim research project on unreached youth.* Toronto: Ontario Department of Education, 1969.
Center for Research and Development for Higher Education, University of

California, Berkeley. Class gap—not a generation gap. *Student NEA News,* 1967, *11* (1), 11. December, 1967.

Douvan, E., & Adelson, J. *The adolescent experience.* New York: Wiley, 1966.

Freud, A. Adolescence. *Psychoanalytic Study of the Child,* 1958, *13,* 255–278.

Friedenberg, E. Z. *The vanishing adolescent.* Boston: Beacon Press, 1959.

Hess, S. *New York Times,* June 21, 1971. P. 29.

Keniston, K. *The uncommitted: Alienated youth in American society.* New York: Harcourt, Brace, 1965.

Kvaraceus, W. C. *Anxious youth: Dynamics of delinquency.* Columbus, Ohio: Merrill, 1966.

Kvaraceus, W. C. Working with youth: Some operational principles and practices. *American Journal of Catholic Youth Work,* 1968, *9* (1), 47–53.

Kvaraceus, W. C. U.S.A. Report for the world social situation of youth. Report prepared for the United Nations. Mimeographed. 1971.

Nixon, R. M. *New York Times,* January 15, 1971.

Drug Abuse as a Symptom of Alienation in Youth

ROBERT E. GOULD

Robert E. Gould, M.D., is the director of adolescent services at Bellevue Psychiatric Hospital and associate professor of psychiatry at New York University Medical Center. He received his M.D. degree from the University of Virginia, and completed his psychoanalytic training at the William Alanson White Psychoanalytic Institute. Dr. Gould has written numerous articles in the field of adolescence. His areas of special interest include delinquency, the problem of suicide in adolescents, the marginally asocial personality (notably the hippie phenomenon), and drug use and abuse in the young. Dr. Gould is a member of the editorial board of the Annals of the American Society for Adolescent Psychiatry, *and is a past president (1967–1968) of the Society for Adolescent Psychiatry.*

EXTENT OF DRUG USE IN OUR SOCIETY

We must be keenly aware of the extent and variety of drug use in our culture today. To say that we are a drug-oriented society is to state the obvious, but to recognize the inherent pathology behind this fact is still a frightening prospect. There is scarcely a family in our society which does not regularly indulge in mood-changing drugs. Alcohol, cigarettes, tranquilizers, amphetamines, often in the form of diet pills, and barbiturates, usually in the form

136

of sedatives or sleeping pills, are staples in many households. What home does not offer one or more of these mood-affecting and ultimately addicting drugs?

That it is now common or average for our young to have grown up in such surroundings does not make the situation any healthier; rather it is a clear indication of how much trouble we are in as a culture, and how deeply.

We are living in strangely difficult and sick (forgive this overused word) times in which the stresses of everyday life, especially in urban America, virtually cry for relief through these drugs and, in many cases, the harder drugs as well. Drugs have become, quite simply, our chosen devices for coping, adjusting, making life more comfortable. If we were living in more simple times and in simpler ways, if we were still capable of enjoying simple and natural pleasures, like Rousseau's natural man, we would have, unquestionably, much less need for drugs. But we are not, and cannot, and do not. The more we build artifices into our lives, the more out of touch with our feelings we become, the more alienated we grow.

ALIENATION AT THE ROOT OF MUCH DRUG USE

It is this alienation which lies at the root of much drug ingestion: the feeling of being out of tune, out of synchronization with the natural rhythms of our true selves and/or our society—institutions, government policies and practices, the goals and styles set for us by the majority culture.

There is an average kind of drug use in the average type of family to help cope with the average kind of alienation we all feel. This average kind of alienation today, with its accompanying drug use (however pathological it really is), is what we see and generally accept as "normal." The ubiquitous cocktail party: what do we really mean when we say that a few drinks break down the barriers between people and allow them to relax and act friendlier faster? It means that our alienation from our fellow-man is such that we need artificial mood-sweeteners to help us relate more warmly to our brothers and sisters. The greater the need and degree of drug use, the greater the incidence of alienation which we try to overcome or hide from ourselves.

The increasingly prevalent use of marijuana and psychedelics among the young often represents their attempt to deal with a society they disapprove of but feel powerless to change. Political action requires a certain temperament and personality-structure; even when these are present, if the action is frustrated and rendered impotent, the alternative is often a turning to drugs. If he cannot change social evils, a young person can, through drugs, make these evils at least bearable, by lessening the pain he feels.

This is alienation on a societal level, but a more fundamental alienation springs from distorted or absent communication within the family setting.

The lack of warmth, love, time, and interest we have to rear our children properly, the hypocrisy and inconsistency so often present when one tries to make a piece of parents' words and their behavior—all this breeds insecurity and various kinds of unhappiness or neurosis in the young. This is the alienation which we, who suffer from it, try to escape. Drugs again become the tempting vehicle to carry us away from what makes us unhappy, or deeper into ourselves.

In the first instance, drugs are used to get out of and away from oneself. One may look for a euphoric high, for feelings of omnipotence, for a numbing feeling of tranquility or nothingness; different problems and personality types will dictate the drug effect one seeks to achieve, but at bottom these are merely variations on the same theme of escape.

Another retreat is to use the psychedelics, such as mescaline, or LSD. Here the user is aware of his out-of-touchness and is desperately seeking his true core, his real self. He is not trying to blot out the whole world, just enough of the noises and distractions and distortions of the *outer* world to let him get deeper into his inner self. He often does indeed break through barriers into the more unconscious processes of his being, but he is rarely able to synthesize or put into effective use what he reaches. It is like plunging into another world, where another language is spoken which you cannot understand. Drugs are powerful agents, and can give you all kinds of "trips" which at least temporarily take you away from yourself. They are all essentially trips without directions or destinations, and so, finally, these journeys serve no useful end.

DRUG USE AMONG THE YOUNG

It is quite important that we distinguish between the drug use just outlined, directly linked to feelings of alienation, and the drug use in which many youngsters indulge themselves for other reasons. The experimenting with drugs in our culture is a normal phenomenon (given the abnormal circumstances characterizing so much of our living). Experimenting with marijuana, for the average youngster today, can be analogous to my generation's sneaking a drink of liquor to do something daring and emulate the grownups.

In many circles one tries pot because it is the thing to do—one's peers are all trying it. In such a case, drug use is a manifestation of being with the group and the mores of that subculture, and is not alienated behavior unless one wants to probe deeper and argue that the more secure and independent youngster may not need to indulge in a harmful or dangerous experiment just because others pressure him to do so. It can be argued that the whole group of experimenters is alienated, and that by mutually supporting and encouraging each other's use of drugs, they are all trying to escape the same feelings of alienation. There are many instances in history to indicate that majorities can support each other in delusionary or destructive behavior. However, although I think that group-induced drug use can represent mass alienation, a condition which undoubtedly exists in our culture, there is also a large group of the simply curious—experimenters who are not basically alienated, but who, at certain stages of their lives, want or need to experience as much as they can. Within limits, this is basically a healthy personality-trait. Such youngsters, though, are not the vulnerable ones who go on to heavy drug use which interferes with the individual's growth and development.

There are other cases in which the individual feels alienated from the majority society but not from himself, and can remain quite free from drugs. For example, consider the Black Panthers. Here is a group, dedicated to the purpose of carving a place for themselves. They have a commitment stemming from a deep conviction of what they are and what they want. Not only is drug use unnecessary to this group, it is banned as counterproductive to their goals.

Similarly, some of the new experimental communes are composed of groups of individuals alienated from the norms of society but not from themselves or the like-minded individuals within their extended "families." These groups, too, live a drug-free life. There are of course other communes of young people in which drugs are used extensively, but here again we would find a group alienated not only from society but from themselves as well.

As a crutch to help the less severely alienated among us, drugs appear to have become too important a part of our life to give up.

The industrial and technological revolutions have eroded some of the naturalness of life, and alienation is part of the price we pay. Television, cars, the quickened pace of activity, and all the other intrusions and jarring elements which have intruded upon the peaceful, secure closeness of nuclear family-living have contributed strongly to personal and family alienation. The government, which has shown itself to be hypocritical and deceiving, unable or unwilling to correct injustices, further alienates our youngsters. A lack of belief and trust in the values and way of life of one's parents and parent country are the seeds of alienation. Only the most independent and secure youngster—and our modern setting is not designed to encourage this kind of strength and security—can escape the feelings of frustration, anger, loneliness, and isolation, and finally the sense of desperation which finds its immediate release in the world of drugs. Only those who can embrace a cause and commit themselves to it seem capable of surviving without drugs.

For many of the poor and disadvantaged, there is no hope in the future and there is no power to change things for the better. The severe alienation among these groups is literally drowned in drugs because, without them, reality is a nightmare.

The middle class has become more and more disenchanted with the value-system and way of life of parents and parent-culture as its members find less fulfillment in interpersonal relations and in relation to the natural world dying all about us; they too suffer from alienation. Affluence, we are finding, is no substitute for love or the belief that one's life is worthwhile.

Drugs increasingly have become the way to mask one's alienated condition. It changes nothing basically and requires ever-larger amounts to keep these feelings out of one's conscious mind.

In a world which advertises quick cures for headaches, tensions, bad odors, pimples (you name it—we promise a drug to cure it), why are we still amazed that our young people would instantly seek a drug to cure alienation—perhaps the most desperately unhappy of existential conditions? Why do we still find it mysterious that more and more drugs are needed by young people who feel more and more alienated?

The ills of our times—nationally, the Vietnam war, together with social, racial, and economic ills, and locally, the disintegration of the nuclear family —are clear. The decay in the quality of living, as we see new signs of ecological destruction in our environment every day, are also clear.

Whether we as a nation and as a people have the courage, the will, the spirit of aliveness, and the ability to care enough to do something about the problem of alienation is a critical question. Our increasing use of drugs is merely a barometer of our state of alienation. We are currently losing the battle. I truly hope that we find the strength needed not to lose the war. Our very survival—in any meaningful sense—is at stake.

Suicide—the Ultimate
in Alienation

CHARLES C. MCARTHUR

Charles Campbell McArthur has earned all of his degrees at Harvard University: B.A. in 1946, M.A. in 1948, and Ph.D. in 1951. Upon the completion of his doctoral work, he became psychologist to the University Health Services at Harvard University, a post which he continues to occupy. Dr. McArthur has been a consistent contributor to psychological journals, with over thirty articles to his credit. He was co-editor with Dr. Graham Blaine of both the first (1961) and the second (1971) editions of The emotional problems of the student.

GENERAL THEORY ABOUT SUICIDE

There exists today surprisingly good theory about suicide. We owe much to the staff of the Los Angeles Suicide Prevention Center (Shneidman, Farberow, & Litman, 1970) not only for their accumulating and sharing great masses of clinical experience (saving hundreds of lives in the process) but also for their bringing together old and new theoretical knowledge and pushing the leading edge of our thinking out in several directions. Not all that we are beginning to know points in the direction of the title of this paper but alienation is probably the *highest* common denominator in our theories that the suicide indeed has his being in a sparsely populated, poisoned-alkali flat of existence.

This is specially so of seriously intended, completed suicides. Suicidal

141

gestures may be something quite other and are worth a postscript in this paper, especially since they are so much part of the college scene.

Of course "alienation" is but the internalized and modernized form of Durkheim's (1897) classical concept of anomie. I remember with what pleasure I, a new student of psychology who thought of himself as a former astronomer, followed Durkheim's masterful focusing and refocusing of his data, holding now this, now that constant, until the reader could scarcely refuse to see meaning in the kaleidoscope of nineteenth-century European public-health statistics. People killed themselves when their world was at lowest ebb: at three in the morning, in February, during a cold drizzle, in a lonely rooming house, after all loved ones had gone. They stopped killing themselves in May, when the sun had risen, by ten o'clock high enough to bring the morning warmth after cold dawn and to bring people out and about, even down the corridors of anonymous *pensions*. As any college health doctor can tell you, our patients stop coming to see us once they have something more valid to do, like flying kites together along the banks of the Charles.

Yet most of us survive our winters, even in New England, and even somehow our nights, though we have to meet these natural shocks all alone. Why do some men find anomie lethal?

LOSS OF HOPE

The classical psychodynamic explanation is depression—and rightly so. There can be no springtime, no matitudinal warming, for a man whose feelings blind him to all that is not black, a man whose rage is directed at himself, and probably unjustly. Yet depression is also a broad category. What seeds of destruction within it are specifically lethal?

Generally, loss of hope. Utter hopelessness is at once a cause and a product of depression. Just as the Russian prince thought it took three generations to make a revolution—one having known better times, one being told about better times, and only the third so unable to conceive better times as to be impelled into Quixotic action—just so the depressive must descend the steps into his black hole before his lack of even the expectation of hope makes him desperate enough to act. But this process can go very quickly. And at that time just having something to do—to take arms against his sea of troubles —just the concreteness of planning an act, even a self-destructive act, gives relief, even a kind of hope. Now he is moribund, for now he will cling to, rehearse, plan in operational detail like a field marshal and connive at concealing this one, false hope: resolution by the act itself. Frequently, in the weeks just before a completed suicide, the victim is reported to have been very happy.

Not every kind of hope is required to keep a man alive. For instance, even in success-oriented America, loss of job or failure in school seldom turns out to have been sufficient cause for a suicide. Triggering mechanisms, yes; but it is something else they trigger. The necessary condition is loss of hope of love.

Hope of love suffers many vicissitudes and, in the sense that the study of suicide is the study of all the ways love can be lost beyond recovery or poisoned beyond cure, the study of suicide is a study in alienation. Loss of even the hope of love is the specific condition for which suicide is the symptom, because it appears to the victim to be a cure.

In our world, where we club our children into line by granting or with-holding conditional love, the child soon learns a feeling of not being able to justify himself. Yet he also sees that he can get love only by meeting the standards of his parents. That is the price. Or so he perceives it, perhaps childishly; perhaps too totally; perhaps with a perception too fiercely primi-tive—or perhaps with true perceptiveness. In the communication of emo-tions, the child may be the one good linguist. At any rate, if he finds he cannot meet his parents' standards, the child is left with no hope of love. Then he, like one of our students who was the first of his extended ethnic kin to go to college, falls down to a B+ in organic chemistry and goes home to hang himself.

UNWORTHY OF LOVE

So suicide is often a disease of conscience, whether the primitiveness of conscience was created by the child or the parent or both. The grown child now shares these primitive and ferocious standards as his own. He comes to feel that he is not living up to what his own innermost feelings tell him is the only measure of being worthy of love. He cannot justify anyone's loving him, whatever that person's overt behavior. He "knows" he is of no worth.

This is often the dynamic of student suicide. Listen to the Sentence Com-pletion Test of a man who was soon to destroy himself by means which left no room for hope of rescue:

> When I was younger *I had a false sense of my worth.*
> The best I can do *is not good enough.*
> I regret *that I have lived so long and learned so little.*
> At home *I am loved for being what I'm not.*

There, of course, was the rub—at least as he saw it. If you feel in your deepest soul that you are worthy of love only as a living sacrifice to the Moloch of National Merit, how is it with you when you also come to feel that your vaunted intellectual prowess has turned out to be all a bluff? You *deserve* not to be loved—and so, in the barbarity of the life of raw feelings, you are beyond hope of any fate save becoming an academic sacrifice.

Hopelessness of being loved or, indeed, lovable, comes to men in a hundred ways: the physically sick patient who concludes that his doctor has abandoned him; or, worse, his family. (How many suicides politely phrased as for surcease of pain were for surcease of a deeper wounding?) The "bottom" an alcoholic allegedly must "hit" includes a climax of unlove, and, often, of suicide. We have not even touched on the effects of losses, leading to suicide as an amalgam of mourning, guilty sacrificing of the self and a wonderfully indirect form of revenge at having been deserted by the lost loved-one. This is also a mechanism often seen in students.

Nor does it relieve alienation to have childishly exaggerated expectations from love. No suicide is more alone than he or she who demands a symbiotic merger of selves between loved ones. Such people must dissolve their own ego's boundaries before they can feel loved. In the end, this becomes a magical, hopelessly unrealistic aspiration, at a level so high as to guarantee hopelessness of its fulfillment.

USE OF DRUGS

We see a lot of this eerie need in young people who turn to drugs. To feel directly one's contact with the cosmos is the ultimate end of a tour of trips with LSD; to attain the "oceanic feeling." There are drugs—psilocybin, for instance—which permit experiencing such a merger of physical bodies. Distressed during his first experiment with the Mexican mushrooms, the young anthropologist Castenada (1968, p. 141) was told by his Yaqui teacher: "Get inside my chest."

For a while, the hallucinogenic drugs seemed to offer us what one youthful speaker today wistfully calls "dreams of chemical love"—dreams from which we awaken. Waking love does not even allow us to enter profitably into the emotional analog of such physical merger. Both partners cannot depend on the other totally, helplessly, as the infant upon his mother's breast. Such pairs are likely candidates for discovering that they have no hope of being (thus cosmically) loved. Indeed, it has been well said (Shneidman, Farberow, & Litman, 1970, p. 444) that the two of them will often be caught up, as a result, in "a mutual race toward suicide by two regressed dependent people."

Nor is this the only dangerous way of loving; the point is that in mature love the ego is not permanently overwhelmed. One must have ego-boundaries to retain hope of being loved.

By whatever route he came there, the person who reaches the suicidal state is too weakened to cope realistically. "I am unworthy / deserted / unlovable / a living sacrifice" are not sentiments calculated to strengthen practical judgment. The ego is deprived of the coping devices most of us use to manage the vicissitudes of living every day. The person suffers a peculiar debility which can be described as a splitting of his ego. Part of him is identified with destructive figures out of his childish perceivings, part of him perhaps with figures he recently has lost, only part of him with his own growing maturity. He is alienated from part of himself, within himself.

ALL SOLUTIONS WILL FAIL

Still, the victim will struggle for life, trying one after another various emotionally meaningful, if not very workable, solutions. The fatal moment comes when it is beyond doubting that all solutions will fail. Listen, through the medium of stories from his Thematic Apperception Test, to a dead man telling us how it was:

> The boy, whose mother always spoiled him, has gotten in trouble. Because he wanted to get ahead fast in order to live up to his mother's expectations, he stole and got caught. His mother can't believe this would happen to her Golden Boy. He is ashamed to tell her about it.
> In the end, he goes away to start all over but getting away doesn't help him. His new life is not better than his first one. Failure continues to haunt him.

Or, much like the man whose sentences we quoted earlier, this boy writes:

> He has been given a new violin because he showed some smidgin of talent. It is time to practice but he is just sitting, brooding, doubting that he'll ever be able to play well enough to deserve such a fine gift. He wonders if he will ever be another Heifetz or if he should just give up. Doubting makes him perform worse. The gift is too much. In the end it spoils for him the very thing he wanted.

Or again,

> These people are going through a wild valley and they are running to get across this gorge before the wild animals behind them catch up with them. When they get across, they come up against a rock cliff and they have to go back the way they came and go through it all again.

In the end, only one solution remains.

ATTEMPT TO REACH OTHERS

Even suicide as a solution usually contains an attempt to reach others. In varying ratios, the suicide is a cry for help, expressing at once the need to die and the need to be rescued. At very least, it is a communication, often a sort of charade, to be read in the language of symbol. Sons die on the anniversary of their father's suicide, and by the same weapon. Lovers pick a sentimental spot.

Before the final act, there will have been warnings. It is as if the suicide casts dice with fate, in one last gamble to see what his gods ordain. He will climb the tower many times before he jumps from it. He will openly keep in his medicine chest his growing hoard of sleeping pills. He will speak of death—"philosophically," of course—to friends and random others. He will write bizarre essays in his hour examinations. All the while, in response to the other half of his ambiguous intent, he is secretly planning The Act, down to its last delicious detail!

The effect of this last, unacknowledged, crude attempt to communicate, to overcome his anomie is that most suicides have, toward the end, many potential rescuers. This is especially true in a university community, where oddities of behavior attract the eye of sadder but wiser deans, university police, or janitors. The young man who is sent down from a belltower by a janitor may evoke concern for his suicidal bent. In a well-staffed university, this can lead to many people's concern and intervention. Yet most potential rescuers come all unwitting to the moment of their nomination. Suicide is not a nice or socially usual thought. All too often, the passerby who might have become a rescuer decides he will do the private errand he was on before he mentions to anyone the odd person he has seen. Sometimes, as in symbiotic pairs, there is something very like unconscious murder. "Oh, she's just sleeping!" the infantile lover defensively concludes. So here is the last irony: the fatal proof of alienation, if the suicide ever needed doubt that he was alone.

UNSUCCESSFUL SUICIDAL ACTIONS

Yet sometimes rescuers do intervene. Often enough, the part of the suicide which needs to be rescued communicates through all of his and of his rescuer's own anomie. Perhaps the suicide himself calls a doctor or an intervention center or a friend whose maturity does not require him to deny the harshness of what he hears. And what then? What can we do after one intervention?

For we know suicide to be a recurring disease. The part of the patient's ego which is bent on dying is going to try to have its way again. How can we foil it?

By massive doses of anti-anomie. By caring and behaviorally showing we care, and by embroiling as many people as possible who are significant to the patient. (The same prescription applies to alcoholism, perhaps insofar as that is also a form of self-destruction.) By providing a people-filled situation which is as difficult as possible to perceive as helpless-hopeless. And meanwhile by some very intensive psychotherapy which moves in on the suicide's immature premises. Or by providing just one relationship of genuine warmth, to give the lie to loss of hope. One good therapist may be enough to keep a man alive.

Interestingly, there are many cases in which the suicide provides its own cure. The sacrifice has been made, the primitively internalized Moloch has eaten his child-victim, the lost person has been symbolically "joined in death," the deserting lover "shown," the world at last reached by an ultimate kind of communication.

There is even, sometimes, a sense of death followed by rebirth. The suicide, seriously intentioned but through circumstance failed, may give himself permission to communicate, to risk hope again. Still, we may perhaps feel that we might have reached out to him to the same effect at earlier stages along his lonely way.

INTENTIONED, SUBINTENTIONED, AND CONTRA-INTENTIONED SUICIDAL ACTS

As I said earlier, not every suicidal action has these dark dynamics. Shneidman (1970, pp. 15–23) rightly distinguishes among suicidal actions which are intentioned, subintentioned, or contra-intentioned.

Intentioned acts are but little ambivalent. Except for the irrational effects of ego-splitting, which enable one part of the suicide to contemplate the end of another part with satisfaction, and except for the unconsciously poor reality-testing of the kind of thinking called "primary process," in which we all become dumb animals who do not know their own death, the intentioned suicide knows what he is doing and carries out his purpose efficiently. There can be little doubt of the intent of a girl who climbs to the attic of a tall building, removes the storm window there, and jumps. Or of a boy who breaks away from his father and the group of boarding airline passengers to walk with measured pace into the whirling propellers of the airplane. Such acts usually turn out to have culminated well-laid plans, even many rehearsals.

Subintentioned acts are more clearly ambivalent; the cry for rescue is visibly part of the wish for destruction. The hoarded overdose is swallowed at the time a roommate usually comes back from supper. But maybe the dose is not quite lethal; these pill-takers often have but a hazy knowledge of the pharmaceutical aspects of their drug. They leave all that just a little up to chance, gambling with death, casting the runes, reading the omens: Russian roulette.

The contra-intentional does not seriously expect to die—only to make the gesture. He intends to communicate. Unhappily some of these gestures cause death. I have in mind the student who planned an elaborate charade for his roommate, who was to enter the room to find him with a huge hangman's noose about his neck, the rope slung over a rafter, while he stood on an orange crate, ostensibly ready to kick it away from under him. An orange crate will not support a two-hundred-pound boy very long.

These differences in intention are not just matters of degree; there are some qualitative differences among them. In particular, many observers have commented on the increased elements of manipulativeness in contra-intended gestures. We see much of these among students, particularly when acts of self-harm take place in the context of immature, often symbiotically toned, love-affairs. Sometimes the result is a kind of *opéra bouffe*. One girl, having the latest of a series of quarrels with her boyfriend, expressed her feelings by slashing her wrists. He, furious, bawled her out in no uncertain terms for childishness, while blood poured onto the carpet. Disgusted, he slammed out the door, remarking as he went that he would put in a call to the college doctors. About the time we got there and began sewing up her wrists, the boy reappeared, ready for the quarrel to be over, and bearing as his peace-offering some sandwiches!

An important element in such gestures is sheer impulsiveness. Lack of impulse-control leads to the choice of adjustment by "acting out," whether in the serious, often bizarre, suicides of psychotics or in the summer storms of contra-intentioned flibbertigibbets among normals.

Often, the character in which a suicidal gesture is grounded is not depressive but hysterical. There is a special intensity about the moment for such people—about almost *any* moment. "I was having a fight with my boyfriend and there was this jug!" says one girl, lovingly tracing the curve of the jug in the air with both hands. The jug was suddenly part of her existential condition. To smash it against its own shelf and slash at her wrists had in that moment the immediacy of any act of perception. "Physiognomic perception" they used to call this kind of immediacy of the given.

A third characteristic of less-than-intentioned acts is that, having survived them, the attempter is uncommonly cheerful. That was a surprise we got when, in a recent year, we tested every known student-attempter. Our attempters were sometimes depressed and visibly affected by recent losses, quite in the classical fashion, but they often were quite the opposite: hypomanic, and scoring so on psychological tests. They would bob into our office chirping away like little sparrows, full of smiles and talk, delighted with themselves and us and life. Such youngsters were usually contra-intentioned in their suicidal acts and often had been using these acts in part to manipulate someone. One soon discovered, however, that a hypomanic may also be in real distress, and be handling it with behavioral immediacy which brooks no time wasted on second thoughts about controlling an impulse. For us to mistake these Cheerful Charlies among suicides for cured would be to fail as rescuers: they were quite capable of repeating their acts.

In the end, it is what we do as rescuers which must break through to the man, woman, or, as is most common, the child lost in anomie. We must have help institutionally and readily available. (The hotline concept does work!) We must have a good medical service there to be called on—often enough by a friend, roommate, or teacher. We must create a knowledgeable and concerned community, in which a passerby feels he should take some action, not pass by on the other side of the road. We must rally around the anomic person many and significant others. We must deal with him in terms of hope. (Maximum-security hospitalization may at moments be a necessary precaution, but it has the disadvantage of showing how frightened we are of the patient's demons and how little hope we feel of defeating them.) We must reach out to the part of his ego which still can grow and is still there— albeit split off from the more primitive parts of him which now have taken over his personality. In all these ways we must offer the self-destructive person a hand and a hope of rejoining a world which can offer him love.

REFERENCES

Castenada, C. *The teachings of Don Juan: A Yaqui way of knowledge.* New York: Ballantine, 1968.
Durkheim, E. *Suicide* (1897). New York: Free Press, 1951.
Shneidman, E. S. Orientations toward death. In E. S. Shneidman, N. L. Farberow, & R. E. Litman (Eds.) *The psychology of suicide.* New York: Science House, 1970. Pp. 3–45.
Shneidman, E. S., Farberow, N. L., & Litman, R. E. (Eds.) *The psychology of suicide.* New York: Science House, 1970.

V
YOUTH SPEAKS ON ALIENATION

Youth Speaks on Alienation

Frank Negron
Stuart Vexler
L Mark Winston
Roger Mooney
Michael Bryant

In this section five young people, representing a variety of viewpoints, present their views on alienation. In order of presentation, Frank Negron, a 19-year-old Puerto Rican former drug addict, speaks on both personal and societal alienation. He is followed by Stuart Vexler who has responded to his own sense of alienation by dedicating himself, as a staff member at Odyssey House, to extricating his contemporaries, caught in the coils of drug addiction. Next is L Mark Winston who speaks for the alienated college student. Mark received his A.B. degree from Georgetown University in 1971 and is now a law-school student. Roger Mooney, a Boston College graduate of 1969, represents post-college alienation. He speaks for the group of college graduates who feel the need to be themselves and who cannot fit into the establishment of adult society. Finally, Michael Bryant, an undergraduate student at Fordham University's Liberal Arts College at Lincoln Center, speaks for the black community and its sense of alienation.

ALIENATION OF A FORMER DRUG ADDICT

Frank Negron
Member, Junior Executive Staff, Odyssey House

I was a drug addict for five years. Even before I became addicted to drugs I was always acting out against myself, stealing or breaking things, disobey-

ing my parents. Many of my feelings of alienation, of inferiority, of inadequacy were turned inward, causing me to be depressed almost all the time.
For me drugs were an adventure, an exciting escape.

Drug addiction was accepted as a way of life by many residents of my
neighborhood and was ignored by the rest of the world outside the ghetto.
Things have changed now. Sons of senators, executive businessmen, and
people from other walks of life have now been reached by drugs. Previously
drug addiction was just the problem of the poor people in America, the ones
who did not have a strong foundation in life. At the time I was using drugs
it did not matter to the authority figures of our nation. But now, since they
are afraid that their own children might be on a "trip," they have decided
to take action against drug addiction.

Most addicts have an alienated feeling toward themselves. They do not
like themselves and turn to drugs to relieve tensions. It is only a short period
of time before they find that they are much more depressed than they were
before they messed with drugs. To many, it will be a problem until the day
they die. Others might find the answers through an experience such as the
one Odyssey House provides.

My history of drug addiction is just a nightmare to me now. I have no
intention of going back to the use of drugs ever in my life. I have been in
Odyssey House for a period of twenty months; never before did I realize
how meaningful life can be.

Besides my alienation as a drug addict, which is now resolved, I had and
still have another alienation. That is the one I feel because of the rejection I
get from many members of society because of the simple fact that I am
Puerto Rican. My people and my family face these prejudices every day.
This brings on aggravation and hostility. This aggravation and hostility are
two factors which have led me and others like me to turn to drugs. Other
young people are becoming revolutionaries and rebelling against American
ways and values in hope of changing the present situation facing the Puerto
Rican people. Some are self-destructive in their revolt. I try to channel my
own frustration toward helping my people.

We have opened a bilingual facility to reach many addicts who have not
overcome the language problems of the Spanish speaker in New York. Too
often we have had these people come into our program only to leave because
of the isolation they felt in the English-speaking atmosphere. Even the once-
a-week group session we held with these residents was not enough.

In my opinion, a person can resolve his alienation by following a meaningful concept of life. I found mine through Odyssey House and its founder,
Dr. Judianne Densen-Gerber.

GENERAL ALIENATION OF YOUTH

STUART VEXLER
Administrator of Spanish Programs, Odyssey House

The other contributors have treated alienation in a very academic manner. Frank Negron does not. He can talk only of his own experience—one which relates only slightly to yours or mine. In Odyssey House we often make use of bridges for persons of vastly different life-experiences to communicate with each other. I will spend a few minutes discussing the alienation of Frank as he became a drug addict in the ghetto and his alienation as he emerges from rehabilitation to go back into the community from which he came.

The insecurities of life with his family and insecurities with himself were prominent problems with Frank. With him and with many other ghetto youngsters there is a foremost need to prove one's manhood. The father figure, when present, is often hung up on his own need to assert his manhood and this is quickly passed on to the son. At about the time of the son's puberty this need can take the form of joining a violent gang or even of striving to be a superior athlete. But increasingly, youths are turning toward the more frightening, more dangerous, and actually more glamorous, use of drugs.

When one goes beneath the surface for reasons for drug abuse one of the most common factors found consists in feelings of low self-esteem, which are too often reinforced in a society in which members of minority groups cannot get jobs, and are sold short on education, public facilities, and public services. Our television culture worships material wealth, while the only money on the block belongs to the pimp or the pusher. In this manner ghetto youth becomes channeled early into an alienation from positive growth.

In the Puerto Rican ghettos of the South Bronx, Spanish Harlem, or Bedford-Stuyvesant, there is an exaggeration of this alienation created by a language barrier, as well as by a cultural barrier. There is a strong tendency to stick with one's own, made even stronger by the familial ties so important to Latin Americans. This has made the residents "block bound," to borrow a term from sociologists. Without direct exposure to it, the greater culture remains alien and the dweller remains isolated.

To one middle-aged mother I know in the South Bronx, 42nd Street is "the Village" and 14th Street is an expensive shopping area she has visited once but which she did not like because there were too many people. She has lived in New York twenty-five years. She cannot feel a part of the affluent society as she spends her welfare check on the block, paying more for her food and other essentials than her middle-class counterpart.

Exposure to young people using drugs—in the ghetto, in junior high school, and in our great universities—has led many of us at Odyssey House to view drug abuse as an outgrowth of man's powerlessness in modern society. What young person can end discrimination against his people, can stop a war three-thousand miles away, can halt the population explosion which begins to engulf us? These are pertinent questions to young people today. A young man in our metropolises is crowded into schools built to house one-third the number they serve, and must spend eight hours a day there no matter how boring it may be. At eighteen he is given a number which may not only decide how he spends the rest of his life, but also how long that life will be. He must assert his individualism. What he says is: "THEY can take away my name, take away my freedom, tell me how I must look and act, but only I have the power to kill my spirit."

At Odyssey, in our Bronx house which is exclusively for Spanish residents, we attempt to cut this alienation at root levels. We provide a Latin ambiance along with the Spanish language. Our house is located in the center of *El Barrio*. The residents feel more comfortable there, and we also want to be, as much as possible, an integral part of the community. The residents learn and grow through interacting and sharing their experience. We hope to return constructive leaders to their community.

I will now turn to my own view of alienation in America—a general alienation which transcends generational barriers and regional boundaries. Twentieth-century man feels no control over his own destiny. Many of the things which he was brought up to believe in have been called lies, and have often been proved to be lies right before his eyes. There is an ever-changing relationship between man and his institutions.

As modernization has come to the Church, an institution many thought dying a few years ago, increasing numbers of young people have rejoined the fold; but what of those who feel that it is sacrilege for a long-haired girl in a miniskirt to strum on her guitar at a folk Mass? They are alienated. As mechanization of much of our lives becomes a reality—as we face a machine where we once faced a face—man becomes more isolated.

Perhaps the most alienating feature of the late 'sixties was the awareness of the fallibility of offices once trusted, of institutions once respected. An example would be the disclosure of President Johnson's Vietnam papers. To many it was a confirmation of statements they had for so long not wanted to believe. For others it was further proof that the members of the press are traitors to our country and are only interested in boosting the morale of our enemies. The two sides have much in common. Both react with increased alienation.

Almost any young person today can spend endless hours rapping about the hypocrisy of the older generation. One is taught from first grade the necessity of respect for the law in our country. As one grows up he finds that everyone in the United States picks those laws he finds it convenient to obey and follows those, ignoring or flaunting disregard for the rest. A presidential candidate running on a law-and-order platform praises breaking of the law if it should deal with integration. A governor who is a superpatriot admits that he has not paid taxes for several years. A lawyer who is our President publicly announces the guilt of a man charged with murder even while his trial is in progress. Those charged with enforcing the law will break the law if it impinges on their right to higher pay. So youth follows—obeying those laws he likes and ignoring the rest. But he carries with him the feeling that it is he against the government—a government whose legislature is a gerontocracy.

Society cannot continue selectively to enforce its laws without paying a high price in the alienation of its youth. The laws in question must be enforced or done away with. All else is a travesty.

My own alienation has been fostered by the assassinations of the three men who most captured the heart of American youth in the 'sixties. The end of the decade made its contribution also. The cause which had most caught my spirit, that of ending the war, was meeting deaf ears in Washington. As disillusionment grew, a movement founded on love, peace, and trust had disintegrated into a modern version of the older generation with its own myths, its own wars, its own failings.

I brought my idealism to the city, where the jobs are and where the action is.

Not long after I arrived in the city fifteen months ago I was riding on the subway and happened to notice the faces of my fellow-passengers. They were all pale, drained, and seemed to fear the future more than to look forward to it. I thought that this was a sick mode of existence. I was happy to be able to forget all these people when I got to the street above.

Then not long ago, I was riding on the subway again. Having nothing to read I looked around at my fellow-passengers. I saw familiar faces: pale, lifeless, afraid. These were the same people. I sat back and looked at myself. I was pale. Then I started wondering whether the subway would make it to the next stop or would die and rest in the dark for a while first. It dawned on me that I was now not too different from my fellow-passengers. It bothered me for some time.

Previously, I had been alienated from them and it was not painful. The last time I was far more disturbed. I felt alienated from myself, from some of my own basic values.

In closing, let me share something I have learned in the last couple of years. At Odyssey House we have developed a highly complex structure with one basic goal in mind: to facilitate communication. Yet communication offers us no assurance of agreement. In American society I find too many of my elders still looking for panaceas—one of the latest being that increased communication will solve the world's problems. It may help or it may be just another beginning which meets a dead end. We must be realistic. There are no wooden ships to carry either generation out of the madness; no drugs, no space programs, no miracle encounter-groups, no organic food—only ourselves.

ALIENATION OF COLLEGE STUDENTS

L MARK WINSTON
A.B., *Georgetown University, 1971*

Alienation is both a process and a condition. It is a process in which the individual moves out from under those values and expectations established by society and its institutions. Often this rejection of common social values results in the alienated state, characterized as much by confusion as by any other quality.

There is no typical pattern to this process of questioning. With some persons it may have been triggered by a particular issue (e.g., the Vietnam War), or by a specific event (e.g., confronting the draft). With others it may come merely from being a witness to the process at work in a friend. The spread of this frustration vicariously is a major factor.

Generally, this skeptical or even cynical attitude is the consequence of the individual's facing conditions which simply do not correspond with the values he was told to expect. He sees those values ignored by the very people who espouse them. He comes to expect the basest of motives in the actions of anyone in authority.

As a reaction to this hypocrisy, the individual turns to the satisfaction of personal needs. He looks at man as an end in himself. This view has some basis in our Western intellectual heritage. The humanists purported to place man at the center of the universe. In some respects today's alienated young person is a humanist who seeks at the same time to place himself at the center of—and apart from—a universe he either cannot understand or understands too well and rejects.

Here, then, is one of the central issues for those of us who intend to analyze the problem of alienation honestly: It may well be that a large number of people do not care even to make the effort to change present social values.

Ordinarily, we consider these people, who in some respects have capitulated, as being the alienated ones. One of the main contentions of this paper is that this is not only misleading, but dangerous. It could lull us into believing, as many people who currently occupy elective office seem to believe, that if we can isolate or placate those few who have "dropped out" we can preserve the existing order. This, however, ignores a large part of the problem.

I believe that to a certain extent we are all alienated. We are all confronted by the incessant contradiction between "the idea and the reality." As Camus might say, some capitulate to absurdity through suicide; others carry on their own style of rebellion. In our advanced society of corporateness, the average individual feels powerless in his quest for personal happiness; how much less his ability to take on important social problems!

The purpose of this essay is not to limit its perspective to those who reject social values and have no desire to change them. It is rather to look at some of the conditions which produce alienation in young people, particularly college students, and view the activist as an alienated person who has not capitulated. The role of this complex personality in the future will also be discussed briefly.

Marx defines alienation as "the contradiction between the interest of the separate individuals . . . and the communal interests of all individuals" (Fromm, 1961, p. 75). This process tends to alienate individuals from the several simultaneous roles into which they are thrust. Man sees how he actually lives and how he would like to live, and becomes alienated from himself. This is exemplified by the story of the people who saved to send their children to college, who saved for the trip to Europe, who waited for retirement, and who upon reaching those golden years were too frail or ill to enjoy what they had waited so long to attain. This is the dilemma of future preference—and when young people see their parents on this treadmill they conclude that they do not wish it for themselves.

Some observers have suggested that those who are alienated reject intimate personal relationships. This does not seem to me to be the case. It is rather that they seek to redefine the nature of their relationships. For example, many of them have lived in a style which eliminates formal bonds of marriage. With such an approach to life, they attempt to expand the sphere in which they maintain maximum personal freedom. "Living every day as it comes," they feel that they approach an ideal level of spontaneous existence —and hence freedom. Often, however, they discover that living each day as it comes is valueless. While they have rejected certain established social values, they have found little more than confusion and uncertainty as a substitute force for their own lives. In a sense, then, we can say that they become alienated from their own alienated response to society.

The hedonism which many decry, exemplified to the critic by "heavy use of drugs, communal sex, and violent criminal behavior," is a manifestation of confusion. While rejecting productivity and "success," these disenchanted individuals have often failed to find a life-style which accords them a sense of personal dignity. They seek free choice and discover instead, in many cases, that dependence on drugs permits them even less personal freedom.

Just as humanism does not flourish in an environment which alienates man from his daily activity, so it does not flourish in an environment which produces confusion.

We have already touched on the alienation of man from himself and from others. Marx has particularly focused on alienation from labor. Simply viewed, this condition is caused by the impersonalization of the productive process itself. One cannot feel creative when one puts in place a screw in an automobile on the assembly-line. He cannot identify, as the medieval guildsman could, with the fruits of his labor. With the increasing specialization of physical labor—not to mention that same trend in the "knowledge industry"—we can expect to find an increase in this kind of frustration.

The student is at the center of the university—a uniquely designed institution in our society. At one time the university seeks to pursue truth by way of creating an unusual form of competition, while it is controlled by a uniquely authoritarian structure. These two factors come into conflict. Within a democratic society, truth is seen within the context of freedom. Within the university, however, there exists a system based on seniority, merit, and specialized competence. Seniority and merit are often found to be the rationale for the authority of the faculty, while specialized competence and legal responsibility constitute the foundation for administrative authority.

Fortunately, the loose organization of the university does not permit the system of meritocracy, seniority, and competence to grow to oppressive proportions for most students most of the time. However, for an increasingly large number of college students three specific problems tend, by their cumulative effect, to alienate the individual from the educational process. Often this is the first step in a chain-reaction leading to a more extensive rejection of socially established values. These three elements are: the curriculum, poor teaching, and the grading system.

The curriculum produces problems when it (a) limits the choice of individuals to determine a sizable proportion of their own academic program, which stifles creativity; and, (b) tends to cause an overspecialization within the learning process which increasingly separates knowledge from anything resembling a unified whole. There is even less justification for this in the undergraduate school of today, simply because most graduate schools want generalists in their specialized areas, and assume that they at the graduate level must teach even the basics of a specialty.

The problem of poor teaching is most difficult. Everyone cannot be a great orator. However, oral communication is not always the single element which disqualifies a professor as a good teacher. Rather it is that the professor is distracted by what he judges to be more *personally rewarding* pursuits—and therefore does not spend enough time in direct interaction with the individual student. The reason that these qualities of being a good communicator in and outside the class are not given pre-eminence is the system of tenure and promotion. This is one of the closed systems of power in the university at which the student must look. Because faculty members are rewarded for research, departmental service, and rate of publication, they have a less-than-significant incentive to consider themselves bonded to undergraduate students in particular. Students sense this and resent it.

Finally, the system of academic evaluation contributes to alienation. As students and faculty members alike speak with cynicism about the arbitrary quality of grades (yet continue to employ them), the student grows to consider most if not all grades as being basically invalid and capricious. Disrespect for this system breeds disrespect for the teacher, brings students into conflicts with parents, and generally undercuts the university's ultimate goal of the pursuit of knowledge as an end in itself. As the contradiction presented by grading emerges, the student increasingly sees a large measure of his labor as make-work and useless. In Marx's sense, then, he is alienated from his labor.

The student becomes more quickly alienated than other people in the society, often because he has more leisure time to consider and to find the contradictions which may drive him to that state.

As I have suggested, some young people withdraw, totally disillusioned by the conduct and institutions of society. Some young people do not withdraw. Instead they commit themselves to a kind of creative rejection: they selectively seek to dislodge those values and reform those institutions which run counter to their needs, and to substitute something better. Often their methods constitute trial and error. Indeed, this has been the method of history.

Why do some people withdraw while others become active? Both types of people have been alienated by many of the same things. Both types have similar opportunities. No explanation seems adequate. I have observed, however, that some people are motivated by fear and others are motivated by irritation. When they meet opposition or resistance, when things do not make sense, they are irritated into action.

I believe that what we have seen on our college campuses for nearly a decade has been a consequence of this irritation: alienated people being forced by many of the very values they reject to work to alter those values and the institutions which support them. Contrary to being paranoid about the meaning of such unrest, our society should reflect on these events as indications of a basic reaction to years of observation. We have observed hypocrisy and wish to confront it. Based on my own experience in such a situation I believe it not likely that this activism will be dissipated. Those who are waiting for that one more class to graduate so as to rid themselves of a problem have a very long wait indeed.

Today's activist will surely grow up a little less emotional than he or she may have been in college. However, we can expect to see that many of the same issues about which we complained while in college will serve as the underpinning for our adult concerns. Such matters as the distribution of power were concerns which dominated the thoughts of many activists. Indeed, it may be said that through the irritation of our college years we were educated in some of these very questions of power simply through the reality of having so little of it. Having had this experience, some of the former college activists will spend some of their lives paying attention to the structure and size of our government and other institutions. In this way we will begin to deal with the basic question of powerlessness of individuals, which plays so great a part in the process of alienation.

POST-COLLEGE ALIENATION

ROGER MOONEY
A.B., *Boston College, 1969*

Alienation in society is a form of segregation, although it is less of a physical absolute and more of a psychological and spiritual problem. Certainly some of those who feel most at odds with "normal" or "standard" behavior patterns or beliefs do leave the pressure points of society and flee to the wild country or slip into the poorest and least-controlled areas of the city. But the greatest number—I would, if pressed, include myself in this category—do not split completely, but rather remain in contact with the mass of people and with the great institutions, although in an assortment of roles and disguises which rarely display true feeling or commitment.

The general cause of one man's alienation from his fellows is a difference in value systems between the individual and society. This difference in values might be voluntary and conscious: the result of scrutiny and comparison of aspects of the culture at large and the open choice to hold opposing views. An example of this is the person who has been appalled by American actions in Southeast Asia and will have no part in the situation. Such a person, and there are obviously many, has come to feel separated from a large portion of national activity. Or, for another example, a man might develop attitudes toward the ownership of property, which are not in accord with legal definitions or the attitudes of most others. This person has certainly created a barrier between himself and society.

By and large, however, alienation is vaguer and less a result of definable particulars. It can often be the culmination of a long period of unexamined uneasiness, or the quiet realization that the individual moves with undue friction through the workings of society, that the individual has not maintained faith in the manifest goals of the society.

There is an important implication in this kind of alienation. Since it is understandably difficult for the individual in many modern situations to zero in on the things bothering him (this age of specialization seems to be one in which we all deny responsibilities for the consequences of our actions), it becomes increasingly difficult to try to remedy specific circumstances and increasingly arduous to alter the attitudes of others. The instinctive desire to fight back, to oppose large methods of state or corporate action, is vitiated, and the individual contents himself with preserving his own personality. What might have been opposed is simply ignored. Frustration feeds the future to the past and one's energies are consumed in exploring oneself. And introspection is a demanding enough task in an era of toppling traditions and theoretically casteless society.

I can think of two ways of relating to the large society outside the individual. One is through direct action, the other through indirect self-expression. I would like briefly to contrast these two approaches and perhaps elucidate the problem of alienation for myself and a significant number of other people to whom I am closest.

Direct action to bring oneself into a more satisfying relationship with society requires political action (in the widest sense of "political"). This means, in a state as grand as ours, working with larger and larger groups of people. The bigger the goal, the more people must come together. Political power still has its roots in the unity of vast numbers of people. (This rule seems to vary greatly from subject to subject and is warped by the pervading pressure of special interests, but I believe that it eventually holds true on all major topics.) However, the massing together of people always forces compromise on the individual and may pervert his particular goals. Ironically, the attempt to change large situations has created a large machine which once again has placed the individual in a subordinate and unsatisfying position. This, unfortunately, has been my experience.

That personal self-expression, however, which is based in honest self-examination and which coerces no one seems to relieve the dull pain of alienation. I am talking less of poetry and modern dance, for example, than of continual, daily modes of behavior: sensibility in satisfying the essential needs of food, clothing, and shelter; the search for work which does not completely smother all one's dignity; a perspective on wealth. I have never seen much joy as the owner of one El Dorado passes the owner of another. I have seen two sandal-wearers stop to compare the way they stitched the straps to the soles. There is here some warmth.

This must sound doltishly simplistic. I do not feel that society must be humane. But it must allow the individual to be humane. I feel that there are too many laws infringing upon the natural rights of the person. A man bound by laws which he considers unwise or unjust will naturally temper his allegiance to the society which maintains those laws, especially when he thinks himself to be without any hope of altering the circumstances. It is no secret that vast numbers of people are daily ignoring statutes which set guidelines

—and promise punishment to offenders—about matters of essentially personal behavior.

If many of us are distrustful of a system which not only advises against some forms of what we believe to be purely personal matters but also makes us criminals for our behavior, it should be surprising to no one. Specifically, I am referring to laws which regulate or prohibit the use of some drugs, and which interfere with the sexual behavior of individuals. Drugs, I believe, are legitimate tools toward the basic understanding of aspects of our humanity. Although I accept the rule that the society we live in must prohibit the use of drugs which turn people into helpless wards of the state—I think heroin should remain inaccessible—I resent the dictates against the use of marijuana.

One's body is primarily one's own property. And for this reason, I also condone freer attitudes toward sex than appear in the law books. The complexities of interpersonal, emotional relationships have always astounded me, and the rather crude efforts by law and by custom to straighten out these complexities leave me dismayed. Once again, I can support some of the laws and attitudes—for example, those against pederasty—and I also have severe reservations about such things as promiscuity. Nevertheless, I approve the loosening of laws about sex, as I do for laws about many drugs. In the meantime, our ignoring as much as possible of restrictive measures in these areas is both a symbol and a symptom of alienation.

Yet even if all my selfish dreams came true and even if all my political attitudes were adopted, if I came to believe that I really did hold some significant power over my social destiny, if law and custom justified my beliefs about the ways of love and chemistry, I still would feel separate from much that goes on about me. It has to do with the intangibles of life-style.

I have said that life should be expressive of one's honest opinions. In this expression, one cannot only reaffirm one's own attitudes and reassure one's own dignity; one must also make a sincere effort to show others one's concern—in short, to bridge the gaps between people and organizations, between people and people: to reduce feelings of alienation. Yet it is our sad experience in this society to see all subcultures parodied, all individual expression popularized, all small achievement prostituted. "The real thing" was once an expression of confirmation, now it is a soft-drink slogan. "Love" is a line of cosmetics, a ginger ale, a string of plastic beads. The commercial behemoth is stomping on everyone. The true emotions displayed, the real feelings expressed are now tools for marketing analysts. When all such honesty is defiled, it is no wonder that so many feel cheated and alienated.

ALIENATION OF THE BLACK MAN

MICHAEL BRYANT
Co-Chairman, MOLIMO, *Black Students' Organization*
Fordham University at Lincoln Center

In America today the black man is the central figure in the interplay of racial forces all across the nation, a social revolution the like of which has never been seen in this country before. This revolution entails a very pronounced recasting of roles and various relationships—racial, cultural, and socioeconomic.

The boisterous outcry of the black man has compelled some to investigate what was under the lid upon which they so comfortably sat. Either they were going to investigate, or the lid of alienation was going to come off and hit them smack in the face. For under this lid lay a considerable population of people. They were people tired of alienation, oppression, repression, and racism. Under that lid was the life of the black man.

In terms of America as a whole, alienation seems to be the wound caused by the rapid growth of technology and the fantastic bureaucracy present in the society. Centralization threatens individuals who do not work for the bureaucracy, and bureaucracy cannot treat people as individuals.

Concentration of economic power and political power threatens individual autonomy. A little more than two-tenths of one per cent of all active corporations, most of which are dominantly owned and controlled by less than one-tenth of one per cent of their stockholders, hold sixty-five per cent of the national corporate income. There is little need for the individual to be an individual, so let him be alienated. The same behavior is found in the government; its alienating tools are wiretaps, conspiracy laws, and just plain, old, simple unresponsiveness.

For all normal purposes, the alienation of the black man was more simply called discrimination. It was found in employment, politics, housing, and education. In employment the use of the authority of law to restrain racial discrimination during World War II was practically nonexistent. In 1941, during a period of increasing labor-shortages because of the war, there remained a large untapped reservoir of black unemployed, who were kept out of the expanding defense industries because of long-established habits of racial exclusion. These patterns had been strengthened and hardened in the cold days of depression in the early 1930s, when blacks were squeezed out of their customary menial, lowgrade jobs as porters, waitresses, and other such unskilled positions. The substantial exclusion of blacks from defense work had led to an outbreak of violence in southern army camps, and in New York, Detroit, and Los Angeles.

A survey showed that seven out of ten blacks at this time believed that they were being discriminated against in employment. More than half in the South felt the same way. On the other hand, surveys of white attitudes in the South showed that only seven per cent were willing to give black people a chance, and only four per cent of that seven per cent were willing to give the black man equal wages. When you cannot get a job because of your color, or only at much less pay than a white person doing the same thing, what is that if not alienating?

One might answer: politics. In politics, the wand of discrimination waves freely. In one Alabama county, only five blacks were registered to vote in 1960. At the same time some 2,200 white persons were on register, even though blacks of voting age outnumbered whites 4,450 to 2,387, or just about 2 to 1. In another Alabama county, blacks make up 80 per cent of the total population. Of these black people, 5,182 were of voting age, but not one registered. This happened in 85 per cent of the counties in the South and you might wonder why the numbers are so gross. If you look, the record is replete with examples. They range from the systematic striking of some thousands of blacks from the voting registry in Louisiana parishes or counties in the 1956 national elections and the resulting refusal of the grand jury to indict under the federal statutes, to a whole catalogue of subterfuges and strategies employed to deprive blacks of the right to vote.

The greatest concentration of denials of the civil right to vote exists in four states of the deep South: Alabama, Georgia, Louisiana, and Mississippi. In 1961, the report of the United States Commission on Civil Rights indicated that in Mississippi only 25,000 blacks registered for the 1960 election, out of a total of 385,000 eligible. In a dozen counties where blacks constituted more than 50 per cent of the population, a total of 21 blacks registered in the 1960 election. In five counties, not a single black was allowed to vote. In Alabama, 66,009 blacks registered, out of 481,320 of voting age. Several rural counties had no black registrants at all. Even the industrial, partially unionized county of Birmingham registered only 1,900 out of 116,160 blacks; the list goes on and on, as it has been going on and on for decades. And now the country cries alienation.

About 1915, the black exodus to the North began, and measures to restrain the black movement were many and varied. Racial zoning and racially restricted housing appeared on the scene to serve the majority power-structure, and vested interests in the black belt joined in this new approach.

Everywhere racial segregation was on the increase. This trend continued and became intensified during the period from World War II to the present. Currently this pattern of population-movement found in the cities of the South, the North, and the West, coupled with inadequate housing-supply and racially restricted markets, has led rapidly to a nation whose central cities are predominantly occupied by blacks and poor whites living in overcrowded, constantly worsening slums, ringed all around by white suburbs and businesses. Deprived of a decent chance to live, constantly engaged in combat with disease, and with no way to move, the slums do know alienation.

In education, one example would show conditions the black man has to cope with. In North Carolina, black students attend school on the average of 67 days per year; white students, 133. The average salary of black teachers, of which there are few, is $112.31; of white teachers, $383.39. Pupil load per teacher, for blacks, is 64 students; for whites, 36. Value of school property per child in the grammar and secondary schools is $2.57 for blacks; $32.11 for whites.

Indeed the process behind alienation is a slow and quite deceptive one. For the black man it is the total isolation from the American dream. Sometimes a black youngster is favored by white teachers, who, recognizing his traditional handicap, give him special encouragement. Social clubs and different charities give crops and bits, and very small donations. Schools give small honors and petty class-offices, and the boy feels no isolation and expects life to be somewhat as sweet as it was in his youth. For a child, it was all right to have a couple of white friends and to know the leading citizens of the town and to watch your sister marry in the style of the middle-class neighbors, even though it put your people in debt for years.

All this is fine and the boy could feel that he was part of things—until he finds out that that job of grocery clerk, or reporter on the town newspaper, or bookkeeper in the bank, or supervisor in the playground is denied him, and that the high aspirations which his high-school honors had stimulated in him were restricted to bootblack or janitor. At this time, it was very easy for him to feel the cold clutches of alienation, or more simply, discrimination. He may then move to the North, where discrimination is more covert. Here he will run into blacks with the same problem; but in addition, their homes are more apt to be broken, fathers more frequently absent, and family atmospheres more negative.

The black man cannot help but maintain an inferior status in mind and a negative self-esteem. He feels that his color is bad, and through mass media and segregated public facilities, he is convinced of it. He perceives himself as an object of derision and disparagement, although he is told by the mighty law of the nation, by religious code, by moral and ethical values, and also by the will of God, that he is equal. But if the situation is still like this, what hope does he have? He feels tied down and cast out, an alien in limbo, a ship without a rudder, and he has been this way for 400 years in a land which claims to offer all a chance for life, liberty, and happiness. But the American way is to deny freedom and justice for the black man, and as things stand it seems that he will never be able to reach or attain any sort of satisfaction.

REFERENCE

Fromm, E. *Marx's concept of man.* New York: Ungar, 1961.

VI
RELIGIOUS ALIENATION

Religious Alienation
on the Catholic College Campus

WILLIAM C. McFADDEN, S.J.

Father William C. McFadden, S.J., is the chair-
man of the department of theology at Georgetown
University. He earned his A.B. degree from
Woodstock College, Maryland, in 1952; his M.A.
from Fordham University in 1957; and his S.T.D.
from the Gregorian University, Rome, in 1963.
Father McFadden writes for religious and theo-
logical journals, and is a member of the Catholic
Theological Society and the College Theology
Society.

I would like to begin by mentioning two authors whose thought has been especially helpful to me in interpreting religious alienation.

Lewis Feuer makes the point that alienation is not specifically modern; it is omnipresent. "What stands out from an historical and comparative stand-point is the omnipresence of alienation; it takes different guises in all societies" (Feuer, 1969, p. 90).

It is also impossible to define alienation with any sharp outline. There are those who define alienation in terms of such notions as powerlessness, meaninglessness, normlessness, isolation, and self-estrangement, and yet "a multitude of alienated persons would be dissatisfied equally with conditions of power-possession, meaningfulness, norm-orientedness, involvement, and self-acknowledgement" (Feuer, 1969, p. 91). There is surely alienation in loneliness, but there is also an alienation in togetherness and overidentifica-tion.

171

Feuer's own attempt at definition shows why alienation takes on so many different forms. Each person has a basic emotional desire to achieve identity, to have a sense of his individuality as distinct from roles which his social groups impose on him. The experience of alienation is the experience of having this desire frustrated in some particular way. Thus, Feuer concludes, alienation is the term used "to convey the emotional tone which accompanies any behavior in which the person is compelled to act self-destructively; that is the most general definition of alienation, and its dimensions will be as varied as human desire and need" (Feuer, 1969, p. 95).

A second author whose work in this area is most helpful is Peter Berger. We cannot enter into his whole theory of the social construction of reality, but let us mention at least this: man produces his social world; it is also true to say that his social world produces man. The relationship between the two is an ongoing dialectical one. Alienation, for Berger, occurs when a man loses the sense of contributing to the construction of his social world and feels only acted upon by it. It becomes for him something fixed, necessary, and fated.

Alienation, then, is a phenomenon of consciousness. It is furthermore not something you fall into during adolescence, but is man's original condition. Berger cites the work of Lévy-Bruhl on the "primitive mentality," and that of Piaget on the thinking of children. Man begins in a state of alienation. At best he develops to a de-alienated condition.

Finally, Berger wishes to keep distinct the notions of *alienation* and *anomie*. Anomie represents a complete break between a man and his world attended by loss of orientation, identity-confusion, and the like. The alienated person, on the other hand, is not separated from his ordered world. He is subjected to it in a necessary fashion from which there seems to be no appeal.

With these pre-notes in mind, then, let us turn to our particular topic.

GENERAL RELIGIOUS ALIENATION

If alienation is taken in a very general sense to mean that condition in which my "self" is strange to me, then religious alienation is a loss of harmony between me and my religiously formed self. Having been to some degree shaped and molded by a religion, I begin to feel uncomfortable with the way of life my religion has been preparing me for. I find it harder and harder to say the things I am supposed to say and to do the things I am expected to do "as a good Catholic." To the extent that I can, I pull back from participation in religious activities. They make me feel like a hypocrite.

The experience of being religiously alienated depends, of course, on the kind of religious education a student has received, but I doubt that any form of religious education could ward it off entirely.

Some students speak of religion as a crutch, implying that it only serves as a support for those who are too weak to stand on their own two feet. A more appropriate image would be that of a body-cast. Religion is seen not merely as the support of the weak but as the binding of the strong. One student summed this up in what has to be a classic expression of the experience of alienation: "The Church is always preventing me from doing things I want to, and making me do things I don't want to."

The above formulation sounds like a typical charge against parents, and I suppose that is fitting, since both parents and the Church play similar roles in the process of educating the young: they are communicating truths and values; they impose discipline; a great deal of their teaching is to be accepted on the basis of authority.

If Peter Berger is right in saying that alienation is not a late development of consciousness and that infantile consciousness develops in an already alienated state (Berger, 1967, p. 86), then all early parental and religious teaching is received in an alienated consciousness and fosters, or at least preserves, that alienation.

As the young person moves through adolescence, the trick is for parents and the Church to aid the individual in moving from an alienated consciousness to a mature self-consciousness. This is exceedingly difficult to do. The adolescent, on the one hand, is likely to be very touchy about anything in your program of education which seems to prolong or restore his state of alienation. The most reasonable regulation may be rejected on the grounds that you are treating him "like a child."

The educator, on the other hand (parent or the Church), has a deep concern that the same truths and values already taught to the young in an alienating way may now be embraced by the mature self-consciousness. This constitutes for the educator an irresistible temptation to manipulate the young person in dozens of subtle ways so that freedom to choose is granted only in those instances where the young person chooses "correctly," i.e., in accordance with the wishes of the educator. This tactic only serves to prolong the alienated state and to postpone the achievement of maturity.

Religious educators are particularly vulnerable to this temptation to manipulate because of the importance, at least to them, of the truth and value they wish to communicate.

We might, then, conclude that the religious alienation on a Catholic college campus is simply an instance of an ordinary and inevitable alienation, indeed a necessary stage in the healthy development of a young person if he is to assume personal responsibility for his religious life.

By and large I think this is so. As self-consciousness develops, any person becomes increasingly aware of how much he has been held under subjection and how much he continues to be inhibited by forces beyond his control. He seeks to be free of them so that he can choose for himself.

SPECIFICALLY CATHOLIC ALIENATION

But suppose that we raise a further question: Is there a distinctly Catholic form of religious alienation? And if so, what are its characteristics?

I would answer the first question in the affirmative; but before proceeding to describe its present characteristics, I would like to make clear that not all students are religiously alienated. In some cases this is a tribute to good parental and scholastic religious-education. It represents the students' growth to a sufficiently mature religious attitude. In other cases a student may not seem to be alienated because he has not yet faced the problem of personally assimilating his religious teaching, perhaps because he is not yet fully aware of his personhood as distinct from his religiously formed self.

In any case what follows is a somewhat bleak picture composed of expressions of religious alienation which I have culled from writings of some students who do feel strongly alienated. No one student said all these things. Few students are completely free of the moods here expressed.

First of all, any institution is in trouble these days with the young, but this is particularly true of one almost two-thousand years old whose procedures for dealing with change are not notably swift. Despite the considerable changes in the content and methodology of religious instruction in Catholic schools, it is still quite common on the college level to hear passionate denunciations of the Baltimore Catechism. There is great anger at having been "spoon-fed, force-fed, brainwashed, and indoctrinated."

Certain Catholic doctrines are a cause of alienation for a growing number of students. For example, today's college student was taught to be proud of the fact that he belonged to "the one, true Church," but he is likely to be embarrassed by those words now and dismiss them as outmoded and "elitist." Today's college student remembers his early religious education as mostly negative: "salvation is something which you attain by not doing certain things." Today he is ill-at-ease with the notion of personal salvation. He responds quickly to the value of working toward the greater temporal well-being of man, especially of minority groups and the poor. But to do this for personal salvation seems self-centered, "an ego trip."

He was taught the importance of assenting to the truth of Catholic dogma, but he does not see much difference whether he assents or not. A great deal of Catholic dogma has no clear and pressing connection with action, although it may serve as a basis for passionate involvement. Students cannot fail to notice that many of those who seek to dig firm foundations of a religious/theological nature never seem to come up out of the cellar to *do* anything.

He identifies easily with the character of Judas in the rock opera *Jesus Christ Superstar* who complains to Jesus, "all your followers are blind, too much heaven on their minds," and who criticizes Magdalene's waste of valuable ointments: "We could have raised maybe three hundred silver pieces or more. People who are hungry, people who are starving, matter more than your feet or hair." And so the student says, "I'm going to work on behalf of my fellow man. If that happens to qualify me for 'salvation,' that's fine, but I can't afford to think much about that."

Catholic moral teaching is generally approved, but not because it is Church teaching. It is simply seen to be a good way to treat your fellow-man.

In the area of sexuality, however, the experience of alienation is particularly strong. Catholic teaching has been strict and detailed concerning the conditions which must be fulfilled for the enjoyment of sexual pleasure to be nonsinful. Young people are more likely to say that the giving and receiving of sexual pleasure is a warm human experience and should be viewed very positively. In any case they will quote the oft-repeated maxim that no one has the right to tell another what he may or may not do in private in matters of sex.

The question of contraception is of particular importance, for the effects of that extended debate go far beyond the issue itself. Many find the Church's teaching on contraception unbelievable. As authority was more and more invoked to resolve the question, that authority itself became unbelievable.

When appeal was made to the rights of conscience, the reply was that in this matter conscience could be rightly formed only in one way. This is understood as requiring that you hand over your conscience to the judgment of another. When the authority invoked has been seriously eroded, religious alienation is inevitable.

Liturgy is an area which some university chaplains view as a strong counterforce against alienation. This is so, at least for small-group liturgies, designed for students, often by students, and with considerable student participation. But what happens when they return home for vacation? Their reaction is to experience an acute sense of alienation. Since for most Catholics the parish Mass is the most important link with the Church, this negative reaction must give cause for great concern.

I have left for last a phenomenon which has greatly puzzled me. It seems to be specific to Catholic religious education. Suppose a student learns in a fifth-grade history class that the invention of the cotton gin was the cause of the Civil War. Then he comes to college and acquires a much deeper and broader appreciation of the factors involved in that war. He ends up with a feeling of satisfaction at having grown intellectually. It never seems to occur to him to complain about his fifth-grade teacher.

The same student reacts differently in theology class. Even students who are not alienated and find new teachings personally satisfying still spend a great deal of time deploring their previous instruction.

I do not know why there is this abiding resentment. I suspect that it is due not so much to what was taught, as to the way in which it was taught. College students of today seem to resent that, when they were young and impressionable, the awesome authority of God Himself was invoked on behalf of teachings which are now seen to be inadequate and even false.

Perhaps this resentment is strongest in those who took religion very seriously and built their lives around it. More precisely, as one student put it, "It's worship that makes the difference. They're asking you to worship Almighty God through their teaching and they ought to get it right."

GOD AND INDIVIDUAL FREEDOM

Perhaps the simplest way to sum up the entire struggle is to say that each person is seeking to realize himself, and the Church, Christ, and God are always getting in the way.

Young people want to test and see how much meaning they can confer on their lives in the world and how much meaning they have to accept as pre-established by some source beyond their control. This sets the stage for a kind of competitive relationship with God: "the more He determines, the less I am free to choose."

Thus they are quick to sympathize with Sartre when he rejects the notion of creation as incompatible with human freedom. He gives this idea vivid expression in his adaptation of the story of Orestes, the Greek tragic hero. Sartre's Orestes stands up to Zeus and refuses to obey him on the grounds that to make someone free, as Zeus did, is to renounce dominion over him. "No sooner had you created me," Orestes says, "than I ceased to be yours" (Sartre, 1949, p. 121). Orestes *is* his freedom; to take it away is to destroy the person of Orestes.

As long as Orestes thought of himself as a *creature,* he was at one with nature and alienated from himself. Suddenly he realized that he was free, and nature sprang back. There was no longer a heaven, a right or wrong, anyone to give him orders. He must blaze his trail alone, for every man must find out his own way.

This catches very well the mood of many a young person who does not see how he can be free in the presence of God. That he can be free is clearly the teaching of the Church: "God has regard for the dignity of the human person whom He Himself created; man is to be guided by his own judgment and he is to enjoy freedom" (Vatican Council II, 1966, n. 11, p. 690). The question remains, how can he be free?

Berger's answer is that, while religion does have an intrinsic tendency to place man in an alienating total dependence, there may also be in a given religion de-alienating or liberating elements (Berger, 1967, p. 96). For example, the God of the Bible relativizes the social order, and His prophets debunk "sacred" institutions.

Man is thus freed from alienating subjection to the world, to the state, or to the Church. But what of his total dependence upon God? Does this not leave him ultimately deprived of choice and alienated from his true self? Thinkers have wrestled with this question over the centuries, and it seems to me that we must continue to do so. Only to the extent that we penetrate and illumine this mystery will we overturn the idol which modern man fears: a God who is in competition with him, who so controls and regulates him as effectively to remove his freedom.

Perhaps no one has gone more directly to the heart of the issue than St. John. The God who is love and whose love was revealed in the sending of His Son to redeem us has loved us, John notes, "first" (1 Jn. 4:19). That we are at all, we owe to this first love.

Meditation on the implications of this fundamental fact can provide a satisfying answer to our problem, at least for someone who has been well-loved, i.e., who has had the experience of love's power to generate your life as yours, to give you to yourself. Such a person has no fear of losing himself in the presence of God who is love. It is rather with God as partner that he hopes to come to a full realization of himself.

But what answer shall we give to someone who has not been well-loved and who still sees others as rivals for the possession of his self?

We reach here a galling limitation. Perhaps we can give no answer, at least at present. You cannot preach the fatherhood of God to someone whose sole experience of fatherhood has been subjection to an irritable and overpowering autocrat. Perhaps the best we can do is to hold out an answer which we know cannot be accepted as such right now. No, there is one thing better, and that is, if we are up to the task, to love such an individual well. For you cannot preach that God is love to someone whose sole experience of being loved has been an alienating struggle over who is to control his life. But you can make a beginning and expose him to the liberating experience of the coordinate and cooperative power of love, that two may join in seeking the good of one.

If we find ourselves dealing in large measure with students who are defending themselves against us in religious matters, this is because the formidable forces of alienation connected with religion have been too little opposed and overcome by the even more formidable force of love.

178   RELIGIOUS ALIENATION

Sometimes I think that God is more interested in our being free than we are. Sometimes I think that God is more interested in our students' being free than we are. Sometimes I think that there is a connection between those two statements.

REFERENCES

Berger, P. L. *The sacred canopy*. Garden City, N.Y.: Doubleday, 1967.
Feuer, L. What is alienation: The career of a concept. In D. Burrows & F. R. Lapides (Eds.) *Alienation: A casebook*. New York: Crowell, 1969. Pp. 87–98.
Sartre, J. P. *No exit and three other plays*. New York: Random House, 1949.
Vatican Council II. Declaration on religious freedom. In W. M. Abbott (s.j.) (Ed.) *The documents of Vatican II*. New York: Herder & Herder, 1966. Pp. 675–696.

Alienation
Among Priests Today

GEORGE V. FOGARTY

Father George V. Fogarty received an M.A. degree from Fordham University in 1952 and is currently a candidate for the Ph.D. degree in classics at the same university. Father Fogarty has served as professor of classics at Cathedral College, Brooklyn; Dean of Cathedral College; and Rector at Cathedral Preparatory School, Elmhurst, N.Y. At the present time, he is the director of the Pastoral Institute of the Diocese of Brooklyn; a member of the Priests' Senate of the Diocese; and the Director of the Diocesan Program of Parish Councils. Father Fogarty also contributes a weekly column to the diocesan newspaper, The Tablet.

In the preface to his recent book, Bernard Murchland says that we live under the dispensation of alienation (Murchland, 1971, p. ix). Indeed the title itself, *The age of alienation,* suggests the prevalence of estrangement in our society. Priests, especially today, are men of their age; hence it is not surprising that alienation affects so many of them, both young and old. We are sure of the problem; of the causes we cannot be so sure. The alienation seems to result from changes in the Church; from forces in society, some of which are hostile to religion, others quite neutral; from misunderstandings and false expectations for which the priests themselves are responsible; and from problems long-unsolved in the Church.

In this paper we shall of necessity limit ourselves to current considera-

179

tions. Priests have always been beset with problems. Whether these have been more numerous or more serious than those which other groups have had to face does not matter so much. The problems of priests are always significant. For when those who are called to service and leadership are troubled, then their people suffer. Again, we can only identify the problems and suggest the causes. But this can lead us to understanding and possibly to solutions.

When we think of alienation among priests today, we are primarily concerned with a kind of social alienation which Keniston describes generally as "a reaction to the stresses, inconsistancies or injustices in our social order" (Keniston, 1965, p. 9). It reflects another notion of Keniston's, that alienation is often synonymous with the feeling that "something is wrong somewhere" and that "we have lost something important" (Keniston, 1965, p. 452). This social alienation easily affects priests psychologically; it seems to be responsible for the malaise which has come over so many priests, even many who, by talent and experience, should be able to be relied upon in this time of change.

For our purposes we shall distinguish two general groups of priests: the one traditional in ideas and in style, more conservative in the face of change; the other advanced in ideas, contemporary in style, and progressive. By way of identification we shall speak of the two as old and new priests. We are all aware, however, that we do not mean to divide them strictly according to age, for there are some young priests who are very traditional, and many older ones who are progressive and are moving forward. The division is mainly one based on vision and spirit.

CURRENT STUDIES ON PRIESTLY LIFE AND MINISTRY

There is an increasing amount of books, studies, and papers on priestly ministry and the problems of today's priests. At the risk of oversimplification we can say that the convergence of evidence identifies three central issues: freedom and authority, personal loneliness, and a lack of satisfaction with the priest's role in the present Church.

As we analyze these issues and as we try to spell out their concrete manifestations, we shall rely especially on the current material provided by the following recent studies:

1. Report on Priestly Life and Ministry of the National Conference of Catholic Bishops.* This is an exhaustive study which has already taken four years. We shall make use of the sociological portion of the study

* Only preliminary reports of this study have been published thus far, but in a letter of December 15, 1971, to the Editor, Dr. Victor J. Heckler, co-author of the Loyola Psychological Study, indicates that the bishops are preparing to make the report available to the public in the very near future.—Ed.

prepared by the National Opinion Research Center at the University of Chicago, under the direction of Father Andrew Greeley (1971). We shall also use the psychological study conducted by the Department of Psychology of Loyola University in Chicago, under the direction of Father Eugene Kennedy (1971a; 1971b).

2. Study of Priestly Celibacy by the National Federation of Priests' Councils. This survey was conducted by John P. Koval and Richard W. Bell of the University of Notre Dame (Koval & Bell, 1971).

3. The Schallert Report. This is an independent work done by Father Eugene Schallert, a Jesuit sociologist at the University of San Francisco, and issued under the title: Some factors associated with voluntary withdrawal from the Catholic priesthood (Schallert & Kelley, 1970). This report contains a good analysis of the problems uncovered in the research.

4. A preliminary summary of the personnel survey made of the priests of the Archdiocese of New York with the professional assistance of four professors of Columbia University.†

5. An attitudinal study of ideas and concepts of the priesthood conducted by and among the priests of the Diocese of Brooklyn who were ordained between 1964 and 1970.‡

6. A schema, entitled: The ministerial priesthood, prepared in Rome for the synod of bishops which met during October, 1971 (Bishops' Synod, 1971).

SCHALLERT'S DROPOUT STUDY

The synod schema, referred to immediately above, focuses the question for us in its opening paragraph: "Today the ministry of Catholic priests is marked by crisis. In many places, the crisis seems serious; and no one denies that it exists" (Bishops' Synod, 1971, p. 1). We can learn a great deal about this crisis from Schallert's study on priests who withdrew from the ministry. It is reported that up to twenty-five thousand or five per cent of the world's priests left the ministry in the eight years from 1963 to 1970. The fact of so many priests' leaving is not the only problem of ministry, but it is a sign of the crisis and an occasion for great concern. The reasons for the departures are important to our understanding of the alienation among priests who continue in the active ministry.

Schallert tries first to identify some of the tensions and contradictions felt by those interviewed. He lists two which relate to the person of the priest: freedom *versus* authoritarianism, and personalism *versus* total-role incumbency. He contrasts the need to grow as a person, to be one's self, and

† A report of this survey, with the title: A preliminary summary of some of the main themes of the personnel survey with illustrative tables, was limited to private circulation, but was reported in the *New York Times*, May 2, 1971, p. 74.

‡ The results of this study were privately issued during February, 1971, under the title: Attitudinal study of ideas and concepts of the priesthood, conducted among priests of the Diocese of Brooklyn ordained between 1964 and 1970.

to exercise responsible freedom with that authoritarianism which seems to control everything and which fosters the idea that "the individual must always think, feel, judge, act, talk, dress, and, in general, behave in such a way that his identity as priest is evident to all" (Schallert & Kelley, 1970, p. 432). So many priests found the traditional role too restrictive for the true mission of the Church.

Schallert then gives some reasons expressed by the respondents which relate more to the Church itself. He notes the difference between a dynamic view of the institution and structure of the Church and a more static one; and between a vital, enriched, personalized message and a rigid dogmatism. The significance of these tensions is that they point up the great expectations created by Vatican Council II and the impatience now felt by so many because of the slowness or lack of change and renewal. In this connection he also notes the human compassion, the understanding, and the sensitivity needed to relate to the world, and contrasts it with a doctrinal orientation which emphasizes rightness, logical cogency, and clarity.

Finally Schallert describes the problems arising from priests' desire for greater democratization, for fuller participation, and for relevance.

Having identified these sources of difficulty, Schallert then describes the process of alienation which develops with the following manifestations:

1. *A sense of powerlessness:* For the new priests this comes from the feeling that they cannot do anything to change and renew the Church. For the older priests it results from the fear of too much change, that things have gotten away from them. For them it is a far cry from "the good old days."

2. *Normlessness:* The goals of the Church and the standards for teaching and acting are not clear. "What is right today?" This is disturbing to older priests; it leaves the new priests without guidance.

3. *Meaninglessness:* In the face of so many changes in the Church and in the world, the priest especially must be a source of meaning for himself, and no one else can really provide it for him. This is difficult for all, and impossible for many. Then the constant questioning by themselves and by others becomes very troubling.

4. *Self-estrangement:* Given the variety of ideas and understandings, the variety of styles of living and of ministry today, some priests feel more and more foreign in the world, others feel foreign in the midst of their primary group, their fellow-priests. This is always difficult and painful.

5. *Isolation:* In this final phase there is the experience of no communication, no common understanding, no sharing of ideas. In the isolation of old and new positions, affecting all aspects of life, priests who are supposed to work together are completely separated. The complaint of the bewildered child is common: "You don't understand." For example, in the Archdiocese of New York survey, referred to above, 52 per cent of the pastors felt that there is a sense of community in the rectory; only 27 per cent of

the assistants shared this feeling. Neither side is misrepresenting; they simply have very different understandings of community. And this is such a crucial matter. It is because of the lack of real community that loneliness becomes a prime problem. Closely connected with the lack of community and the resulting loneliness is the whole issue of celibacy.

AMERICAN BISHOPS' REPORT

If we turn to the sociological section of the American Bishops' Report we find a listing of much the same problems. In the summary of the report (Greeley, 1971), almost all the points mentioned are potential causes for disaffection and alienation.

Greeley speaks first of all of the large number of priests who are dissatisfied with the way the ecclesiastical structure is shaped and the way in which decisions are made. He notes that new and old priests differ in their thinking about Church authority and that these differences are rooted in ideological differences about the very nature of the Church and of religion. In general, he says, the leadership of the Church does not share the dissatisfaction of the priests.

This leads him to speak of "a serious and potentially dangerous 'gap' between the priests and the hierarchy" (Greeley, 1971, p. 2). There were systematic and substantial differences between bishops and priests on almost every matter studied. This was particularly true in matters of sex—birth control, divorce, and celibacy. Further, the study showed that the condition of associate pastors—usually, of course, the younger priests—is poor. Job-satisfaction in this group, he says, is generally lower than that of unskilled workers. His final but telling point has to do with the decline among priests in enthusiasm for vocational recruiting. Greeley comments that this is a phenomenon which may be more serious than the resignation rate.

Turning to the psychological report, we find that Father Kennedy in his summary has expressed the implications of the research findings in terms of two questions which are of the greatest importance, for they get to the root of our problems:

1. Do you put first priority on assisting American priests to achieve greater personal maturity and therefore greater effectiveness as priests?
2. Do you rather put priority on American priests' adjusting themselves to the expectations of the institutional priesthood even at the price of not developing themselves? [Kennedy, 1971b, p. 1].

It is good to keep this conflict of points-of-view in mind as we note the main points made in the psychological report itself. There is special emphasis on the point that the priests of the United States are ordinary men. This is true, despite the fact that, as the survey indicates, approximately two-thirds of those studied are not developed to full maturity. For it must be added immediately that this is the same proportion which would occur in any cross-sectional sample of American men.

Conflicts and challenges arise for priests because they have to live as if they were *not* ordinary men. The expectations for them are too high, expectations arising from the institution of the Church, from the myths which Catholic folklore has built up around priests, and from expectations coming from the priest's own image of himself.

The report notes that priests tend to conformity, to passivity toward regulations and toward authority, and to willingness to stay away from many normal developmental experiences such as dating and a normal social life. These are understandable since in the period of the priests' training the institution especially rewarded these qualities.

Significantly, the report observes that priests use high-order defenses to handle the problems of psychological underdevelopment—for example, intellectualization. They do not confront their lack of growth or deal with it directly, but they are adept at smoothing it over through their skilled use of this intellectual defense.

This issue is seen in the matter of the priests' interpersonal relations. These are frequently distant, highly stylized, and unrewarding both for the priest and for the other person. The defense was to enunciate a principle: the priest by his very calling should remain at a distance from people. Two conflicts arise from this stance today: the defense breaks down because people simply challenge the principle and because in a new style of life, new relationships are thrust upon priests; and, through the defense, there is no growth, the priest does not relate, and this prevents his getting through to people. This is very hard for a priest to face.

Two final points made in the report can be treated here briefly: So many priests perform adequately, but this is not the same as performing with a sense of, or an aspiration toward, excellence. There is no spark, no spirit. Again, priests are ambivalent toward authority, wanting its protection and direction on the one hand, while they resent it on the other.

The conclusion of the report should be quoted here:

> In summary, the ordinary men who are American priests are bright, able, and dedicated. A large number of them are underdeveloped as persons with a consequent lack of fully realized religious and human values in their lives. They are not sick; they are not fully grown. They seem to need a broader, deeper, and genuinely freer experience of life to overcome this lack of development. There seem to be minimal risks in increasing the active options in their lives and, therefore, increasing the areas in which they must become more fully responsible for themselves and their work.
>
> The priests of the United States are clearly adequate in their function;

they could be far more effective personally and professionally if they were helped to achieve greater human and religious maturity. The basic therapy for this kind of problem is the opportunity and encouragement for a deeper and freer participation in life itself [Kennedy, 1971a, p. 11].

OTHER MANIFESTATIONS OF TENSION AND CONFLICT

The various other studies available to us usually reinforce the points which we have made. They do, however, contain some further issues which cannot be overlooked.

Priests of all ages are distressed that fewer Catholics go to Church, that they subscribe less to religious teaching and practice, that many so-called active Catholics no longer relate to the structure of the Church, and that a recent Gallup poll reveals that so many Americans discount the influence of religion today. These factors make priests question themselves and the meaning of their religious service.

When the New York Archdiocesan survey was reported in the *New York Times,** the headline read: "Study Finds Priests' Morale Here is Low." It went on to indicate that a majority of the priests had lower morale and less job-satisfaction than that of comparable groups of professionals. The sources of the discontent were that the priests had little responsibility, that their work lacked challenge and meaning, that their talents and skills were not used, and that they were overoccupied with time-consuming but routine work. There was clearly a divergence between their expectations for priestly work and the reality, and between the demand made on them and their own concept of their role.

In the replies, only 27 per cent of the curates found high satisfaction in their work; added to that, only 50 per cent of the pastors found high satisfaction. There is much confusion and varied understandings of priest's work. In a number of reports, and in informal discussions, we learn that each group of priests, old and new, believes it works hard and the other one does not.

In the Brooklyn survey of young priests, 75 per cent of them were found to be dissatisfied with the pace of change. Eighty per cent of the respondents made this dissatisfaction the prime factor in the withdrawal of priests from the active ministry, since they could no longer live within the structure of the Church as currently constituted. It is notable that in this survey twelve proposals on restructuring the Church were given for evaluation. Eleven of the twelve were approved by at least two-thirds of the respondents. However, in only three cases did even one-half of the respondents expect to see the proposals worked out. This is evidence of a distressing lack of confidence in the Church's willingness to adapt to change.

* May 2, 1971, p. 74.

Again, in seeking to understand the interplay of new and old priests, the book of A. J. Moore (1969), *The young adult generation,* is very helpful when we realize that the young priests and some not so young—perhaps a higher percentage than in other professional groups—belong to or include themselves in the young-adult group of today. A first problem for the priests is that so many of the young adults have opted out of organized religion. To older people this reaction seems to be a loss of faith, to the younger ones it is a rejection of superficial faith and a search for meaning and commitment in life.

In contrast to traditional, institutional religion, Moore (1969, pp. 83–84) sets out the new alternatives which move the young adults. For them, the essence of spirituality lies within human experience. They are concerned about the recovery, or discovery, of community and the sacredness of relationships. They put priority on the quest for the spirit and emphasize self-expression and self-realization.

Young priests generally relate to all this, they wonder about the official Church's attitude, and they often fear that they themselves will compromise and fail to preserve these live values. In a very strong article in *Newsweek* following the Spring 1971 meeting of the National Conference of Catholic Bishops, the religion editor, Kenneth Woodward said, "It is sad to watch them [priests] turn sour in a Church that I believe unnecessarily inhibits their deepest Christian instincts" (Woodward, 1971, pp. 74–75).

A special problem of our day, particularly in our metropolitan areas, is the priests' ministry in the inner city—their service to the blacks, the Puerto Ricans, and other poor minorities. The priests who devote themselves to such work take on new attitudes, develop new life-styles, form new allegiances which easily isolate them, always in feeling and often in fact, from the diocese and from their fellow-priests. At the same time such priests often find it next to impossible to be fully accepted in the new community which they come to serve.

CELIBACY

In the course of this paper, we have touched on the issue of celibacy more than once. It needs a more specific treatment. All the studies reported in this paper indicate that a majority of the priests of the United States—and the plurality increases greatly among younger priests—would favor optional celibacy. The report on the survey of the National Federation of Priests' Councils sums up the situation in this way:

> The majority of the clergy favor optional celibacy. A greater majority favor the ordination of married laymen. Most think the celibacy law will eventually change; they are divided as to when. . . . Those who oppose

the above changes are generally over 50; those who support them are generally under 45 [Koval & Bell, 1971, pp. 6–7].

This position is most understandable as a response to the concern of priests for freedom and personal responsibility, for meaning in all aspects of living, and for solutions to the problem of loneliness.

It is important to recognize, however, that almost all priests affirm the value of celibacy for priestly life and ministry and only a very small percentage would anticipate marrying, if permission were to be granted. This latter fact seems to indicate that the celibacy issue is a symptom, that it is a dramatic issue, and that it is a sign that substantial changes are needed in the structures which affect the lives of our priests today.

CONCLUSION: TROUBLE AND HOPE

To do as we have tried to do in this paper, to search out and line up the manifestations of alienation among priests, is not calculated to present a bright picture. Yet if we see the elements presented as difficulties to be corrected and as demands for renewal, then there can be hope.

Moore in his book on the young adults calls them a prophetic generation. He says:

In their protests and demonstrations as well as in their general style of life young adults are trying to tell us something. They are trying to say that there are some things basically wrong with life in our times, and they are pointing out the pitfalls as well as the possibilities for life in the future [Moore, 1969, pp. 150–151]

Our young priests, among whom we find more signs of estrangement than among those who are older, also are a challenge to all of us. With strong voice and in response to the Spirit they point the way to what can be a better future for the Church.

Keniston reminds us of an important point in the section of his book where he asks: "Is alienation good or bad?" There he says:

It cannot simply be said that society is right and the alienated wrong; alienation may point more to a society that needs "treatment" than to an individual in need of therapy [Keniston, 1965, p. 413].

The results of the many studies of priestly ministry reveal not so much deep-seated personal psychological alienation as a social estrangement and a disaffection and widespread malaise. The problems are many and serious, but there are also increasing efforts to meet them, as a part of the general renewal of the Church. The understanding of the problems and their causes can lead us to solutions, both in helping individual priests and in working to effect new structures in the Church.

REFERENCES

Bishops' Synod. Synod schema on the ministerial priesthood. *Documentary Service*. United States Catholic Conference, Press Department. April 29, 1971.

Greeley, A. American priests: Sociological study by the National Opinion Research Center. Summary report. *Documentary Service*. United States Catholic Conference, Press Department. April 19, 1971.

Keniston, K. *The uncommitted: Alienated youth in American society*. New York: Harcourt, Brace, 1965.

Kennedy, E. C. (M.M.) Loyola psychological study of the ministry and life of the American priest. Text. *National Catholic Reporter*, April 30, 1971. (a)

Kennedy, E. C. (M.M.) Loyola psychological study of the ministry and life of the American priest. Summary report. *Documentary Service*. United States Catholic Conference, Press Department. April 20, 1971. (b)

Koval, J. P., & Bell, R. W. A study of priestly celibacy. Summary of final report. *Priests USA*, 1971, *1* (9), 6–7 (April, 1971).

Moore, A. J. *The young adult generation: A perspective on the future*. Nashville, Tenn.: Abingdon, 1969.

Murchland, B. *The age of alienation*. New York: Random House, 1971.

Schallert, E. (S.J.), & Kelley, J. Some factors associated with voluntary withdrawal from the Catholic priesthood. *Lumen Vitae*, 1970, *25*, 425–460.

Woodward, K. A priest is as a priest does. *Newsweek*, May 10, 1971.

Alienation Among Members
of Religious Orders

GERALD A. MCCOOL, S.J.

Father Gerald A. McCool, S.J., has two de-grees from Fordham University, an A.B. (1940) and a Ph.D. (1956), and three degrees from Woodstock College, Maryland, a Ph.L. (1946), an M.A. (1947), and an S.T.L. (1953). He has published articles in such journals as Theological Studies, Thought, Modern Schoolman, Interna-tional Philosophical Quarterly, Continuum, *and* Re-view for Religious. *Father McCool has been on the faculty of Fordham University since 1955, initially at the College of Philosophy and Letters at Shrub Oak, and since 1969 at the Rose Hill campus, where he is currently associate professor of philosophy. He has been active in retreat work with religious and in various institutes devoted to religious renewal.*

In this paper alienation is used as a descriptive term to indicate, in loose and summary fashion, the progressive loss of identification with their in-stitute experienced by religious in the turbulent years following Vatican II. Religious order will be taken to mean, again loosely, institutes of common life to whose constitutions members commit themselves by the public vows of religion. We have long been conscious of the distinguished history of religious life in the Orthodox and Anglican communities and, through increased personal contact and through such books as those by Biot (1963) and Heijke (1966), we are becoming more and more aware of the remarkable renewal of religious life in Lutheran and Calvinist communities which has taken place in the past three decades. Nevertheless, limits of time—to say nothing of the writer's competence—require that our discussion be confined to Roman Catholic groups.

THE PROBLEM OF ALIENATION

Alienation from their institute has become a major problem for Catholic religious because of its widespread nature. There were always religious who withdrew from their institute or lived restlessly inside it, either because they no longer felt within themselves the power or the willingness to shape their lives in accordance with its demands, or because they had reached the conviction that its life of rule was not the life of service which God wished them to lead within His Church. Their cases were exceptional, whereas in the last decade defections from religious congregations have grown to disturbing proportions. Furthermore, religious who continue to live in their institutes are upset, not only by the departure of respected confreres, but by the feeling that they have lost the peaceful, almost instinctive, identification of their commitment to God's service with the goals, ideals, and practices embodied in their congregation as a concrete social and ecclesial reality. Their congregation has become a questionable entity over against which they now stand consciously in judgment. The pressures, conflicts, and compromises of the past decade have desacralized it. Interiorization of its ideals once constituted the highest operative value of their lives. Yet, as its human weaknesses have been progressively exposed, often in bitter and recriminatory debate, they have been made to ask themselves whether the goals toward which their institute is striving in practice do not tend to diminish rather than to increase the spiritual strength of its members, and whether the social pressure which its common life exerts on them does not tend to weaken rather than to intensify the generous charity with which a Christian should give himself to the service of God in the Church.

Open divisions among religious over the manner in which their interior commitment to God and the Church should objectify itself in action have weakened the sense of union which links members psychologically to their institute. When radical and polarizing schisms become an enduring phenomenon in a congregation, there are many words and actions of superiors and fellow-members with which a religious who disagrees with them cannot identify, and from which, at first silently and later overtly, he dissociates himself. The peace, support, and pride which he once found in being "one of the congregation" have been diminished. Now he is inclined to think that either he stands alone in what matters most to him, or that his real community is his informal grouping with the religious who "feel as he does."

In either case his bond to the visible totality of his institute is no longer what it was and his normative goals and ideals cease to be sought through conscious identification with it. Psychological divorce from his institute is seldom a happy situation for the alienated religious. Frequently he complains that this is not of his own choosing. For his own part, he would like to identify with his institute as once he could, or hoped he could. "They," however, be they subjects or superiors, are making it increasingly impossible for him to do so in good conscience. Sometimes he wonders whether his public identification with a group from whom he has become interiorly dissociated is a living lie, and whether his continued membership is a sign of weakness rather than of fidelity to God.

THE SOCIAL AND ECCLESIAL ROOTS OF ALIENATION

Directors of conscience have become very sensitive to the damage which alienation from his institute can do to the individual member. It disturbs his peace of soul, saps his energy and enthusiasm, and diminishes his hope for the future of his congregation. Until very recently, however, directors of conscience felt quite frustrated in their efforts to deal with the problem on an individual basis. Since its roots were social and ecclesial it could not be treated simply as a personal difficulty, much less a personal aberration. Alienation was often overreaction, but it was reaction to a genuine, objective problem of the type about which psychiatrists tell us we should be worried. It was a psychological and spiritual response to the complexus of radical changes in the tightly woven net of interior and exterior relationships which bind a religious to his institute. These changes occurred too rapidly for religious, either individually or collectively, to accept them intellectually and emotionally. Not only were individual religious thrown off balance. Congregations were shaken in their own self-understanding, and, as their lack of emotional and intellectual equilibrium rose to the conscious level, an unsettling distrust in the group's ability to hear and answer the call of God became a collective phenomenon.

In a period of ecclesial and theological revolution in which so many new, and often opposed, ideas clamored for immediate recognition, how could a congregation clearly and rapidly define itself? Yet, if it could not, how could it help the religious to define his own relation to it? What goals, aims, and ideals could it present to him for his interiorization? What understanding of spiritual life and apostolic service could it advance to justify the many concrete and fundamental changes which he as a member was asked to accept in virtue of his commitment to the central purpose and ideals of his institute? The history of the early stages of *aggiornamento* was the history of growing alienation among members of religious orders which were unable to retain a spiritual understanding of their total life and role in the Church broad enough to serve as a satisfactory norm for the changes they were making and clear enough to justify these changes as genuine developments of their communal life and work. There are, however, encouraging signs that congregations are beginning to arrive at such an understanding and to reassess more clearly the changes made and still to be made on the basis of their perduring commitment to the life of the vows. It is early yet, but it would seem that in the progress of the *aggiornamento* which produced the problem we are beginning to find the elements of its solution. My reasons for thinking so are based on my reading of the history of religious congregations during the past ten years.

CONNECTION WITH THE GENERAL PROBLEMS OF THE CHURCH

The problem of alienation in religious cannot be considered in isolation from the general history of the *aggiornamento* Church. Religious have lived through the violent upheaval which accompanied the Church's change of stance toward liturgy, apostolic witness, and discipline, and her reevaluation of secular activity, the married state, and non-Catholic religions. They have shared the inevitable problems of a rapidly changing Church in interaction with a rapidly changing world. As they reassessed their relation to the Church, and her authority and doctrine in the period of revolutionary ferment so vividly described by James Hitchcock (1971) in his controversial account of the American *aggiornamento,* religious found themselves in conflict with other Catholics whose views and actions contradicted their own understanding of genuinely Catholic life and witness. As teachers, pastors, and social workers, they have become increasingly involved in the cultural and social revolution through which secular society has passed in the last decade. They have shared its hopes and fears, its divisions and alliances. The conflict between the individual and authority, the controversy about the nature of priestly and apostolic ministry, the breakdown in communication between orders, classes, and generations in the Church have disturbed and divided religious as they have other Catholics, and have colored the specific problem which they have about their identification with their institute.

THE VECTOR RESULTING FROM THE RAPIDITY OF CHANGE

In a religious institute, however, there is a tightly woven unity of family life and institutional activity, of interior prayer and discipline, and of external apostolic work. A change in one element in the life of a religious has repercussions in all the others. In institutional as well as in physical dynamics there is a "resultant vector," the combined thrust of which is the outcome of the interplay of many individual forces. Determining its strength and point of impact takes careful calculation when the forces at work are many and complex. Unfortunately, little attention was given to anticipating what might be the impact on the institute of the combined thrust of such a resultant vector. Powerful psychological and social forces were set loose when changes in the life and work of the institute were introduced piecemeal in reaction to the pressures of *aggiornamento*, without time to consider their cumulative effect on the total context and quality of religious life. Consequently, the changes set off a chain-reaction of response which no one had anticipated.

Most of our congregations date from the period of the Counter Reformation or the nineteenth century. Their histories are closely linked with the educational, missionary, charitable, and social institutions through which the Church rallied the faithful against the Reformation and nineteenth-century rationalism, and converted millions of Asians and Africans to the faith. In the minds of members of active congregations staffing these institutions, this was their work. It was the vocation which justified their sacrifices in the service of the Church. Today, the solid cultural and theological reasons why the Church's apostolic work could no longer continue in the form which had proved successful from Trent to Vatican II have been advanced many times in the balanced and nuanced discussions of competent theologians and can be more generally appreciated. Yet shattering changes in their relation to social and educational institutions were demanded of religious, before those who questioned them had the time to consider and appreciate the reasons for their necessity, and before their advocates had the time to understand them clearly and to formulate them in a balanced and convincing way. The result was resistance, often stubborn and emotional, followed by polarization of the institute and—under pressure for a quick decision—by confrontations and political solutions by compromise or *coup de main*. Misunderstanding was succeeded by distrust and a vague sense of betrayal, of being compromised through association with institutional activity whose connection with the religious' interior consecration to God's service was not as clear and intimate as it had been in the past.

To the disorientation caused by the altered relation between the exterior work of religious congregations and their inner life was added the shock of rapid changes in the inner life itself. Liturgy, life-style, prayer, and religious discipline were all affected. Some of the changes were comparatively superficial. Others were profound in their effect on the nature and structure of religious life. Yet these changes, too, had to be made before the religious who asked for them or were asked to make them had the chance to sift, clarify, and formulate the religious and theological reasoning which supported them. Confrontations within communities were violent and, understandably enough, resentment against compromise solutions was bitter.

In the intellectual confusion and the emotional polarization produced by poorly understood changes which revolutionized the nature of their life, religious, trained to a life of hierarchical obedience, could not master quickly and employ successfully the psychological and sociological techniques for decision-making which they were asked to use in coming to community decisions about their life and apostolate. Nor is it surprising that superiors, seeking the voice of the Spirit in a whirlwind of conflicting opinions and unsure of their own role in new institutional structures, were unable to exert the new type of leadership which many of their subjects demanded (though few could specify the form which it should take). And so, disappointment with community efforts at renewal became the deciding factor which fixed many a religious in his attitude of thorough-going alienation from his institute.

FACTORS CONTRIBUTING TO THE CURE OF ALIENATION

"Too much, too fast," the confusion, polarization, and psychological paralysis attendant upon radical changes made before they could be understood and accepted—these, it would appear, are the social and ecclesial roots of alienation in religious orders. Are there signs, however, that congregations are beginning to overcome their intellectual confusion and emotional division and to arrive at a common understanding of their life and work with which the alienated religious can again identify? We have reason to think so. In the forces at work in religious life there are a number of factors which are beginning to contribute to a movement in that direction.

1. *Time.* The first is time. Time contributes to clarification of thought. The rush of new ideas which overwhelmed us at the beginning of *aggiornamento* has slowed down. Theology is beginning to regain its balance, to weigh, reject, and develop the new ideas proposed about the Church, the life of grace, and the apostolate. The basis for a sound theology of the religious life is being laid on which religious may rely for the reconstitution of a total vision of their life. Time is the tester of initiatives and experiments. The results of successes and failures are becoming known and add empirical verification to the more theoretical conclusions of the theologians concerning the religious vocation. Time allows emotions to cool and changes, good or bad, to be accepted as facts of life rather than as rallying points for factions. Time brings into communities young religious untouched by the battles of the past whose positive endeavor to commit themselves to the life of the institute encourages and reunites older religious. There is a positive resultant vector in these sobering effects of time. Religious life has not been swept away. A total vision of its meaning and role in the Church seems a

possibility again, and the intellectual and emotional conditions for cooperative work by religious in finding it seem capable of being realized.

2. *Supernatural Realism.* The second encouraging factor in the contemporary movement of religious institutes is the growth of supernatural realism. The attrition of *aggiornamento* has taught religious that renewal is a slow and difficult business. Scientific and sociological techniques, though important, are not enough. Theological and historical studies, like those of Clarke (1970, 1971), Futrell (1970a, 1970b), Lonergan (1970), and Rahner (1964, 1971), have shown that communal discernment has as its condition a genuine spirituality of obedience to God which demands faith, prayer, and purity of heart. And once again, the theoretical reflections of the theologians are finding confirmation in the experience of the religious themselves. Many recent meetings of religious communities have been notable for the absence of the facile, secular-city optimism of early *aggiornamento*. Unity is emphasized once more as a grace to be won through the discipline of supernatural faith and prayer. With the development and dissemination of the spirituality of obedience to God in communal discernment, the spiritual director will find his ability to help the alienated religious notably increased.

3. *Clearer Understanding of Religious Renewal.* Another factor contributing to the better climate in religious communities is a clearer understanding of the nature of the religious renewal of the Church. Even in an age of secular involvement when the value of anonymous Christianity has gained acceptance, there is an essential role for the specific witness of the believing Christian in the visible Church. Religious through their special faith-commitment of the vows have a vital part to play in the specific witness of the visible Church to modern man. Yet, in an age in which, as Lonergan (1967, 1968, 1969) has shown, the Church is passing through a cultural crisis, that specific witness and apostolate must be redetermined. With the hierarchy and the theologians, religious are called to the slow and patient work of determining the details of its new form. The work will be long and painful. But for a religious, who can see once more the relation of that work to his personal commitment to God in the vows, its difficulties and dislocations become a challenge to generous united action with the fellow-members of his institute rather than a cause for alienation from it.

PROSPECTS FOR THE FUTURE

It would appear therefore that the clearer understanding of the nature and demands of *aggiornamento* which religious are beginning to acquire will enable many of them to shake off the disappointment and discouragement which underlie much of their alienation. Renewed appreciation of the supernatural nature and demands of religious renewal, the cooling of emotions, and increased appreciation that community discernment requires a vigorous, self-denying spirituality and not just techniques, may through their resultant vector enable some, if not all, communities to unite themselves once more in their life and work. A movement in that direction is visible. In many communities, however, it is still slack tide. Strong and enlightened leadership and the example of successful communities will be required to dissipate the inertia, distrust, and cynicism of religious whose alienation has become deep-seated. Even today, however, a spiritual director who has his eyes about him can give an alienated religious a clearer picture than he could some time ago of the causes of his malaise, and can point to the hopeful signs which may help him to overcome it.

REFERENCES

Biot, F. (o.p.) *The rise of Protestant monasticism.* Baltimore: Helicon, 1963.

Clarke, T. E. (s.j.) Religious community. *The Way,* 1970, *10,* 103–112.

Clarke, T. E. (s.j.) Jesuit commitment—fraternal covenant? *Studies in the Spirituality of Jesuits,* 1971, *3,* 69–101.

Futrell, J. C. (s.j.) Ignatian discernment. *Studies in the Spirituality of Jesuits,* 1970, *2,* 47–88. (a)

Futrell, J. C. (s.j.) *Making an apostolic community: The role of the superior according to Saint Ignatius of Loyola.* St. Louis: Institute of Jesuit Sources, 1970. (b)

Heijke, J. (c.ss.p.) *An ecumenical light on the renewal of religious community life: Taizé.* Pittsburgh: Duquesne University Press, 1966.

Hitchcock, J. *The decline and fall of radical Catholicism.* New York: Herder & Herder, 1971.

Lonergan, B. (s.j.) Transition from a classicist worldview to historical mindedness. In J. E. Biechler (Ed.) *The role of law in the church today.* Baltimore: Helicon, 1967. Pp. 126–133.

Lonergan, B. (s.j.) Theology in its new context. In L. K. Shook (c.s.b.) (Ed.) *Theology of renewal* (2 vols.). New York: Herder & Herder, 1968. Vol. I, pp. 34–46.

Lonergan, B. (s.j.) The absence of God in modern culture. In C. F. Mooney (s.j.) (Ed.) *The presence and absence of God.* New York: Fordham University Press, 1969. Pp. 167–178.

Lonergan, B. (s.j.) The response of the Jesuit, as priest and apostle, in the modern world. *Studies in the Spirituality of Jesuits,* 1970, *2,* 89–110.

Rahner, K. (s.j.) *The dynamic element in the church* (trans. by W. J. O'Hara). New York: Herder & Herder, 1964.

Rahner, K. (s.j.) *Chancen des Glaubens.* Freiburg im Breisgau: Herder, 1971.

VII
OTHER MANIFESTATIONS
OF ALIENATION

Alienation
Among the Aged

CHAIM GRUNWALD

*Chaim Grunwald received a B.S. degree, with
a major in sociology, from Brooklyn College in
1961, and an M.S.W. degree from the New York
University School of Social Work in 1963. Mr.
Grunwald has had extensive social work experience and, except for a two-year interval (1955–
1957) when he was in Israel, he has had a continuous connection since 1955 with the Educational Alliance, since 1966 as assistant executive
director. This is a Settlement House on the Lower
East Side in New York City, founded in 1889 to
serve the increasing number of Jewish immigrants
arriving from Eastern Europe. Today it maintains
extensive social, cultural, educational, and recreational services for all age and population groups
(including a residence for the elderly), as well as
programs for special problem-populations (e.g.
drug abusers, the mentally ill, delinquent youth,
etc.). In view of the topic of his paper, it should
be mentioned that, among numerous other commitments, Mr. Grunwald has served as a member
of the Task Force for Region I for the White
House Conference on the Aging.*

And so I learned that familiar paths traced in the dusk of
summer evenings may lead as well to prisons as to innocent,
untroubled sleep.—ALBERT CAMUS, *The Stranger*

Before addressing my subject directly, let me attempt to clarify the meaning
or meanings within which I will try to use the terms "Alienation" and "The
Aged."

199

Erik Erikson uses the term "alienation" to describe a basic attribute of man. He urges us to recognize and accept

> . . . the universality of the problem of technical estrangement which started with the creation of tools and the development of a self-conscious brain at the beginning of mankind [Erikson, 1964, p. 105].

In this sense, then, alienation is attributable to the nature of man as a self-aware creature who has developed tools and a technology, which have permitted him from the very beginning an ever-increasing degree of control and manipulation of his environment, and the self-awareness, tools and technology which have interposed themselves between man and his environment. Our ability to think about ourselves, to observe ourselves, and to make judgments about ourselves has caused us to become alienated from our sources, our roots, our original being. For the aged, of course, the awareness of our mortality is the most significant aspect of self-awareness.

For the purpose of this presentation, I will divide the theme into two parts: alienation from the societal point of view—alienation of the aged as a population group within society from the rest of society; and alienation from the personal, psychological point of view—alienation of the individual old person, which means the effect of the societal differentiation, societal alienation, upon the individual living within the population group called "The Aged." By societal alienation of the aged I will mean the estrangement of a total generation from society as a whole, whose opposite is societal integration—the ability to be part of the whole. Personal or psychological alienation will mean the estrangement of the individual aged person from himself, and the impairment of his ability to continue to play meaningful roles in relation to others and to society.

It may seem superfluous to define the term "aged." But though there is some agreement on its meaning (age 60 or 65 and over), and some of my discussion will address itself to this population as a whole, it will be helpful to think of the aged not only in terms of years, but in terms which functionally distinguish them from other groups—that is, in terms of *changes* in status, roles, and social participation *related to their age*. When we speak of alienation of the aged we speak of people who *because* of their age have in some way achieved a new status in their lives. They cease to be what they had been up to that point, up to that period, and become something else. The change affects their relationship to society, their relationship to what they are and do, and their self-perception. Winston Churchill was aged, but that does not say too much about him; Pablo Picasso is an old man, yet to say that is not very descriptive of him. Other characterizations, which are not considered attributes of old age, describe these and many other old people much more significantly.

Finally, when speaking of the contemporary aged I will not have in mind the severely disabled, incapacitated, senile—their alienation will have to do with specific disabilities—but that vast majority who are well enough physically and mentally to consider themselves and to be considered within the norm for their age group.

HISTORICAL REVIEW

The question before this Institute is whether alienation is a plight particular to or characteristic of modern man. I think that as far as the aged are concerned it is not. Throughout man's long history the place of the elderly in society has been rather precarious. The Bible exhorts us to honor our elders, and old age no doubt did confer status and authority in Biblical days. Yet the outcry "Cast me not off in the time of old age; forsake me not when my strength faileth" (Ps. 71:9) and the admonition "despise not thy mother when she is old" (Prov. 23:22) show that concerns similar to today's existed then. In primitive societies, certainly, the aged have never fared too well. Even though only a very small number survived to old age it was an almost universal custom—and one fully accepted by the aged themselves—to kill or abandon to death those who could no longer contribute to or move with their group, family, or tribe. In a sense, this was the ancient approach to the problem of overpopulation. G. W. Sumner discusses this in a chapter entitled, significantly, if none too subtly, "Abortion, Infanticide, Killing the Old" (Sumner, 1960, pp. 265–283), where he shows that some of these practices continued in Europe well into the Middle Ages. He speaks, for example, of Wales, where

> . . . sons pull their fathers out of bed and kill them to save the disgrace of dying in bed [Summer, 1960, p. 280].

and of Sweden where

> . . . the "holy mawle" . . . hung behind the church door which, when the father was seventy, the son might fetch to knock his father on the head as effete and of no more use [Sumner, 1960, p. 280].

These customs and practices were, of course, based on an economy of scarcity. When there is not enough, those who cannot contribute become a burden too heavy to bear, or, as Sumner puts it, the survival of one may endanger the survival of all.

We see then that alienation, if alienation means estrangement, if it means not having a place in your own world, has been the fate of the aged since the beginning of human life. Of the different economic stages man has gone through, agriculture has been the most congenial to the accommoda-

tion, maintenance, and social integration of the aged. In pre-agricultural *
societies (fruit-gathering, hunting, herding-nomadic), the enfeebled elderly
could not keep up; in post-agricultural * societies (mercantile, industrial,
automated), the elderly, even when well, have found themselves less and
less needed for societal or economic purposes. Therein may lie some of
the difference between the alienation of the modern aged and that of their
predecessors.

I mentioned an economy of scarcity. With the relative abundance in
the modern life of the Western world, with the rapid advances in medicine
and sanitation, in science and in technology, more and more people live
to be old. Another distinction, then, between the aged in primitive and
ancient societies and those of today is that today there are so many more
of them. The few who survived into old age in the past did fulfill a number
of crucial social functions: they were the transmitters of accumulated
knowledge and of the group's history and identity. They were also, because
of their long life and experience, likely to have the best basis for making
judgments and arriving at decisions. It may also be assumed that those who
lived longer under the harsh conditions of primitive life were the rather
sturdier and better-endowed part of the population to begin with, and that
therefore the aged deserved the respect and authority they enjoyed not only
by virtue of their age but also because they were in fact superior in ability
and knowledge to the general population.

In the West today, the aged face a loss in this respect in two ways:
many more survive, which perhaps lowers their average level of ability
and certainly their social standing—how many "wise elders" does a society
need? And then, the role of transmitting knowledge and tradition has been
usurped by technology. The transmission of knowledge today is not only
beyond the capacity of any individual or group of individuals; it is done
much more effectively, thoroughly, and perhaps reliably by means of books,
films, tapes, and so on. There is also, of course, the rapidity of change
today, so that knowledge which was valid 60, 40, or even 20 years ago
may not be nearly as valid today. This realization contributes to the
feeling, widespread among the young, that the knowledge and the wisdom
of the aged may not be as valuable today as it has been in the past. This
is, of course, an oversimplification. There are kinds of knowledge which
cannot be transmitted by books or mechanical means, but only through
personal contacts: the knowledge of life-experience, if you will. The
question here is whether as individuals and as a society we are capable of
leaving open, within the deluge of mechanically conveyed material which
we have to face daily, channels for such personal transmittal from one
generation to another.

* These are meant in a developmental, rather than chronological, sense.

SOCIETAL ALIENATION

It seems that, beyond that of wise elders, no role for its aged * has been
defined with any degree of clarity or depth by any society to date. We are
all obliged to seek our directives for living, and our identity, from outside
ourselves. Lacking such directives, the aged among us find themselves without a task, without a socially recognized purpose. This is the only age-
group for which no formal initiation is provided by society. Society has
established formal steps acknowledging our progress through the ages of
life—ceremonies, rites of passage. These rites not only mark the stages of
our lives—birth, puberty (confirmation), adulthood (graduation, marriage)
—but also spell out in a formal way societal norms, expectations, and
demands for each stage. They define us and our age-group in relation to
our general society and to other groupings in society. No such ceremony,
no such rites, no such steps exist in relation to the aged. We pass into old
age unnoticed and uncelebrated. (Very often, of course, the individual
does not wish to acknowledge the arrival of old age any more than society
does.)

There are therefore, in truth, no norms, demands, and expectations which
society imposes upon its aged. The aged have to make their own definitions,
define their own norms. There are positive factors in this state of limbo
in which the old person finds himself—the opportunity for choice and self-
determination—which I will come back to, but the old among us find themselves in the extremely difficult situation of not being responsible—not being
made responsible—to society.

I see a parallel here, incidentally, between old age and youth in our
society. Youth, too, has been left stranded by the advances of technology.
Our expectations of man focus, in the main, on his economic productivity,
on his ability to contribute to the material and social wealth of the nation,
and we are waiting longer and longer before demanding the productive
contribution of our young. Our elaborate and protracted school-systems
can be viewed as mechanisms for keeping youth "on the shelf" as active
contributors to our economy and society. This long and growing period of
"uselessness," of waiting is, no doubt, one of the major causes of alienation
among the young today. They too have no particular societal expectations
put upon them until they actively enter productive life. The difference here
between the young and the old is, of course, that there will be a point in
the young person's life when he will reach the stage of being a contributing

---

* In our own society, residual evidence of such definition appears in the use of the
word "senate" to designate the "upper" house of our legislatures. Webster has: "Senate
(from Latin . . . *senex*, gen. *senis*—old, an old man). 1. Literally, an assembly of
old men or elders; hence . . . a council with the highest deliberative and legislative
functions . . ." (Webster, 1950).

and recognized and appreciated member of society. The aged person has no such future to look forward to—and this may well be the most significant distinguishing mark of this age-group.

Another aspect of the problem the aged as a group (and the youths waiting to enter their productive stage) face here is that of leisure—the problem of the use of time for purposes other than work, or for purposes not sufficiently prescribed or regulated by society. Margaret Mead has suggested that one solution of the problem of leisure time for the aged is for them to return to school, to share the school bench with youth and thereby gain both by renewed study and involvement in the questions of the day and by becoming aware of the new and different approaches and world-views of the young. The young, too, would benefit in this scheme through their association with the old. No doubt this idea has merit, but it also serves to underline the "cold storage" function of school in our society.*

The connection between old age and leisure time raises a host of other problems which bear closely on the question of alienation. Time is a very central, value-laden concept in our culture, and its uses are intimately connected not only with our status and position in society, but with our perceptions and feelings about ourselves. Much of our education and training goes toward assuring a use of time which we will be able to account for —first to society and then to ourselves. Furthermore, industrialization and mechanization have brought about a view of time determined by that mechanical device, the clock. Sebastian de Grazia points to the fact that for most of history—until not much more than a hundred years ago—the vast majority of people even in the Western world lived not by the clock but by the sun and the moon, not by the ticking away of minutes (or seconds) but by the change of day and night, the passage of weeks and months and of the seasons. The machine, de Grazia points out, has given us time free from work; but it has changed our concept of time in such a way as to rob it of this freeness—evident in our thinking of free time as time free from work but still measured by the clock which also measures work. But "clocked time cannot be free" (de Grazia, 1964, p. 310). For the aged, the retired, the clock has suddenly stopped ticking. They find themselves with an ample supply of that most valuable commodity—time; but in their hands it has turned to ashes. They suffer, to borrow a term from economics, under an extreme and somewhat artificial inflation.

But there is another aspect of our view of time as measured by the clock which turns the very idea of leisure into a psychological threat—leisure being time without structure:

* It may be of interest to mention here that the word "school" derives from the Greek word scholē, meaning leisure, and hence that in which leisure is employed; a disputation, a school (Webster, 1950).

> Apparently the schedule of the work day, the fact that it has definite things to do, that as long as one goes to work or to the office the day can be chalked up on the side of virtue—these things reassure many persons of their productiveness, sociability and place in the community. They need not fear having to evaluate their own activities—and perhaps change and choose others—as long as the routine itself sanctions it. . . . The lack of structure to the (free) days opens them up to choice . . . leads them to a feeling of not knowing how to act, of existing without a purpose. . . . Wide open time, like space, is frightening [de Grazia, 1964, pp. 259–260].

The aged, of course, are confronted with this problem more than any other group, and they are faced with it, again, without the aid of a socially approved system of directives and norms. They are, in this respect, cut loose from the main body of society, thrown upon their own resources and resourcefulness—alienated as a population group.

Societal alienation, then, stems from the increments in longevity and leisure time, the creation in fact of a whole new population, and the time lag in the development of social norms and roles for this population. Fundamental to the establishment of these new and necessary norms will be a change in much of the value system determining our view of man and of life and its purpose. Or rather a shift within our value system toward what we profess—the view of man as an end in himself, as the justification of his own being, as his own purpose—from much of what we practice, which sees man more as a means toward purposes outside himself and which therefore requires of him a justification for his existence outside himself: a justification which the aged are hard-put to provide both for society and for themselves.

Some of this shift in emphasis on values is taking place even now. Among the young today we see efforts toward moving away from the value to time, from the value of production, the dedication to the clock, as supreme arbiters of the worth of man. Societal demands with respect to the use of time and schedules are also becoming more flexible. The negative phenomenon of dropped-out youth is not approved, but neither is it forcibly suppressed. This small degree of sanction may well open the way for new and more positive explorations for new uses of our time and for different ways of valuing our use of time. When today's youth reaches old age, perhaps it will become the first generation in recent, Western civilization to live without the exclusive need to follow the clock, without the need for accounting for every minute, for justifying its use of time solely in terms of production; perhaps it will find a new kind of productivity which has new social and personal, but not necessarily economic, value.

Without such shift in ethos we face a rather bleak future. As industrialization and automation develop, even less of our time will have to be used for production, for the provision of our needs, and more and more of us will be free, but unneeded and undefined by society. Thus Western society itself, not only its aged, will one day find itself in an automated future in which man will be a superfluous appendage to his own machines. Having lost the role of being his own provider he will also have lost that which heretofore has been his main rationale for being. This would be a rather dramatic closing of the cycle: from animal existence, after millennia of human development through self-awareness and the use of tools, back to an animal—almost foetal—existence devoid of the need— and the reason—to struggle for life and survival.

There is a challenge here, and an opportunity and, perhaps, a paradox for today's aged. The same factors which have cut the aged loose from the rest of society can also set them free. They find themselves in a situation which we all dream about at times: perhaps they are the first really free people. Assuming their physical well-being and sufficient means for existence, society puts no expectations upon them, no demands, no norms, sets them free to develop their own definitions, to make their own determinations. Is this not one of our dreams, one of the goals we strive for? The crucial and perhaps most painful question is: can we handle this; is this something we are capable of doing? Can we as individuals and as a society define ourselves in terms different from those with which we grew up and those which surround us?

PERSONAL ALIENATION AMONG THE AGED

At present, however, there are the millions of aged living today and tomorrow and in the foreseeable future in a society which takes rather reluctant notice of their existence. How do they fare? What pangs of alienation do they experience?

Obviously, the social matrix and the dominant value-systems play a determining role here. The individual's group memberships profoundly affect his feelings and views about himself and his psychological well-being. But much of what has been said so far about the aged as a population group has been in the nature of theory, of general sociological discussion. It is in the actual experience of the individual that these sociological phenomena come to life, assume flesh and blood and meaning. It is within our own, individual lifespan that we must reconcile our past, our present, and our future: that which we are with what we were and, in this context most importantly, with that which we strive to be.

With the rest of his age-group, each individual reaches a period in his life at which he is considered—by a variety of criteria—to be old, and at which he faces the sociological implications of this fact. But whether or not he will personally feel alienated, the degree to which he will consider the advent of old age a serious or severe disruption and disorientation in his life will depend upon a series of intricate internal and external processes and events.

The individual at this point faces the threat not only of societal alienation —estrangement from others—but also of alienation from himself. One of the major difficulties encountered by the individual in this period is the threatened psychological discontinuity between his past and his future, a threat to his very identity. Erikson defines identity as ". . . the capacity of the ego to sustain sameness and continuity in the face of changing fate . . ." as well as ". . . the resilience of maintaining essential patterns of change" (Erikson, 1964, pp. 95–96).

The "press of change" upon the aging is often so great that it becomes difficult to maintain such continuity and resilience. A major factor here is the individual's realization that a point has been reached at which what has been a vital component of his whole life—the future—has now come to be bereft of much of its significance. Throughout his life he has had a future not only as a dimension of time, but in the sense of being able to believe in the possibility of modifying his life, of changing and correcting those elements of his life which he found problematic or unacceptable. He now can no longer expect to do this, but must face his life as it is and as it has been. And at this juncture, so crucial to psychological well-being, research clearly indicates that the advantage belongs to those who have been strong and successful all along. Kutner states, in his discussion of the self-image of a group of old people, that

> The prevailing optimism and sense of well-being of those holding high social and economic status suggests that possession of the cultural marks of attainment, position in life, and other material evidence of success may serve to overcome some of the effects of handicapping conditions of the later years [Kutner, Fanshel, Togo, & Langner, 1956, p. 54].

Investigators disagree on the importance of various age-connected disabilities, including declining health, to the morale of the elderly. The ability to accept one's life, to derive satisfaction from one's past and present, is often seen as the determining factor. Each student of the problem states this in his own way. Lowenthal & Boler, for instance, find that ". . . it is the socially affluent who can afford to withdraw without damage to their morale" (Lowenthal & Boler, 1965, p. 370). Tobin & Neugarten (1961, pp. 344–346) establish a Life Satisfaction Rate Scale (LSR) for the aged, whose most significant points are one's ability to regard life as meaningful and to accept "resolutely that which life has been" (p. 345)—the feeling of having achieved one's major goals. Marvin Koller identifies "successful aging as personal satisfaction with past and present life" (Koller, 1968, p. 51). He finds that the well-developed, organized, capable person ages successfully, while the immature person, habitually unable to deal with reality, does not. Thus the ability to maintain one's identity, to ward off major psychological discontinuities in one's life—to avert alienation—with the advent of old age, in a large measure is a blessing bestowed upon the blessed and denied to many who have been deprived of success and satisfaction throughout much of their lives. The solution to the despair of many of the aged lies in their past and, therefore, beyond their reach. This is of importance to those of us who work not only with the aged but in the helping professions in general: self-acceptance on the part of the individual is a crucial factor in his ability to accept old age, and it can often be achieved only prior to old age.

Our view of death, of course, affects our feelings about old age most crucially. Where a belief in the afterlife prevails, old age not only loses much of its sting, it may be seen as the last step toward final fulfillment. In societies in which the dead (or ancestors) are worshipped, the aged enjoy the reflected glory of their future status. In our society, death is widely viewed as the ultimate alienation—not only as the end of life, but as retroactively robbing life of meaning. This, too, reflects upon our view of old age and the aged.

The aged as a group have a kind of immortality—indeed, they are increasing. Each of us, however, must face his old age as that period of life which ends in death. The ability to view death with a degree of equanimity, and to derive meaning and continuity for ourselves from our accumulating lives in all their ramifications, will be needed to combat a sense of alienation in old age. Crucial to this capacity is the ability to see old age as part of life, rather than as just the prelude to death. And this is something which usually has to be achieved long before old age, and involves, again, a need for a change of values. Let me close with another quote from de Grazia:

> The life of the aged is what it is largely because they have been turned out to stay around and then die quietly without disturbing anyone. Youth is so well advertised that once past it seems to be the only time one had for living. . . . If it were believed that in length of days there is understanding, or better yet, that this understanding is more important than having been trained to work the newest machines, the problem of the aged would be less troublesome, and perhaps in a paradox, so would that of youth [de Grazia, 1961, p. 146].

REFERENCES

Camus, A. *The stranger* (trans. S. Gilbert). New York: Random House, 1964.
De Grazia, S. The uses of time. In R. W. Kleemeier (Ed.) *Aging and leisure.* New York: Oxford University Press, 1961. Pp. 113–153.
De Grazia, S. *Of time and leisure.* Garden City, N.Y.: Doubleday, 1964.
Erikson, E. *Insight and responsibility.* New York: Norton, 1964.

Koller, M. *Social gerontology.* New York: Random House, 1968.
Kutner, B., Fanshel, D., Togo, A., & Langner, T. S. *Five hundred over sixty: A community survey on aging.* New York: Russel Sage Foundation, 1956.
Lowenthal, M. F., & Boler, D. Voluntary vs. involuntary withdrawal. *Journal of Gerontology,* 1965, *20,* 363–367.
Sumner, W. G. *Folkways.* New York: Mentor Books, 1960.
Tobin, S., & Neugarten, B. L. Life satisfaction and social interaction in the aging. *Journal of Gerontology,* 1961, *16,* 344–346.
Webster's new international dictionary of the English language. (2nd ed., unabridged) Springfield, Mass.: Merriam, 1950.

Alienation Among the Poor

STEPHEN M. DAVID

Stephen M. David received a B.A. degree from Columbia University in 1956, an LL.B. from the Harvard Law School in 1959, and a Ph.D. from Columbia University in 1967. After receiving his law degree he worked for a year as a research assistant for the New York State Commission on Governmental Operations of the City of New York, and then from 1962 to 1964 he was a teaching assistant in the department of public law and government at Columbia University. In 1965 Dr. David joined the faculty of Fordham University, where he is currently associate professor of political science. A member of the New York State and the American Political Science Associations, he has contributed articles to professional journals and to volumes dealing particularly with race and poverty issues. In 1971 Dr. David co-edited with Jewel Bellush the volume: Race and politics in New York City: Five case studies in policy making.

The 1960s were a decade commonly referred to as one in which America rediscovered its poor. News about migrant farm-workers, poor whites living in Appalachia, Chicanos, and, especially, black slum-dwellers, became almost an every-day occurrence. The last group evoked the most concern. From the sit-ins and freedom rides of the early 'sixties to the more massive protests, rioting, and small-scale guerrilla warfare which took place in Northern cities in the latter years of the decade, black Americans were the most visible of our poor. The behavior of these groups was widely interpreted as manifesting their discontent with the political system—as well as with other aspects of American society.

Some analysts (Aberbach & Walker, 1970) have argued that the attitudes held by some of the poor and reflected in their behavior represented, not the mild disaffection or cynicism toward politicians which is widely held in America, but a level of disapproval usually associated with concepts such as political alienation. Political alienation has been defined by a well-known political scientist, Robert Lane, as "a person's sense of estrangement from the politics and government of his society. . . . It implies more than [lack of interest]; it implies a rejection" (Lane, 1962, pp. 161–162).

Attitudes which can be used as empirical indicators of alienation include the feeling that one is powerless to influence governmental policies and that the government is not responsive to one's interests. Unfortunately, the extent to which poor persons during these years held attitudes which are symptomatic of political alienation appears never to have been reliably determined. In the absence of these data, we will assume that "significant" numbers of the poor fell within this rubric, and proceed to its major theme. During the course of the article, the "estrangement" of the poor from their government will be described by terms such as alienated, discontented, and disaffected.

The theme of this paper is to describe and explain how political elites or influentials in our society reacted to these developments. The elites comprise, among others, many of our leading elected officials, many of the leaders of the industrial, financial, and commercial worlds, many of the leaders of organized labor, and other executives of large institutions.

This topic is selected because the behavior and the actions of those who most influence the direction of our polity are widely misunderstood. The shock which greeted the release of the Pentagon Papers stems, in part, from the failure to understand the perspective of the leaders of a political system. This failure extends, not only to the general public, but also to many influential segments or groups within our society. One of the segments can be called, for lack of a better word, the helping professions. This group includes, among others, social workers, psychologists, most academicians, and, of particular import to this Institute, most clergymen. Our intent is to shed some light on the perspectives of political leaders; the hope is that a fuller understanding of the workings of a political system will lead to a more just resolution of the conflicts within the system.

The core of the problem which members of the helping professions have in understanding the actions of political leaders is that they approach social, economic, and psychological problems from a different vantage point. The helping professions responded to the rediscovery of the poor by seeking solutions to alleviate their problems. The poor were a group to be aided; the recognition of widespread poverty by many in the general public was an opportunity to promote societal changes desired by members of these professions (who differ among themselves as to the "correct" solutions). Those who opposed such changes were branded as enemies of the poor.

ALIENATION OF THE POOR AS A POLITICAL PROBLEM

The political elites perceived the actions of the poor from a different orientation. The alienation of the poor was approached, not as a social or economic problem requiring remediation, but as presenting political problems. The manifestations of their discontent were seen as threats to the regime or political system; threats which needed to be managed or controlled. The disaffection of the poor was presenting a problem for the political system to deal with.

A number of political scientists have written about this orientation of political leaders. These writers agree that the elites are highly concerned about the levels of support and opposition to political objects existent among groups or classes within a political system.* Political influentials care if "significant" numbers feel that the government is indifferent or neglects them or that they are unable to influence public officials on behalf of their interests.

The reasons for their concern are twofold. Obviously, an increase in the number of discontented or alienated citizens represents simultaneously a threat to the *status quo* and a force for change. Generally, the political elites are satisfied with the workings of the political system. While they may be competing for "relative advantages" in the allocation of resources made by that system, few, if any, desire serious disruptions in its processes and decisions. Deep and widespread discontent threatens to lead groups into behavior which may seriously upset the delicate arrangements that have been arrived at by the elites: arrangements which assure them of a significant share of the desired resources and values of our society.

The behavior of alienated groups can range from apathy and non-participation in the political system at one end of the spectrum to the use of violence and the promotion of separatist programs at the other end. In the light of the importance of knowing the consequences of political alienation, it is surprising that the literature is very sparse on the subject.† Moreover, apathetic behavior by discontented citizens at one point in time may be a precursor of more active and "extreme" behavior at a later date. The best-known example of this behavior was the increased electoral support received by the National Socialist Party in Germany as the number of voters increased.

* For a concise and useful summary of this literature, see Gamson, 1968, pp. 39–42.
† For good reviews of this literature, see Crain, Katz, & Rosenthal, 1969, ch. 3; and Aberbach & Walker, 1970, pp. 1200–1202.

There is a second, less discussed, reason for political elites to be concerned about the level and scope of political alienation. It relates to their effectiveness to govern. The leaders in all political systems want to be able to commit resources, both human and financial, on behalf of their decisions. They want to know that their citizens will respond to their legal responsibilities. If their decision is for increased taxes, they want to know that the payments will be made. If the decision is to initiate or enter a war, they want to know that the members of their system will fight.

If the level and scope of discontent is low, then the political elites can be confident that their decisions will be implemented. On the other hand, if alienation is deep and widespread, the elites will find it difficult to commit the human and financial resources of their political system. They will discover that their freedom of action has been seriously curtailed. Instead of making decisions in accord with their perceived responsibilities, they will find that their highest priority will be to deal with this discontent or alienation. One could argue that this has occurred with respect to our government's policy in regard to the Indo-China war. Whatever its own policy preferences may have been on this matter, it appears that the major concern of the administration has been to devise a policy which would mollify critics of the war on both the left and the right. In short, political influentials are concerned about the level and scope of alienation because it presents dangers to existing arrangements and curtails their freedom to govern.

In managing such discontent, political elites are confronted with two fundamental choices or strategies.* The first is to take actions intended to weaken or undermine the *sources of power* of the alienated groups. The intent is to deprive these groups of the ability to impose change upon the political system. Such actions will be called control measures. The alternative is for the political influentials to modify some of the decisions made by the system and to provide the disaffected groups with certain desired objectives. The expectation is that, by providing alienated groups with a little at the right time, this will prevent more massive changes in the political system at a later date. These actions will be called decisional changes. As a general rule, political elites would prefer to resort to control measures in handling discontent. They will only change the content of their decisions as a last resort.

CONTROL MEASURES EMPLOYED

There are two primary control measures used by political influentials. One technique is to deny groups access to resources which are needed to exercise

* Much of the following discussion is heavily indebted to the insights of William A. Gamson on this subject (Gamson, 1968, ch. 6). However, it should be noted that the author diverges from Gamson's analysis at a number of points.

influence within a political system. An example of this technique were the acts of white Southerners in preventing blacks from acquiring sufficient skills and knowledge necessary for achievement and success in American society. Colonial powers have used a similar strategy. Another example is to keep the members of a discontented group physically separated. This strategy— particularly useful before the development of mass means of communications—was intended to retard the growth of a sense of common interest among group members and to present hurdles in the way of any attempt to organize and mobilize the group for political action.

The other major control measure used by elites is the application of sanctions against members of the alienated group. Individuals who act in a manner "unacceptable" to the political leaders can find themselves imprisoned, physically harmed, or even put to death. Less severe sanctions would include loss of employment or deportation. On the other hand, "responsible" behavior is rewarded by the influentials.

DECISIONAL CHANGES

These two control measures are ordinarily preferred by elites in dealing with discontented groups. However, there are situations in which the political influentials will resort to decisional changes. This will occur when the elites perceive the threat to the political system from alienated groups to be of considerable magnitude and that the control measures, for one reason or another, cannot be expected to diminish the danger. There are two types of decisional changes which can be made. One is to invite members of the alienated group into selected arenas of the political system. The expectation is that the effect of participation and the exercise of influence on decisions made in these arenas will lead to an identification with and commitment to the system. This technique is known as cooptation. The other is for the political influentials to change the content of the decisions themselves. All decisions made by a political system favor some groups (or individuals) at the expense of others. The allocation of valued resources made by a political system always reflects a bias. By changing the content of some of these decisions, the elites are, of course, in a sense, redistributing the discontent. They are choosing to give some groups or classes more at the expense of other groupings. However, in seeking to manage the discontent of an alienated group, they may decide to allocate more resources to this group as a means of relieving pressure. The intent of the influentials is that by offering conciliatory outputs to this group, they can head off more-serious threats to the system.

The strategy of cooptation is a very complex one. It involves bringing selected members of the alienated group into certain decisional arenas of the system. These members will participate in and exert some influence on the choices made. Elites believe that the very participation of hitherto-excluded groups will promote the acceptance of the decisions made in this arena. They also believe that the resultant content changes in the decisions will increase the identification and commitment to the political system. Moreover, once the discontented group is a participant, its members can be rewarded by the system for "good behavior" and deprived of rewards which they are now receiving for "bad behavior."

From the perspective of the political leaders, cooptation does not always succeed. The representatives of the alienated group who achieve access may not change their attitudes and behavior toward the system. Another risk is that these representatives may be perceived by the disaffected group as having "sold out," and thus lose their ability to control the actions of group members. Lastly, the technique may result in the alienated group's changing the content of the decisions more than the elites desired.

The elites can also decide to change the content of some of the decisions made by the system without involving the participation of the disaffected. By providing the discontented group with more of the desired allocations, their identification or commitment to that system can be expected to increase. At the same time, their exclusion as participants in such decisions ensures the elites of complete control over its determinations. The political influentials can thereby decide the amount of ground they wish to yield and which segments of the society will be disadvantaged by these decisions. On the other hand, the elites lose the advantages of participation. This involves, not only the previously discussed effects of promoting commitment to the system, but also the ability of the elites to influence the selection of the "leaders" of the alienated group. The political influentials can usually play an important part in determining the process to be used in selecting the representatives of the disaffected group. Since all such procedures have their own biases, the elites can influence the choice of these leaders.

CURRENT STRATEGY CALLS FOR DECISIONAL CHANGE

At this point in American history, it appears that many of the political elites have decided that the management of the alienation of the poor, particularly of the black slum-dweller, calls for the use of decisional changes rather than social-control measures. Their present debate appears to be over which method of decisional change—cooptation or changing decisional content—should be followed. The most discussed use of the technique of cooptation is popularly known as community control. Changes in the content of governmental policies usually involve public services intended for the poor and the redistributive aspects involved in the financing of these services. As a means of illustrating the concepts described above, the orientation, vastly oversimplified, of the elites to these proposals will now be described.

Community control is promoted by some of the elites as a means of developing an indigenous leadership for the black community (Long, 1969, pp. 31–44). Their argument stems from the consequences of slavery and the post-Civil War experience of American blacks. The effect was to leave the blacks without any leadership of their own. Whites, in their roles as police officers, social workers, teachers, and businessmen, were the only governors of the ghetto. Middle-class blacks served no leadership role; they either sought to leave or ignore the ghetto or were on white payrolls and hence distrusted by the slum-dwellers. The result was "the dominance of the ghetto by lower-class Negro culture, the only authentic culture it has" (Long, 1969, p. 33). By the 1960s, the costs of this dominant slum-culture —its political volatility, its unproductive labor supply—were becoming too high for the elites. Their solution was to develop a black leadership which can come to dominate this lower-class culture. Community control of various aspects of urban government provides a vehicle for this purpose. Black leaders, selected by the community, can use these bureaucracies to change the ethos of the ghetto. Self-pride will replace dependency; a previously alienated, apathetic, and potentially violent community can be made into one which is productive and achieving within the context of the dominant culture. As a result of this development of an indigenous leadership with the capability of controlling its lower-class culture, social stability will be assured. In other words, community control is perceived by the elites as the use of the technique of cooptation; leaders of an alienated group are given access to certain decisional arenas as a means of securing stability for the larger political system.

Other political influentials promote changes in public services as a preferable alternative for dealing with the discontent of the poor. They argue that the placement of blacks in positions of authority within urban bureaucracies is alone insufficient to insure stability. It is not enough to create a black middle class; it is necessary that this class have control over sufficient financial resources to improve significantly the condition of the lower class before they can be accepted as leaders. In other words, these political elites argue that our political system cannot escape the necessity of a major redistribution of wealth in order to manage this alienated group. Programs promoting more participation by the poor may quiet the discontent in the short run; it will, however, eventually fail if it does not result in increased tangible benefits in the lives of the poor. Proponents of this point of view argue for major federal efforts in areas such as job training, job development, health and medical care, housing, and education.

As suggested in this discussion, there is a significant division among American elites on how to deal with the alienation of our poor, particularly the urban black. The difference, it should be noted, is not one of orientation or objective; both groups of influentials are concerned primarily with achieving the objective of managing this discontent. The division is over strategy. To oversimplify vastly, elites emanating from the business community are more likely to be found promoting community control, while leaders from organized labor are more likely to be promoting an expansion of public-service programs.

This conflict—as well as other differences—among the elites is resolved through a bargaining process (Allison, 1969, pp. 707–712). Elites differ about what must be done. Conflicts occur among political leaders when they differ over the ultimate values which should determine the matter at hand, or when it is not clear to them which programs are most instrumental in achieving their purposes. These disagreements are resolved in a process in which the power of each proponent and the skill with which he employs his resources determine the outcomes. Power consists of such resources as control over money and credit, control over the means of violence, status, control over jobs, formal legal authority, and popular support. The outcomes often differ from what any of the actors intended.

ROLE OF THE HELPING PROFESSIONS

This review of the workings of the political elites—their objectives, their techniques or strategies, and the process used to resolve their differences— was intended for an audience to which this maneuvering is quite foreign. If the objective of the elites is social stability, that of the helping professions is perceived to be social justice. If the techniques of the political influentials aim at control and management, the treatment methods of those whose primary function is to provide assistance are directed toward emotional peace, economic security, and personal freedom. If the process of resolution among the elites can best be characterized as bargaining, that of the helping professions can be characterized as problem-solving.

The very role of members of the helping professions calls upon them to be concerned with and to ameliorate the conditions promoting the alienation of the poor. Most members of these professions are agreed that this will require some changes in public policies, though they, too, are in sharp conflict over the types of change needed. This effort for change will necessitate an involvement with the members or representatives of the political elites. It is necessary that the helping professions understand the workings of these elites if they desire to increase the possibilities of influencing their decisions. The political leaders are open to persuasion. However, they will be convinced only by arguments directed toward their concerns. Alternatively, the elites can be pressured into accepting change. This strategy requires that those who serve the poor become knowledgeable about the sources of power in our society and skillful in their application. It is hoped that the effect of an enlarged role in public-policy formation by members of the helping professions will be a polity reflecting greater concern for social justice. The healthy state is one which strikes a "balance" between the goals of stability and justice.

REFERENCES

Aberbach, J. D., & Walker, J. L. Political trust and racial ideology. *American Political Science Review,* 1970, *64,* 1199–1220.
Allison, G. T. Conceptual models and the Cuban missile crisis. *American Political Science Review,* 1969, *63,* 689–719.
Crain, R. L., Katz, E., & Rosenthal, D. B. *The politics of community conflict.* New York: Bobbs-Merrill, 1969.
Gamson, W. *Power and discontent.* Homewood, Ill.: Dorsey Press, 1968.
Lane, R. *Political ideology.* New York: Free Press, 1962.
Long, N. Politics and ghetto perpetuation. In R. L. Warren (Ed.) *Politics and the ghettos.* New York: Atherton, 1969. Pp. 31–44.

Alienation and
Homosexuality

ROBERT J. CAMPBELL

Robert Jean Campbell, M.D., is associate direc-
tor, department of psychiatry, St. Vincent's Hos-
pital and Medical Center, New York City. In
addition to this principal position, he is also direc-
tor of the division of community mental health at
the Hospital. His previous positions at the same
institution included those of chief, inpatient serv-
ice, Reiss Mental Health Pavilion (1956–1961),
and director, division of training and education,
department of psychiatry (1956–1969). Dr.
Campbell's B.A. degree (1944) is from the Uni-
versity of Wisconsin, his M.D. degree (1948) is
from the College of Physicians and Surgeons of
Columbia University, and his Diplomate in Psy-
chiatry (1957) is from the American Board of
Psychiatry and Neurology. Dr. Campbell is a Fel-
low of both the American Psychiatric Association
and the New York Academy of Medicine. He is
the author of approximately thirty articles in pro-
fessional journals, and is the editor of both the
third and the fourth edition of Hinsie & Camp-
bell's Psychiatric Dictionary.

To know oneself, to describe the culture and society of which he himself
is a part, to move with the tide and yet not be engulfed in it, to fathom the
plight of modern man as one is sinking with him—such tasks as we have

set ourselves in this Institute require that we be uncommonly objective, to some extent aloof, certainly detached, and possibly even alienated. We can only hope that we do not share the ill-defined fate of the mental patient who, having "lost his mind," can therefore have no mind with which to appreciate the fact that it is lost. We must assume that, no matter how far down the path of alienation we have traveled, we can yet turn back, or at the very least look back, to see what it is we have come away from.

GENERAL DISCONTENT AND DISRUPTION IN SOCIETY

As we scan the world about us, our eye is caught by flares of discontent, dissension, and disruption. Whether they signal evolution or revolution, victory or defeat, is increasingly difficult to decide; aware that we are not at all certain of where we are going, we are beginning to understand too that we are unsure of where we want to go. Modern science has catapulted us into tomorrow before we learned how to cope with today. We can send men to the moon with greater dispatch than we can send them across Manhattan during the rush hour.

We can decipher the genetic code, transplant vital organs, and transform inert chemicals into living matter; yet our quest for peace in our time, our promises of equality and tolerance for all men for all time, and our planning for the future of our species seem as fruitless as the alchemist's search for gold. The science and technology from which we had expected so much have begun to fail us. The very core of our modern society, the forces we have for so long lauded as the natural end of democracy, seem now to constitute the seeds of that society's destruction.

The telltale signs of enlightened individualism are there—mass production, mass culture, mass democracy, increased suffrage—and thus in one sense we feel confident that we have approached the ideal we had sought. But now that we are almost upon it, what have we gained? Can we claim that we have reaped a harvest of freedom and liberation, of autonomy and independence? There are many who would register a loud "Nay," asserting that instead of political freedom we have a tyranny imposed by the mass, that individual autonomy has been crushed by the weight of mechanical robotization and spiritual homogeneization, that the discipline of taste, judgment, and moral values has been superseded by mass opinion and regimentation.

The individual may have some vague notion of the fragmented roles he is forced to play in his society, but very little certainty of his worth in any of them. He is unsure of his status and place in society, uneasy in his sense of identity and purpose, uncomfortable in his loss of continuity with his own past. His memories of that past grow dim, but what few glints remain are enshrined as precious relics. Nostalgia exerts a mysterious attraction, so much so that in time it becomes a marketable commodity to be sold at premium prices to hordes of isolated robots—who hope to find in "No, No, Nanette," "70 Girls 70," and "Follies" some key to the puzzle of who they are and where they fit.

Surveying the current scene, it is difficult to remember that de Tocqueville died in 1859. His cautionary notes are frightening in their prescience—that uncritical tolerance of mass opinion makes independence of mind impossible; that significant and relevant issues are swept away by preoccupation with the useful, the finite, the average; that concentration on dexterity, technique, and craftsmanship makes the laborer more adroit but less industrious, an improved workman but a degraded man; that a conviction that everything in the world can be explained leads one to deny what he cannot comprehend, and to ignore philosophy and theorizing in favor of applied science, technology, and commercialism (Nisbet, 1966).

On all sides, we see people who are uprooted, alone, separated from themselves as much as they are separated from society—whose remoteness, impersonality, complexity, and inability to recognize the individual except as a tiny cog in an enormous organization have made life forbidding and inaccessible. It is no wonder, then, that from this seething cauldron of social and scientific change have emerged voices of dissonance and revolt, skeptics who challenge the belief that only slow progress is acceptable progress, leaders who demand that the ambiguities and pragmatism of past and present give way to a more humanistic impulse. Some have been so rash as to suggest that model cities be planned for people and not automobiles, and that the well-being of those people replace the gross national product as a measure of society's worth.

The revolt has taken no single form but has surfaced in a bewildering variety of shapes—the black social movement, population control and ecological balance, consumer protection, drug-taking, women's liberation, and any number of groups concerned with freedom of expression. Today's generation insists that it be allowed to do its own thing and let it all hang out— in dress, in hair-do, in use of leisure time, in life-style, in value-setting. It finds supervision, control, and censorship insupportable, even immoral, when pursued only for their own sakes. Inevitably, this press for freedom has come to include sexual behavior, and here what the youth consider liberty is likely to be classed as license by the traditionalist. It is not my purpose now to explore the so-called sexual revolution, except to say that, whatever it does, it does not confine itself to quantity and timing of sexual behavior. It extends also to varieties of sexual experience, and one of them is homosexuality.

SOCIETY VIEWS HOMOSEXUALITY AS A DEVIANCE

Homosexuality presents a fascinating problem to the student of human behavior. To begin with, the student is a member of the society which labels homosexuality a deviance, and thus he himself has been conditioned and programmed to perceive certain kinds of behavior in the way his culture defines them. Too often, we believe that it is only the experimental subject whose attitudes and behavior depend upon his culture and society, ignoring the fact that the observer's perceptions, attitudes, values, and behavior are equally dependent upon the organizational conditions of the life around him. Those social organizations and groups structure and prescribe, explicitly and implicitly, much of the individual behavior which happens within them— the kind of research the scientist does, the kind of behavior his subjects show, and the kind of reaction the community at large will have to his results.

Every society has norms of sexual behavior which have developed over a long period of time, during which, presumably, they proved themselves advantageous from the point of view of survival of the society. In defining the sexual rights and obligations of their members, most societies have linked sexual norms with the rest of the social structure, and especially with the family. Such a linkage was quite understandable when survival of the species was, in fact, an issue. But now that too many of us threaten to survive, and now that the family has lost most of its functions of a century ago, one wonders if such survival-oriented norms can long be maintained. Homosexuals were among the first to question the linkage of sexual norms with maintenance of the family and the indulgence of mindless reproduction, and this may account for some of society's reaction to them.

It is assumed by some that sexual norms are solely a matter of prejudice among the unenlightened, and that truly natural behavior would require the lifting of all sanctions and prohibitions. It is interesting, though, that even the most liberal of the self-styled "enlightened avant-garde" have never seriously questioned all sexual norms. Rather, they agree with the people they would label as puritanical on various sanctions, such as against incest, sexual abuse of children, white slavery, and rape. Their plea for a change in standards is typically in reference to very particular aspects of sexuality: the prevention or interruption of unwanted pregnancy, the extent of erotic display permitted in public, and forms of sexual activity which takes place outside of marriage—premarital intercourse, prostitution, and homosexuality (Davis, 1966).

Our society labels homosexuals as deviants, and once the label has been applied society accords them the treatment considered appropriate for homosexuals. The problem is that neither society nor science has yet been able to define what homosexuality is. As Schofield (1965) points out, four errors are commonly made in approaching the subject—first, failing to distinguish between an emotionally indifferent episode of genital activity between persons of the same sex, at one extreme, and at the other a dedicated commitment both physically and emotionally to a partner of the same sex; second, assuming that homosexuality is the same as pedophilia, and that the person who at any point in his lifetime has engaged in any form of homosexual action is forever after a menace to children of his own sex; third, accepting as representative of all homosexuals those who are convicted of homosexual offenses (even though the likelihood of conviction is less than 1 in 550, and the likelihood of imprisonment less than 1 in 3,100); and fourth, defining homosexuality as an illness and considering it in only medical or psychiatric terms, even though most homosexuals will never be, or need to be, in treatment for their sexual preferences. It is hard for many to see that nonconformity and mental illness are not synonymous.

VARIABILITY WITHIN HOMOSEXUAL BEHAVIOR

When one considers the magnitude of variability within the class of homosexual activity, it is clear that societal reaction is as much a determinant of what is labeled deviant as the behavior itself. How, for instance, does one label and in consequence react to a couple of mutual-masturbation sessions in a prep school? Is the label different if the participants are 40 years old and in jail? Does the type of activity make the difference? Is the anal penetrator more or less homosexual than the fellator? And would the label change if he did it one way today, another way tomorrow? Would he be less homosexual if he happened also to be married, and responsive and sexually gratifying to his wife? Would he be more or less manly if he received a watch, or a dinner, or a $20 bill from his sex-partner? And what if he stole the money or the watch—would society call him sick, would they jail him as a criminal, or would they be amused by his antics? The fact that there is no single correct answer to such questions—and a hundred more like them could be posed—serves only to underscore the futility of attempting to mark every homoerotic thought, feeling, wish, propensity, or action with the rubric of disease. To argue on the basis of proportionate incidence or frequency is at best specious reasoning whose illogicality is fortunately abandoned when the scientist turns his attention to eye color, body build, handedness, and blood type. Is being black an illness, because in America whites outnumber blacks?

While sickness may be defined as the failure of function, it would not be correct to say—as some have—that a person is ill when he is chronically unable to function in his appropriate gender identity. Certainly no such claim could be made for those who function at a high level in every other area of their lives. Most homosexuals, in fact, do just that; they function as well as their non-homosexual counterparts in every vocational area—arts, sciences, business, labor—and by no means are they capable only as hairdressers or fashion designers. Furthermore, they reach those high levels of functioning against almost insurmountable odds. Until recently, at least, organized religion stigmatized and ostracized them for their unmentionable sin, the law persecuted them for their heinous crimes, and psychiatry has defined their sickness in such a way as to provide society with still another rationalization for discriminating against them.

Today's American homosexual, if he is sick at all, is likely to be reacting to society's treatment of him as an outcast. Of all the charges leveled against him, the one which seems to have some substance in fact is that the homosexual tends to be more promiscuous sexually than his non-homosexual counterpart. If that is true, it may be because society's attitude to his preferences, with its demand that he deny himself any satisfactory outlet, has lessened the respect he has for social mores. It may also be that a sexist society which attempts to force him into a role which he feels is unnatural to him makes his sexual feelings the central issue, and forces him into excessive concentration on sexuality. It may also be—and none of these possibilities excludes the others—that, in a society so reluctant to grant him status at any level, he seeks status within his homosexual peer group as a "successful" sexual object.

Related to what may be promiscuity is another fear which society has: because the homosexual is promiscuous, he is always trying to convert non-homosexuals into his camp. Most homosexuals are not proselytizers, but seek only to make contact with others already of the same persuasion. And the fear that heterosexual men are in such danger of succumbing to homosexual overtures, unless they get a heavy helping hand from the law, is not a very winning argument for the naturalness or superiority of heterosexual intercourse. Whatever the rationalizations, society quite typically denies homosexuals whom it recognizes as such the social, economic, vocational, and legal rights accorded other citizens. They are objects of public ridicule and scorn—now that ethnic jokes are out, "fag" jokes are in. While there is nothing in the nature of any occupation which makes it male or female, homosexual or heterosexual, homosexuals are barred from many jobs, or dismissed from them even though their work bears no more relationship to their sexual preference than to their religious preference. They are subject to blackmail, harassment by the authorities, and are driven to become involved with the criminal syndicates which operate the only places where they have freedom to assemble. It is little wonder that most homosexuals try to "pass" as normal-heterosexual to avoid the societal oppression to which they are subject. The consequent necessity to lead a double life certainly takes its toll, but the alienation, role-confusion, self-doubts, and self-hate which may develop can hardly be imputed to homosexuality. The blame lies instead with society's reaction.

Since that reaction depends so much upon how society comes to "know" that a person is homosexual, it is interesting to see what constitutes adequate evidence. More often than not, the evidence is indirect—a person hears and accepts a vague rumor, or an acquaintance tells him that there was something "funny" about his last meeting with So-and-So, or the person concludes that So-and-So is homosexual on the basis of his associates, his predilection for certain activities or his avoidance of others. The suspected homosexual may get the definite label if his behavior fails to conform to the usual activity of other members of his group—such as the sailor on shore leave who goes to a concert instead of the wharfside bar and bordello. Sometimes the conclusion is reached on the basis of direct observation, but observers show enormous differences in how they interpret any bit of behavior. Kitsuse reported an interview with a 20-year-old subject who had affixed the label homosexual on an acquaintance:

SUBJECT: Then he asked me what I was studying. When I told him psychology he appeared very interested.
INTERVIEWER: What do you mean "interested"?
SUBJECT: Well, you know queers really go for this psychology stuff [Kitsuse, 1969, p. 595].

The homosexual has also been reared in the society which trains its members to discriminate against people whose sexual role and behavior are perceived as inappropriate to their ascribed sex status. He—or she—is unable to accept fully the limitations imposed by society's sex-typing of him. The recognition that he is not meeting social expectations makes him feel guilty, but at the same time he is driven to question the values and standards which the rest of society accepts without demur. He must begin to weave his own pattern of life and find ways to cope with the loneliness which nonconformity brings. The part of him which is loath to accept himself for what he is leads him into attempts to pass as straight, to try to accept the illusions which society defines as reality. Like most non-homosexuals, he rolls with the punches, tries not to make waves, tries not to get himself into a position where he is fighting city hall. The part of him which questions society's standards fills him with resentment against his prejudiced oppressors. But even should he take courage to rebel openly, he is in a highly vulnerable position: the self-proclaimed experts in behavior (the guardians of morality in a culture which no longer listens to its clergy) will pronounce him sick, or insane, or a criminal. At the very least they will claim that as a homosexual he is too biased to be able to say anything credible or pertinent about homosexuality (but will ignore the question of who is competent then to speak about heterosexuality).

Some do rebel, even so; but they must be very special people, quite aside from being homosexuals. I suggest that it would be as unwise to equate all homosexuals with those crusaders as to equate them with child-molesters. Homosexuality as a term is relatively meaningless. It certainly is not a diagnosis of a condition, but only suggestive of a piece of behavior. The persons who, at any point in time, demonstrate such behavior will be found to run the gamut of all types of persons in the world. Some will be psychotic and homosexual; some will be neurotic and homosexual; some will be character and personality disorders (like all of us) and also be homosexuals; and many will be as normal as anyone but still show a preference for sexual contact and love relationships with persons of the same sex. As the homosexual community itself has become organized—largely within the past two decades—its members have become increasingly vocal and its leaders increasingly articulate in their pleas for a new interpretation of homosexuality within the existing social structure.

GAY LIBERATION MOVEMENT

In New York, we saw the birth of Gay Liberation as a formal entity in June 1969. It happened at the "Stonewall" on Christopher Street—a gay bar in Greenwich Village which had enjoyed some measure of "protection" for many months. One night the police arrived to "raid" the bar—a harassment maneuver which is the rule rather than the exception for the ghetto establishments catering to homosexual patrons. The different thing about this raid was that, probably for the first time in history, the homosexuals fought back, and there ensued a riot which threatened to overwhelm the police. Implicit in that action were an insistence that homosexuals have a moral right to become, to be, and to remain homosexual, and absolute rejection of the notion that homosexuality is pathology. Homosexuality is instead to be considered ". . . a preference, orientation or propensity not different in kind from heterosexuality and fully on par with it" (Kameny, 1971, p. 22). The homophile movement approaches homosexuality not as the homosexual's problem but as a sociological problem in bigotry and prejudice identical to that leveled against other sociological minority groups. As Kameny notes:

> Assistance is needed, therefore, not to change homosexuals to heterosexuality, but to reinforce the homosexual in his homosexuality, to restore or establish his self-esteem and self-confidence—in sum, to undo the damage done him by a hostile society [Kameny, 1971, p. 26].

Even though the homophile movement in general (and not without reason) is antagonistic to psychiatry, not all psychiatrists subscribe to the general view of homosexuality as sickness. Weissman, for instance, writes:

For the ultimate truth is that we have not as yet resolved all the mysteries of the final evolvements of man's bisexual nature to which Freud alluded. Whatever our future understanding will be about why heterosexuality or homosexuality dominates in any given individual, we must in the meantime become increasingly liberated from our traditional intolerance and prejudices in these matters [Weissman, 1971, p. 27].

As Halleck states:

Psychiatrists must examine certain myths that they have accepted as facts and must stop perpetuating them in a manner that oppresses blacks, women, the elderly, the poor and those who have unconventional sexual tastes [Halleck, 1971, p. 99].

MASCULINE-INSPIRED SEXISM

It is difficult to appreciate the extent to which sexism, and particularly masculine-inspired sexism, dominates our thinking. When one is speaking in the third person singular about humanity in general, does she speak about her tendency, or does he speak about his? Imagine that all the voices on radio, and all of the faces on television, at least at prime times and on programs dealing with the most burning and significant issues of the day, are women's voices, women's faces. Imagine that there is just one male senator representing all of us in Washington. Remind yourself that it is the woman who is the born and natural leader; during pregnancy, she devotes her whole body to the preservation of the race, and to balance her contribution nature has decreed that the male fulfill himself through nurturing children and caring for the home, which is to be woman's refuge from the heavy demands of politics, government, business, and industry. We can see how biologically this was meant to be. The woman's reproductive system, after all, is compact, internal, and protected from harm by her entire body. The man, on the other hand, must be ever on the alert to attack on his exposed genitals. He requires sheltering engulfment in the protecting body of woman; to deny these needs is to deny his masculinity. Should he persist in that denial, treatment is indicated to assist him in adjusting to his own nature. One of the most successful treatments thus far described is an encounter group on "Being a Man"—led, of course, by a woman (Wells, 1970).

The feminist movement which has thrown a scorching beam on the discriminatory practices of our society has also—it is claimed—stepped up the requirements for masculinity. As a result, a number of men whose hold on masculinity was only a tenuous one have had to flee the field and escape into homosexuality. Now whether one believes that or not, the question it poses is worthy of consideration. If homosexuality is dependent not only on early-life experiences of the person but also on the attitude of society toward homosexuality and on the controls which limit it or encourage it to develop in a certain way, it would be tempting to say that the complete answer lies in a decision to change society's attitudes. Yet such changes as might be required would not necessarily be changes for the better. In the suggested example, would the solution for homosexuality be to reverse the feminist campaign and deny equal rights to women?

CONCLUSION

The solution, instead, might be to accept homosexuality as a different behavior which cannot be eliminated without changing society in adverse ways; then the goal of the helper—be he psychiatrist, psychologist, social worker, legal counsel, clergyman, or teacher—will be to prevent homosexuality from damaging the homosexual in other ways, in other areas of his living and functioning.

In common with the physician and psychologist, the clergyman has accepted as one of his primary responsibilities serving the needs of the people. All of us have been made acutely aware of the differences between serving people and trying to force people into roles which a not-always-relevant society would have them assume. Like the black movement, the homophile movement is resisting, repairing, removing, and preventing the alienation with which society whips its minorities. The movement is not a self-effacing apologia which begs pity for its members; it is a bill of rights which reminds society of its obligations to people, which reminds its members of the worth of their own individualism. If truly we are to help, it behooves us all to familiarize ourselves with what is happening within the movement, if for no other reason than to find out what reality actually is. This might be the first step in a painful process of self-instruction, wherein we learn how to stop playing God, how to relinquish our credo that all others should be fashioned in our image.

REFERENCES

Davis, K. Sexual behavior. In R. K. Merton & R. A. Nisbet (Eds.) *Contemporary social problems*. (2nd ed.) New York: Harcourt, Brace, 1966. Pp. 322–372.

Halleck, S. L. Stimulus/response therapy is the handmaiden of the status quo. *Psychology Today*, 1971, *4* (11), 30, 32, 34, 98, 100 (April, 1971).

Kameny, F. E. Gay liberation and psychiatry. *Psychiatric Opinion*, 1971, *8* (1), 18–27.

Kitsuse, J. L. Societal reactions to deviant behavior: Problems of theory and method. In D. R. Cressey & D. A. Ward (Eds.) *Delinquency, crime and social process*. New York: Harper & Row, 1969. Pp. 590–602.

Nisbet, R. A. *The sociological tradition*. New York: Basic Books, 1966.

Schofield, M. *Sociological aspects of homosexuality*. Boston: Little, Brown, 1965.
Weissman, P. Honest homosexuality in the theatre. *Psychiatric Opinion*, 1971, *8* (2), 25–28.
Wells, T. Woman, which includes man, of course. *Newsletter, Association for Humanistic Psychology*, December, 1970.

VIII
RESPONSES TO ALIENATION

Response to Alienation
from Psychiatry

PHILIP J. GUERIN

*Philip J. Guerin, M.D., is director of training,
family studies section, Albert Einstein College of
Medicine, Bronx State Hospital. He is likewise
adjunct assistant professor of psychology at Fordham University, and director of liaison for the
program in college and family psychiatry of the
Albert Einstein College of Medicine and Fordham
University. Dr. Guerin's B.S. degree is from Fair-
field University and his M.D. degree from the
Georgetown University School of Medicine. In
addition to the above-mentioned commitments,
Dr. Guerin is also visiting lecturer in family psychiatry at the Virginia Commonwealth University
School of Medicine, and engaged in the private
practice of family psychiatry in New Rochelle,
New York.*

It is somewhat ironic that I have been asked to speak for psychiatry. The
irony lies in my own mild to moderate degree of alienation from the con-
ventional values and ways of establishment thinking of my own discipline.
In many ways I might be termed a professional outsider. But then again
that all depends on your point of view.

I could mystify you in this presentation with one abstraction after another; however, I would rather share with you a clinical experience. I
hope that, by relating this experience, I can demonstrate my view of an
appropriate response to the phenomenon of alienation.

233

THE CASE OF JIM

Jim was a nineteen-year-old white male. On my first meeting with him he was on a leave of absence from a midwestern university, his father's alma mater. He had been an outstanding and creative student in primary and secondary school and his parents harbored high expectations for his future accomplishments. His first three semesters in college had, on the surface, been more of the same: dean's list, and an award for excellence in the writing of a series of one-act plays. At the end of his third semester, instead of boarding a jet for semester break at home, he gathered his resources, purchased a used motorcycle, and headed for the West Coast to join a former highschool classmate who had "dropped out" two years earlier. In his months on the West Coast Jim experienced communal and other forms of less-than-conventional habitation.

After seven months he returned home unannounced, almost as if to look around again to make sure that he had not overlooked the thing he sought and was convinced was missing. After he had spent six weeks at home—weeks filled with negativism, isolation, and resentment—Jim's parents sensed that he was itching to head out for nowhere and pleaded with him to seek professional help at least once.

Initial Session with Jim. Jim presented himself in a skeptical, apathetic, negative fashion. Frustrated with the value system and institutions of the world around him, he felt helpless to change himself and hopeless that anything around him would change. He was quick to remind me that I, too, was someone not to be trusted too quickly and that our meetings were at best a last-ditch token to his parents, poor victimized bastards that they were.

I listened for quite a while and attempted to clarify a few things with a brief question here and there. I finally volunteered the idea that when young people reached his age both cultural and biologic demands were made on them to define themselves as adults, and that this was a difficult proposition. As I saw it this demand presented two major pitfalls: that of overadherence to the programmed code of belief, or that of counterpositioning oneself to every aspect of that code of belief.

As he listened Jim's eyes slowly moved upward until upon completion of my speech their gaze was ceiling-high. His verbal response was that my "little homily had to be the most brilliant piece of deductive reasoning ever to come forth from the mouth of man." I assured him, that if I were not such a superior judge of character, I might think he was being sarcastic, but since I knew better I wanted to congratulate him on the concurrence of his opinion with the multitude of others who had in the past appreciated my brilliance. He brought his eyes down from the ceiling, looked me straight in the eye, frowned, and allowed himself a soft chuckle. I cautioned him to be careful about smiling; it would really mess him up. He looked at me rather quizzically and asked "Well, where do we go from here?" I said that, if he were ready, I'd fire off homily number two. He nodded, and I offered from my experience in talking with young people that those who talked most about the overwhelming fecality of the world about them seemed at times to be avoiding a look at self and the state of their important personal relationships, i.e., their family.

"What's there to say?" was Jim's response; "My father is a big-shot, tread-mill executive. My mother is a frustrated, hovering bitch who can't mind her own business. My sisters—well, they don't know where they are at yet. I guess they are basically good kids though."

In the remainder of our time together Jim provided his descriptive perception of the relationship between his parents. He viewed it as moderately conflicted, but on the surface "they seemed happy with it." He also volunteered that he had never had much contact with either side of the extended family and that the grandparents and uncles and cousins were strangers to him.

In closing I asked if he thought his folks would come in for a session. "You mean with me here too, at the same time?" he responded. "Well, I guess they'll do anything for their little Jimmy, but I don't think I can cut it." "Okay, then send them in by themselves next time," I said. In closing, I added that he had better get his motorcycle revved up, because by the time his parents and I finished hatching a conspiracy on him in that session there would be no escaping. So he had better leave now while the leaving was good. We shook hands and parted.

Session with Jim and his Parents. A week later Jim showed up in my office with his parents, Bob and Joan. Bob stood 6'4" with the shoulders of an all-pro tackle. He smiled easily, although from beneath his meticulous exterior a trace of perspiration betrayed his discomfort. Joan was an attractive slender 5'3" brunette who appeared anxious to get on with the proceedings. Jim was markedly more anxious in their presence than he had been even initially with me. It almost seemed that one could register the static in the open space between Jim and his mother. I started by filling the parents in on my first session with Jim and my reasons for requesting their presence. I then asked for their definition of the problem.

Both of them defined Jim as the problem and described their dismay and disbelief at the present state of affairs with this once-ideal son. Mother's explanation had as its major theme bad company. Father concurred while adding a dash of overbearing motherhood to this explanation. Both glossed over their relationship as non-problematic. At this point I avoided wrestling or reasoning at their seeming denial. Instead I chose to pass on with the comment "that I like to be educated about the better-working marital relationships in this world so that I'd want to know more about theirs later." I then began to question the location and frequency of contact with extended family members.

Father gave me the ages of his father and mother as 72 and 69, respectively. His parents lived 40 miles away in the town where he had been born and raised. Both were in fair health. Mother complained a lot and father turned his ever-increasingly deaf ear. He described his perception of his parents' relationship as non-combative, but distant. For years father worked long hours in his business, and mother invested most of her time and energy in her children. Since his retirement four years ago, his father spent a lot of time at their summer place where mother did not choose to go very often. Bob said that he saw his mother and father about twice a year and that his mother would telephone every once in a while. He had a brother in California and a sister in southern New Jersey, neither of whom he saw very often. He viewed his father as unreachable and his mother as overcontrolling. He added that his wife had strongly resented his mother's interference in the early days of their marriage. This he thought had led to his gradually decreasing his contact with them.

Joan described her parents as impossible. She and her mother were predictably at each other within ten minutes of their occupying the same time and space. They lived in a small town in Illinois. She saw them only on their semi-annual pilgrimage to New York. The last time she had been back to Illinois was twelve years ago for her youngest sister's wedding. Her two sisters, both married, lived in Illinois. Joan viewed her parents' relationship as a distant one in which her mother was a nag, constantly alternating a barrage of questions with firm statements of the truth. Father was seen as pleasant and tolerant, somewhat distant but "who wouldn't be in face of mother's onslaught?"

I asked if it would make any sense to them to make an attempt at improving their relationships with each of their parents. The mutual reply was that "maybe they weren't the greatest relationships in the world but there was not much chance of improving them, so why stir it all up?"

I asked: if it were semi-predictable that, unless they were able to work things out in a better way with their own parents, there was at least a 75 per cent chance that they would have the same situation to contend with in three out of their four children, would it then make sense?

Both parents looked somewhat stunned, and Jim focused his gaze on me in a quizzical way. I offered that "well, at least it was something to think about." I then moved to investigate the feeling-tone and anxiety-level present when all three were together.

Joan responded that she felt a great distance between herself and her son. It both frightened her and gave her an empty feeling which frequently forced her to the point of tears. Jim smirked, and responded that he just felt bugged in their presence and a great deal of pressure coming through from his mother. Father said that he did not feel anxious but could sense the trouble between Jim and his mother. I ended the session with the request that the parents come alone to the next session.

Sessions with the Parents. During the next several sessions, I met with the parents. The following process was spelled out during that time. Mother's major complaints about father were that he was overinvolved in his work, tuned out, and emotionally unavailable to her. He did not share with her his personal thoughts and feelings, and when she was most upset he would not meet her on a feeling level, but would attempt to reason at her. In face of this, Joan could not understand why at other times it took him so long to make a decision. Over the years she had tried to reach him but had given up in frustration. Now it did not seem to matter much what he did or did not do.

Joan became aware that in her reactive distance to Bob she had become hyperinvolved with her children, and especially involved in Jim and his accomplishments. She also recalled that over the years Jim seemed the most sensitized child to the flashes of static in their marital relationship. She also remembered that at times even recently she had pushed her husband to try to get close to Jim, and vice versa. But it seemed that the more she tried the less it happened.

Bob at first defended himself, and placed the problem squarely in the relationship between mother and son. Gradually, however, he began to look at his own ways of feeling, thinking, and operating. He began to log some clear ideas about his marital relationship. He gained some appreciation of his own difficulty in fielding the personal thoughts and feelings of his wife and kids. His reaction to them was to pull away into himself or to over-invest in his work. His highly developed, selective tune-out mechanism became an issue and was defined. Bob felt that, despite the obvious conflict between his wife and Jim, there was a closeness there which was missing in his relationship with Jim, and that both Jim and his wife did not value or appreciate him very much.

The Plan which was Developed. A plan was developed wherein mother was to make an attempt at decreasing her movement toward and degree of involvement with Jim. While doing this, she would not press her husband but would maintain a distance and would encourage any movement by him to close up the distance in the father–son relationship. Father was going to attempt to be more tuned-in and emotionally available to his wife; to make "I" statements about his personal thoughts and feelings, and to meet his wife on a feeling level on an occasion or two. In addition, father

238

was to try moving in on Jim and just spending time with him in the same physical space, and observing what happened. The purpose was not just to accomplish the plan but rather, while enacting it, to observe the effect of it on the people involved and on the insides of the people making the moves. In the course of events, mother initially became significantly depressed. Father, after several aborted attempts, was able to open up the relationship with Jim. In three months' time, Jim's symptoms began to fade somewhat and he managed, while remaining at home, to re-enroll in college and to improve greatly the functioning of his relationships both in his family and in his social network. Mother finally moved back into her extended family and opened up relationships there which at the beginning she doubted could ever exist.

The marital relationship reached a level of functioning higher than it had ever attained in the past. At present the family is continuing to work on it. The contour of the road is still rough but the potholes are less deep and consequently less destructive.

CENTERLESS-WEB VIEW OF ALIENATION

This tale might easily be labeled a hero-story or even a fairy-tale. Obviously not all the situations I have dealt with involving alienation have moved as quickly as this; some have not moved at all. I have used this tale to illustrate a way of thinking about the problem of alienation. This is important because it is one's way of thinking about a problem which should determine one's response to it. Keniston, in his work *The uncommitted*, a study of alienated youth in American society, uses these ideas to crystallize an approach to the problem of alienation. He writes that

> . . . It would be comforting to think we could find *the* cause of alienation in possessive mothers, the bureaucratization of modern man, or the decline of Utopia. It is confusing to begin to see that *all* these factors, and many others, are simultaneously involved. And confusion is compounded when we realize that each of these partial causes is itself interconnected with all of the others: that possessive mothers may be made more possessive by the limitations of their husbands' jobs, that the decline of Utopia may be related to the quality of men's work. Faced with such real complexity, the search for causes must yield to a search for connections; and the primitive causal model of dominoes toppling each other to the end of the row must be supplanted by the concept of a centerless web, all of whose threads are related to, are influenced by, and influence, all of the others [Keniston, 1965, p. 10].

If one adopts the centerless-web model for viewing problems like alienation, one can no longer look in isolation at any one relationship or facet of an emotional process, but must keep a systematized view of the intricate interconnectedness of all related factors.

In a recent discussion I had the pleasure of having with Kenneth Keniston, much of what was said related to a dyadic or intrapsychic model. I called this to Keniston's attention along with the preceding quotation. He remembered his centerless-web statement well, but said that he had great difficulty keeping his focus on a centerless-web model. As he saw it, because of his training in psychoanalytic thinking, he quickly moved to dyadic and intrapsychic models for describing his clinical experiences.

ALIENATION: A MULTI-RELATED RESPONSE

There are many psychological theories and ways of viewing emotional problems. For the sake of simplicity, I would like to break them down into thinking in terms of one's, two's, and three's. In the preceding clinical description, if one thinks in terms of one's, there would be careful focus and attention paid to Jim's intrapsychic process, defenses, fixation levels, etc. If one thinks in terms of two's, i.e. mother–son, there would be careful scrutiny of the dyadic relationships and the effect of the intrapsychic structure of one on the other. If one thinks in terms of three's, one can no longer view the relationship between mother and son without also taking into account the relationships between father and son, and father and mother. One can no longer view Jim's alienation without also connecting his father's distance and his mother's attempts at other-control. Jim's family very classically demonstrates the family process present in clinical situations involving the symptom of alienation:

1. A distant father over-involved in work, reactively under-involved with the personal workings of his family.
2. A mother who responds to anxiety by moving in, taking over control, and directing the situation from a position of truth.
3. A son the target of mother's investment, somehow sensitized to the negative emotional charge in his parents' relationship. The son chooses in some way to remain hooked in and symptomatic. Often symptomatic behavior in an offspring seems to be the only issue around which parents are pulled together into some semblance of a relationship.
4. A clear cut-off of contact and dealing with the emotional process from both sides of the extended family.

In view of these factors it makes no sense to me to define the problem of alienation as situated within a person, and to isolate and fix it there. Neither does it make sense to externalize it out of home base to the ultimate boogieman, the "greater social system." It has been both my personal and my clinical experience that, when relationships in a three-generational

family system are working well, the obstacles presented by the greater
social system can be dealt with and, I have reason to hope, even changed.

The response entailed in this way of thinking calls for each person to
view the problem of alienation from a vantage point which includes self
as a part of the overall emotional process which produces the symptom of
alienation. Specifically on a personal level, this means defining and taking
responsibility for one's own part. Clinically, it means taking responsibility
for one's own behavior, thoughts, and feelings in dealing with the symptom.

REFERENCE

Keniston, K. *The uncommitted: Alienated youth in American society*. New York:
    Harcourt, Brace, 1965.

Response to Alienation
from Political Science

JOSEPH CROPSEY

Joseph Cropsey received all his degrees from Columbia University: his A.B. in 1939, his M.A. in 1940, and his Ph.D. in 1952. His teaching career has been devoted to the University of Chicago where he is currently professor of political science. Professor Cropsey is the author of one book, Polity and economy *(1957), and editor of three others:* History of political philosophy *(1963),* Ancients and moderns *(1964), and* Hobbes's dialogue *(1971).*

Alienation is a word of numerous meanings, many of which will not concern us. We will confine our attention to the state of otherness or apartness, or the sense of being in a state of otherness or apartness, which the word commonly conveys. We must take note of the fact that alienation so understood is thought to be a problem, especially a problem with a political bearing. Our task will be to assess the view of it which sees it as a problem, and to judge of the aptness of the view which sees it as having a political bearing.

It must immediately appear strange that a man's sense of his otherness, of his distinctness from all those whom he must know to be "other," is regarded as a thing to be deplored and overcome; for one of the first things that any animal, and surely a man, must learn is where he ends and all else begins. Without such a consciousness of his own "otherness," he could have no sense of his own identity or boundedness. In the perfect confusion of himself and the All, he would, it is true, have no occasion to know

in interest and sentiment which are opened up between each and all by the rules of society. Is it unfair to say that for the condition of distance between one and other there are two antidotes? One antidote is to overcome the distance by abolishing the difference between the one and the other, making a one out of two or more, which I call integration; the other antidote is to bring on a state of mind in one, such that it will cease to prefer itself to the other and might in the end prefer the other to itself, which I call altruism. Let us consider these in their political bearing.

According to its own self-understanding, the United States is a one which has been made out of many. No one could deny that there is and has always been an element of metaphor in this description of the federal union. For the moment, we are less interested in the question whether a perfect political integration is impossible than in the question (at least as old as Plato's *Republic*) whether such an integration is desirable. Is it of the essence of the political association that it contain elements irreducible to each other—bodies and souls, lower and higher, nobility and wisdom, to say nothing of male and female and young and old? If the political community is composed of such elements, as it surely is, then "integration" as the antidote to alienation must be understood merely figuratively. The one which is constructed of the many derives its unity from the fact that the diverse many are ordered and ranged in an articulated whole, composing a one in the way in which diverse fractions can add up to one. While it is easy to speak about such ordering and ranking, it is very hard to arrive at the principle of it, which is called justice. Apart from the difficulty of saying what justice concretely requires, the fact emerges that, when the radical remedy of integration is proposed for the disease of alienation, the disease itself is shown to have been wrongly diagnosed. The psychological formulation in terms of alienation replaces unserviceably the formulation in terms of justice, and deserves to be ejected by it.

What of altruism as the antidote to alienation? If altruism means a proper regard for the concerns of others, a rational abstention from making a special case of oneself, it is in itself wholly unexceptionable but is, like "integration," simply an aspect of justice and has nothing particular to do with alienation. If altruism must be given its more radical meaning—namely, a serious replacement of self-preference by preference for the other—then it is particularly important that it be examined by the light of claims which have been made on behalf of its contrary, namely, egoism.

There is, to begin with, a famous species of argument which appeals to preconventional nature in order to prove that the deepest and strongest drive in a man is toward the preservation of his life. When you see a man striving singlemindedly in his own interest, you see true man as he really is—undissembling, sincere, untinted by mere convention, undeflected by culture or society. Callicles, Hobbes, and Nietzsche have seen something along these lines. Is there not at least a likelihood that nature dictates egoism and is a stranger to altruism? If so, only by the most violent conventionalism could men be transformed into altruists—a prospect which can only repel the alienationists. This *démarche* is particularly awkward, for the political expression of sincere naturalism, unconfused by sham professions of care for others, proves to be familiar capitalism.

Thinkers who surveyed the egoistic tendencies of classic modern doctrine were sometimes offended by what they saw. The preservation of life in the easily understood sense was proving inimical to the true vitality of men: their enjoyment, their virtue, the keenness of their genuine self-life. Thus Rousseau in his way, Kierkegaard in his, Nietzsche in his, and all to some extent anticipated by Spinoza, pointed toward a heightened level of life based on a deeper understanding of "self-preservation" than the one which moves through the thought of Hobbes, Locke, and Adam Smith. In no case could this understanding be said to adopt radical altruism as a principle: rather the contrary. The doctrines of the self, in their early and, I believe, even in their derivative states, are primarily egoistic and exploit a relation with others for the sake of the happiness and vitality of the one, not of the other. A serious and by no means obviously base claim is thus raised on behalf of the individual man precisely in his contradistinction from others, a claim which deserves to be recognized as a reservation against radicalized altruism.

Arguments and claims which arise out of self-interest are rightly scrutinized with suspicion. We can do little more here than allude to the possibility that there are good men whose interests may rightfully be the basis of extensive claims and arguments. If worthy men advance their own measured claims, and the political society is organized to give those claims respectful and sympathetic attention, is the correct description of the regime "egoistical" or "just"? It is doubtful whether the alienationists are well equipped to give an impartial answer.

BASIC PROBLEM NOT ALIENATION BUT JUSTICE

We have been glancing at the proposed antidotes to alienation, and have found that something can be argued in support of the contraries to those antidotes. I wish to suggest now that there are reasons for doubting that alienation, or conscious "otherness," is simply and in itself the ultimate social evil. In the first place, as was already said, there could be no sense of being self without a sense of being other. Moreover, if there were no strong sense of barrier or gap, the human species would fall into the carnal chaos of unregulated herd-animals. Let us if necessary remind ourselves that the all-time illustration of man overcoming the generation gap is Oedipus. Akin to this thought is the popular wisdom that familiarity breeds contempt very often, and the insight that the ugliest work of art might well be a representation of beauty seen by a proximate eye. As it appears, both virtue and beauty demand distance.

We must be careful not to prove too much, not to seem to deny, for example, that a state is defective in some way if many of its citizens have the sense of being excluded from the community's life, with the result that they are lost equally to ambition and to shame. Still, common experience teaches that when a distance exists between two beings, including men, it is necessary to look impartially into the circumstances. A lamb which puts a distance between itself and a lion is not atrocious, nor is a man who separates himself from a snake or from a cannibal: the initiator of the distance may or may not be fair and reasonable. On the other hand, the one who feels himself kept at a distance might be under the influence of what is vulgarly called paranoia, or a pathologic sense of being rejected. If he correctly apprehends his rejection, what is the manly way for him to deal with it—in a spirit of envy, resentment, and vicious truculence; or with dignity, pride in neglected achievement, perhaps withdrawal to a fortified if invisible height? The answer evidently bears upon the justice or injustice with which the distance has been created. Of one thing we can be fairly certain: distance or "alienation" by itself is not a diagnosis. It is at most a symptom.

My aim has been to propose that, for purposes of understanding and discussing political life, "alienation" is partly unhelpful and partly misleading. It is not simply useless, but it has the decisive defect of distorting or obscuring the properly political issue, which is not whether a certain public act causes pain but whether it is just. These two criteria cannot be made to coincide except on the premise of gross hedonism—namely, that whatever gives pain is immoral and unjust because pleasure is the sovereign good. This premise does not necessarily conflict with the alienationist premise that love and intimate unity are the supreme goods, but it gives it a base or repulsive color, and I doubt that it is publicly or wittingly owned by the alienationists. None of the foregoing is meant to dispute the fact that a regime which engenders vulgarity, hurtfulness, mutual indifference, moral shiftiness, mendacity, or cruelty among its citizens is to that extent a failure. It is meant to argue that sounder progress is likely to result if we replace the question of "alienation" with the question "What is justice?"

Response to Alienation
from Social Science

JOHN L. THOMAS, S.J.

*Father John Lawrence Thomas, S.J., is a widely
known sociologist who has an A.B. degree from
St. Louis University, an M.A. from the University
of Montreal, and a Ph.D. from the University
of Chicago. He is a prolific writer and is the
author of nine books, the most recent of which
are* Religion and the American people *(1963)*
and Looking toward marriage *(1965). He has
also contributed numerous articles to various
European and American journals, such as* Stim-
men der Zeit, American Journal of Sociology,
American Sociological Review, Sociological Analysis, America, *and* Commonweal. *From 1949 to
1965 Fr. Thomas was on the faculty of St. Louis
University, and from 1965 to 1971 he was research associate at the Cambridge Center for Social Studies. Currently, he is research professor,
Jesuit Center for Social Studies, Georgetown University, Washington, D.C.*

Alienation has become something of a "weasel" word, its meaning changing with its contexts; and further to compound our semantic confusion, it
has also become a "nomad," moving from one denotation to another even
within the same general context. During the nineteenth century and the
first half of the twentieth, accepted usage tended to confine the concept
of alienation within three major categories: juridical, to signify loss of
property rights; psychopathological, to indicate a deterioration of mental

247

faculties; and Marxist-Hegelian, to designate the deleterious consequences of the industrial worker's deprivation of ownership and control of the means of production (Gabel, 1970). For roughly the past two decades, however, the concept has been enjoying widespread popularity in theology, philosophy, and most of the social sciences; yet in none of these general disciplines do we find it used consistently or with the precision required for useful research and discussion. A cursory review of the literature indeed reveals that the phenomena dealt with under this rubric include everything from original sin to the generation gap, from existential Teutonic *Angst* and Gallic *nausea* to social deviance and cultural disaffiliation, from cosmic disenchantment to low participation in various social processes (Seeman, 1959, 1967; Nettler, 1957; Keniston, 1965; Israel, 1971; Schacht, 1970; Dean, 1961; Lang, 1967; Fromm, 1941, 1955, 1961).

Why the concept of alienation finds such resonance in the contemporary *Zeitgeist,* or why writers in such diverse disciplines now tend to characterize in terms of alienation whatever they feel to be currently amiss, are fascinating questions for the sociology of knowledge, but I raise them here only to emphasize that the current almost cavalier use of the concept is leading many social scientists to question its value. Some (Israel, 1971) feel it should be replaced by several more-specific, less-ambiguous concepts; some (Gabel, 1970) would retain only one of its nineteenth-century usages though in a revised Marxist-Hegelian frame of reference; still others (Keniston, 1965; Seeman, 1959) find it useful if given a multidimensional definition, arguing that in this respect its meaning is no more ambiguous or vague than such widely accepted terms as "frustration," "aggression," or "anomie."

THEME UNDERLYING ALIENATION

The assigned purpose of this paper limits it to discussion of sociological responses to alienation; but, given the present confused state of the question, I feel that it will be helpful to preface my responses with a brief description of the problem as I at present conceive of it. Hence these introductory observations will relate to those peculiar aspects of the concept which in my estimation go far toward explaining its perduring though seemingly protean character as well as its inherently normative context.

As its long history clearly attests, alienation is a significant archetypal concept associated with and focusing on one of those important underlying *themata* which despite all change and progress of human knowledge remain relatively few, and in one guise or another persist as major mainstays of man's creative imagination and concern down through the ages. Overarching concepts of this type have the merit of drawing attention to the structural similarities of a wide variety of behaviors which might otherwise appear to have little in common; yet at the same time they have the disadvantage of obscuring distinctions and dissimilarities which may prove crucial in certain contexts. To obviate this difficulty, we must take the time to "unpack" such concepts through careful analysis; that is, we must try to identify and define their essential specifying components and thus delimit the behavioral phenomena falling within their legitimate scope. Applied to the concept of alienation, this means that we must be able not only to specify the unifying *theme* underlying its various constructs but also to identify the normative postulates or presuppositions providing the criteria on the basis of which a given form of behavior is judged to be a manifestation of this *theme*.

A critical overview of past and current varieties of alienation reveals that they revolve around and focus on a common underlying *theme* which includes two basic considerations: first, somebody or some group is estranged, disaffiliated, or separated from something; and second, this estrangement, which may refer to a state or a process, is regarded as a deprivation—that is, an undue lack of something—or as a deviation from a human condition thought to be normal. This second consideration points up an essential, specifying component of the *theme*. Not all forms of estrangement fall under the rubric of alienation—some are regarded as an emancipation or a liberation. Further, since rational judgments regarding deprivation or deviation can be made only on the basis of normative criteria relating to the nature, or some aspect of the nature, of man, society, and their interrelatedness, it seems clear that concepts of alienation necessarily involve a set of normative presuppositions and can be fully understood only to the extent that these postulates are made explicit. Failure to recognize or acknowledge this point accounts for much of the obscurity and confusion plaguing most contemporary theories of alienation. Theorists who ignore or make light of any concern with such normative presuppositions must explain why the idea of alienation merits serious consideration in the first place; and if they persist in making use of the concept, they ought at least to inform us on the basis of what criteria they characterize a given form of behavior as indicative of alienation. Because there has long been a tendency among American social scientists in particular to attempt to make their work appear more scientific by leaving their value-premises unstated, we need to remind ourselves frequently that all psychological and sociological theories of an empirical type are based on postulated normative notions which precede and consequently delimit their scope and content.

PSYCHOLOGICAL AND SOCIOLOGICAL APPROACHES TO ALIENATION

An additional source of confusion if not controversy in contemporary discussions of alienation relates to the fact that the phenomenon of alienation may be analyzed from two different points of view, or, perhaps better, on two

different levels—psychological and sociological. Those who consider alienation to be primarily a psychological problem will define it as a psychological
state or complex of psychological states experienced by an individual: for
example, "powerlessness," "meaninglessness," "normlessness," "isolation,"
"self-estrangement," and so on (Seeman, 1959). In studying the degree or
extent of the alienation experienced by an individual or a group, one can
attempt either to measure the phenomena empirically by operationalizing
these psychological dimensions in attitude scales (Seeman, 1959) or to define
the experience more precisely by providing a detailed description of its actual
manifestations based on interviews, trained observation, and so forth. Although those who follow this psychologically oriented approach are chiefly
concerned with the actual awareness or felt experience of alienation (that is,
with subjective phenomena) they may also view the situation objectively and,
as trained scientists, present their own analysis of conditions, based on the
assumption that the behavior they observe manifests alienation—even though,
as a result of what Marx called "false consciousness," it may not be experienced as such by the participants themselves. This assumption on the part of
the observer clearly implies a number of normative postulates regarding the
nature of man, society, and their interrelatedness; yet these presuppositions
are seldom stated explicitly, with the result that it is often difficult to ascertain
to what extent the peculiar ideology of the observer has affected the selection
of data and the interpretation of their significance.

On the other hand, those (Israel, 1971) who consider alienation to be
mainly a sociological problem will define it in terms of social processes which
are judged to be structured in ways which inhibit man's self-fulfillment or
self-realization and lessen his possibility of controlling his life in a conscious
and responsibly intended manner. The etiological significance these theorists
attribute to social processes and structures in explaining alienation is predi-
cated on a concept of human nature which sees man as a profoundly *zoan
politikon,* that is, as a political animal not only in the Aristotelian sense of
the term but also as one that can develop into a human individual only in
society. The wholly society-centered orientation of their analysis does not in
itself imply any presuppositions regarding social or cultural determinism,
but, in contrast to the psychological, person-centered approach mentioned
above, it serves to situate the strategic locus of concern in social processes
and structures rather than in psychological states. In other words, although
these theorists acknowledge that man is both the creator and object of the
intricate web of social processes constituting his social environment or
"world," they maintain that a given individual operating within a sociocultural system characterized, for example, by corporate bigness, structural
complexity, occupational specialization, bureaucratic organization, and the
ideological dominance of formal rather than substantive rationality—to use
Weber's enlightening distinctions—becomes primarily an "object," subjected

to "blind" forces within the system which largely determine his available options and consequently diminish his possibilities for directing and controlling the course of his life in a fully conscious, freely chosen way.

These two approaches are not incompatible and may usefully be combined in studies of alienation designed to describe the various psychological and social factors associated with the phenomenon in a given situation. However, once the practitioners of these two approaches proceed beyond mere description and try to identify the multiple causal relationships thought to be operative in generating alienation, they tend to diverge sharply—with the important result that, in devising therapy or assigning therapeutic priorities, they come up with markedly different responses.

Thus, psychologically oriented theorists tend to view therapy in terms of individual adjustment and adaptation which they seek to promote by means of counseling, conditioning, dialogue, and the resolution of conflicting interests through reasonable compromise. Their sociologically oriented colleagues regard such therapy as a stop-gap measure at best, or, what is worse, as a manipulative human-relations technique designed to induce conformity to what they regard as the humanly destructive demands of the established order. Consistent with their own definition of the situation, therefore, they maintain that there can be no remedy for alienation unless existing social processes and structures are so changed or modified that modern man can regain some direction and control of those quasi-autonomous forces in society which now dominate his life. How or if this reform of social institutions can be accomplished without notably diminishing present material standards of living or even jeopardizing the stability of the entire economic system is admittedly far from clear, though the sociological practitioners counter such conservative concerns with the sobering reminder that the alternative to reform—that is, the uninterrupted continuance of current fast-moving trends —will be a "mass" society increasingly subservient to the exigencies of impersonal social processes and structures, or, what is more likely, to the manipulations of a utilitarian-minded power elite.

HISTORICAL DEVELOPMENT OF THE CONCEPT OF ALIENATION

By way of concluding these introductory remarks I would like at least to call to your attention several aspects of the historical development of the idea of alienation which have special relevance for our understanding of the present state of the problem. Briefly, inasmuch as the sources, interpretations, and actual awareness of the deprivations which can be associated with or attributed to the human condition obviously differ from one historical stage and/or one sociocultural system to another, it is now rather generally recognized that alienation has appeared in a number of different forms or modalities, has received a number of different interpretations or explanations, and has occasioned a number of different therapeutic responses. But what is frequently overlooked in reviewing the historical and cultural variations developed around this central theme is the significant fact that each successive new notion is based on a different set of normative postulates or presuppositions relating to the nature of man and the world.

In other words, changes in the concept of alienation always reflect changes in the way men come to view and define the human condition. This complex, multifaceted and multidimensional phenomenon has, as we learn from history, successively been viewed from three different perspectives and has consequently been defined in terms of three different frames of reference, which we may broadly categorize as theological, philosophical, and empirical-scientific.

These different approaches, or ways of viewing and defining, are not mutually exclusive—the conceptual framework of each is based on a different set of presuppositions, each precedes and therefore delimits the specific aspects and dimensions of the human condition which can legitimately be included within its scope, and each responds to a different category of questions which men are impelled to raise and somehow to answer as they strive to make sense of all aspects and dimensions of their human condition. This leads us to conclude that all three of these approaches not only can be, but if we are to achieve a comprehensive view of reality must be, developed equally and concurrently within the same cultural complex.

As a general rule throughout the past, however, we find that only one of these approaches has provided the dominant perceptual or cognitive paradigm operative in a given culture during any major stage of its development, while the other two were not yet fully articulated, or persisted as latent cultural residues perhaps to be reactivated later in somewhat different form, or retained full acceptance only among those individuals or subgroups which for one reason or another remained impervious to prevailing cultural trends. Now inasmuch as it is the specific type of paradigm currently dominant in a society which largely determines the kinds of estrangements or deprivations which come to be regarded as of primary significance, it follows that general awareness of and concern with the phenomenon of alienation at any given stage of cultural development have primarily been focused on only those sources and manifestations of deprivation identifiable within the limited scope of the dominant paradigm. Other sources and manifestations were either simply disregarded as trivial or rejected as spurious, while those which were recognized were made to provide the sole explanatory basis for what was felt to be wrong with man and his world at the time. This explains why each major historical period of man's cultural development, up to and including the present, is characterized by its own distinctive though limited concept of alienation.

Stated in somewhat different terms, historical changes in the concept of alienation imply a previous shift of dominant cultural paradigms; and in the Western world, at least, these shifts have evolved according to a definite pattern in the sense that dominance has shifted from a theological, to a philosophical, and finally to an empirical-scientific paradigm. Considered from the viewpoint of the historical development of the human species, each successive step in this process may be interpreted either as the zero-sum progression which Comte and his numerous modern followers have assumed or as the manifestation of a different aspect and the actualization of a different power of the species' total human potential. These two interpretations have radically different implications for a theory of alienation.

The first makes the *a priori* assumption that when these historical shifts occurred (for example, from a theological to a philosophical, or from a philosophical to an empirical-scientific approach), the new dominant paradigm not only completely replaced the previously dominant one but also rendered invalid or meaningless the total conceptual framework within which it had been formulated and the entire category of questions to which it had attempted to respond. All previously developed concepts of alienation consequently became outmoded since the kinds of deprivations with which they dealt were now regarded as spurious or non-existent. The second interpretation, on the other hand, maintains that as historical man gradually became aware of new aspects and dimensions of his human condition, he proceeded to develop new conceptual frameworks on the basis of which he attempted to make sense of his progressively deepening insights and expanding experiences.

The successive steps in this historical process were cumulative, each shift of dominant paradigms reflecting a distinctive stage of cultural development. Hence the historical emergence of a new dominant paradigm neither invalidated all previously acquired approaches and conceptual frames of reference—though they were necessarily affected and had to be modified accordingly—nor rendered obsolete all existing concepts of alienation, though it lessened their relative cultural saliency by focusing attention on new aspects and dimensions of the human condition and consequently on new potential sources of deprivation.

Lest these sketchy, somewhat theoretical considerations should be thought to throw little light on the contemporary phenomenon of alienation, I shall add a few concrete instances from history to show why I judge them to be highly relevant. For example, among those archaic cultures of which we have knowledge, the definitions of the human condition expressed in their symbols, rituals, and myths postulated some type of primeval warfare among cosmic powers, as well as some form of human estrangement from an original paradisiacal state; and within this quasi-religious or theological frame of reference, alienation was experienced as a state of complete dependency upon arbitrary transcendent beings which had to be propitiated by appropriate cultic acts.

On the basis of a somewhat similar definition of the human condition, members of so-called primitive cultures apparently believed, as we may conclude from their numerous and elaborate *rites de passage,* that the journey through life, and the major transitional stages of the life-cycle in particular, involved man's exposure to a variety of potentially alienating powers or beings which had to be ritually neutralized at every step of the way.

Coming closer to the historical roots of our own Western culture, we find evidence of a marked shift from a theological to a philosophical frame of reference. Although this new way of perceiving the human condition was expressed in a wide variety of relatively sophisticated philosophical systems of a Pythagorean, Platonic, Stoic, Orphic, or Gnostic provenance, its essential premise was the postulated ontological dichotomy of spirit and matter, while its cultural manifestation was a pervasive sense of disenchantment and personal estrangement.

Into this amazingly diversified cultural amalgam the Judaeo-Christian tradition, with its novel beliefs relating to creation in time and *ex nihilo,* the primal fall, original sin, redemption and rebirth in Christ, introduced its own distinctive sources of deprivation. As these came to be formally articulated in the light of, or in opposition to, contemporary Hellenic philosophies and later sociocultural influences, there gradually developed a comprehensive Christian worldview within which a theological concept of alienation played a strategic role. Thus, as a result of Adam's fall, nothing in the present world is as it should be; life is a brief pilgrimage set in a statically conceived, though ephemeral, secular world having significance primarily as the stage for the human moral drama; man is born in a state of estrangement—from God, from his fellow-men, from nature, and even from himself in the sense that his "carnal" passions and this-worldly desires wage constant war against his "spiritual" self.

Although this definition of the human condition provided the unquestioned *point de départ* for Western man's thinking on alienation up to the middle of the eighteenth century and—with its inherently pessimistic secular import progressively toned down or conveniently overlooked—for the practicing believers of all Christian denominations down to the present (Thomas, 1963), the beginnings of a profound cultural shift toward an empirical-scientific frame of reference were clearly discernible during the preceding century. But the mature actualization of Bacon's conception of empirical science as the *novum organum* which would revolutionize man's approach to nature required, among other things, time for much further development of technology and the mathematical sciences, as well as for that moral and intellectual discrediting of the entire Christian heritage of the West which resulted from the scandal generated by the prolonged sordid wars of religion, the persistent refusal of churchmen to discard their bitter inter- and intradenominational rivalries, the relentless attacks of the rationalist *philosophes* of the Enlightenment, the uncritical acceptance of positivism, and the pervasive spread of a pragmatic business mentality or climate of opinion which made much of the Church's teaching seem psychologically unreal and its concern with transcendental explanations of life simply irrelevant. By the end of the nineteenth century, however, dominance of the empirical-scientific paradigm was assured, at least north of the Alps and particularly in the United States, where it seemed tailored to the needs of the emerging "healthy-mindedness" of liberal Christianity (James, 1902) with its notions of universal evolution, general meliorism, inevitable progress, and manifest destiny under a benevolent divine providence.

The concept of alienation, meanwhile, had also been undergoing change. As a result of seventeenth-century scientific discoveries and eighteenth-century skeptical philosophies, the axial or cardinal point of emphasis in Western culture shifted from concern with teleology, divine providence, and the future life to concern with secondary causes, the laws of nature, and man's terrestrial vocation. The sources and manifestations of depriva- tion identifiable within this new conceptual framework were varied but almost exclusively anthropological in scope and content. For example, convinced that they were witnessing the end of a cultural epoch, English and French rationalists as well as influential German romanticists (Regin, 1969) looked forward to a bright new world freed from religious and po- litical tyrannies and open to the full development of secular man. Being somewhat more perceptive, Hegel regarded the alienating conflict between the one and the many as inevitable, but since he had divinized the one, he resolved the conflict by urging the many to submit to the State as the manifestation of the Spirit in history.

Influenced by the current Hegelian and German romanticist presupposi- tion that man must fulfill himself through creative work, the young Marx located the basic source of alienation in the capitalist mode of production and the worker's consequent loss of freedom to control and direct his life, even though in his mature writings he placed major emphasis on the "fetish- ism of commodities," "false consciousness," and what we would now call "reification." Treating roughly similar ideas, other classical theorists such as Simmel, Weber, and Durkheim differed considerably from Marx in regard to their presuppositions and explanations but not in their exclusion of an explicit theological or philosophical frame of reference. The recent revival of interest in the phenomenon of alienation, on the other hand, reflects a much more diversified set of concerns, suggesting that the adequacy of an exclusively empirical-scientific approach to the problem is now beginning to be questioned.

CONCLUSIONS FROM THIS HISTORICAL REVIEW

Several summary conclusions follow from this brief review. First, since concepts of alienation are largely determined by the specific conceptual frameworks within which they are formulated, and since each of the basic frameworks—theological, philosophical, and empirical-scientific—includes only limited aspects and dimensions of the human condition, no concept of alienation formulated solely in terms of one of these approaches can encompass the varied types of deprivation which modern man is capable of identifying and experiencing. Second, it follows that the currently dominant concept of alienation, which is concerned with only those sources and manifestations of deprivation identifiable within an empirical-scientific frame of reference, is seriously lacking in comprehensiveness. Third, what is more important, this arbitrary consideration of only limited aspects and dimensions of the human condition leads to an exaggerated estimate of their causal significance as sources of alienation, and they consequently become the exclusive focus of concern when prescribing antidotes or devising therapeutic programs, with the result that false expectations are raised and subsequent frustrations become greater.

CURRENT SITUATION

Thus during the past two centuries the Western world has been exposed to an endless series of prophetic secular panaceas promising freedom from almost every form of traditional want and tyranny; yet it is precisely in those societies in which such programs have been most successful that the phenomenon of alienation appears most pervasive. This results not primarily because even well-planned and well-intentioned practical programs of action may have unanticipated deleterious consequences but because the successful achievement of freedom *from* something does not necessarily imply a corresponding development of freedom *for* something. Particularly in our rapidly changing, technologically advanced society the maintenance of this "freedom for" requires, at a minimum, the progressive formulation of a relatively integrated set of common or shared goals, objectives, and value-premises which take into consideration all aspects and dimensions of the human condition—a requirement which can be met only if this condition is viewed within a theological and philosophical as well as an empirical-scientific frame of reference.

This all adds up to saying that modern man, especially now that he has "come of age," can no longer postpone that characteristically human search for ultimate meaning and significance from which his nineteenth-and twentieth-century predecessors were temporarily distracted by the heady successes initially achieved through total dedication to an empirical-scientific approach. The widespread cultural malaise and sense of deprivation currently reflected in the advanced societies of the West stem not from lack of scientific knowledge, technology, or natural resources, but from lack of shared significant meanings, of goals judged worthy of lasting commitments, and of a unitary system of common beliefs and credibilities, justifying society's institutions, underpinning its normative standards, and supplying its moral energy. In this sense, modern Western man resembles the classic hobo of whom it was said that he had attained his freedom but lost his sense of direction—he did not know where he was going or what he was free for.

LIMITATIONS OF A PURELY SOCIOLOGICAL APPROACH

I have devoted so much time to these preliminary considerations because I feel that it would be quite misleading to attempt to discuss the sociological implications of contemporary forms of alienation without taking into account relevant components of the historical and cultural contexts within which these forms developed and in terms of which their comparative social significance must be judged. If my observations are substantially correct—namely, that different concepts of alienation reflect different ways of perceiving the human condition, and that there are three distinctive basic ways of viewing this condition—we may safely conclude that a purely sociological explanation of alienation will reveal only limited aspects of the phenomenon. The explanatory model usually employed by sociologists and social psychologists in analyzing alienation is relatively simple. One assumes that a given sociocultural condition, state, or process gives rise to specified kinds of feelings, dispositions, or attitudes which in turn result in characteristic types of behavior. To the extent that the resultant behavior is judged to be undesirable, therapeutic programs may be designed either to change social structures and processes or to foster adjustment and adaptation by modifying an individual's feelings or attitudes.

For example, if we feel that current rates of juvenile delinquency, school dropouts, marital breakdown, and so on, are indicative of alienation and should be lowered, we may proceed to analyze the socialization process in family and neighborhood, the structure and function of the educational system, the institutional aspects of marriage, and so forth, and recommend changes accordingly; or we may investigate feelings of disaffiliation and withdrawal of affect among social, educational, marital, or other alienated "deviants," and then propose more effective ways of "selling" them on law, education, marriage, and so forth. The first approach locates the sources of alienation primarily in social structures and processes on the assumption that they inhibit the full development of the individual; the second takes current social structures and processes for granted or regards them as necessary under present socio-economic conditions and consequently locates the sources of alienation in the individual's failure to adjust to the inevitable on the assumption that human nature is almost infinitely adaptable. It should be noted that both approaches involve definite though generally not clearly stated presuppositions regarding the nature of man, of society, and of their interrelatedness.

In the practical order this means that if our sociological approach to alienation is to proceed beyond trivial description to the proposal of positive therapeutic programs of action, we are forced to be explicit regarding our underlying assumptions; and when we attempt to do this, we discover that we are dealing with aspects and dimensions of the human condition which fall within the scope of philosophical and theological conceptual frameworks. This discovery would cause little difficulty in a culturally integrated society, and there seems little doubt that American sociologists, at least, have avoided making this discovery until recently because it was popularly assumed that all Americans shared a common value-system.

IMPLICATIONS OF CULTURAL PLURALISM

Perhaps because of the dominance of the Protestant establishment, the spatial and social segregation of minorities, and the uncritical acceptance of the acculturative efficacy of the "melting-pot" process, the American people have been remarkably slow to recognize the profound implications of cultural pluralism. In particular, while acknowledging the ethnic, racial, social-class, regional, and religious diversity within the nation, they have uniformly assumed that the vast majority of Americans shared a common value-system, in the sense that the values serving as their criteria for judging individual and societal actions, as well as for ranging a number of conflicting values in a hierarchy, were roughly similar. This assumption is no longer tenable, given the widespread, organized, socially disruptive outbursts experienced during the past decade. Yet many Americans are just beginning to discover that relatively large segments of the population have developed or are now developing life-styles and value hierarchies which reveal no common value-system.

Undoubtedly, this discovery that the melting-pot process has not fused us into a nation of like-minded equalitarians proves so upsetting because it undermines another widely held myth. When dealing with social conflicts Americans have typically assumed that all men are motivated by interests, and these can be compromised or accommodated without jeopardizing basic values. Hence rational behavior implies that conflicts be resolved through discussion of differences and mutual compromise of interests. But an analysis of the conflicts arising within a context of pluralism reveals that men are motivated by values rather than interests; and further, that the contending parties hold mutually incompatible value-systems. In such situations, the resolution of conflict through mutual compromise would constitute heresy or apostasy, not rational behavior. Conflicts originating in pluralism are basically conflicts of values, and conflicts of values necessarily lead to confrontation, as recent experience both at home and abroad clearly demonstrate. When conflicts occur between individuals or groups, confrontation can be avoided only if the contending parties share a common system of values and valuing.

The recognition that men can be motivated by values as well as by interests, and consequently that there can be conflicts of values as well as conflicts of interests, has special significance for contemporary Americans. Many are beginning to suspect that the uncritical acceptance of the industrial revolution and eighteenth-century Enlightenment social philosophy, with its promises of progress and utopia through technology and science, has produced some highly ambiguous gains. In an industrial civilization—and historian Perry Miller reminds us that this has been the dominant theme of American history for well over a century—the entire social system becomes progressively geared or oriented to the ever-increasing production, marketing, and consumption of material goods.

Efficiency becomes the overruling criterion of judgment, and in our large, resource-rich country imbued with the Enlightenment's pragmatic, *laissez-faire* individualism this has led to the development of huge economic and financial power-centers characterized by bureaucratic organizational complexity, intensive functional specialization, impersonal relationships (since a participant is judged and valued only in terms of his specific contribution to the enterprise), and unprecedented productive capacity. It has also led to the ruthless exploitation of natural resources and powerless minorities, widespread environmental pollution, increasing involvement in international power-struggles, and the cancerous growth of an immense military-industrial complex which, as President Eisenhower warned us in his final message to the nation, has grave implications for the maintenance of our liberties and democratic processes.

Because of the sheer size, baffling complexity, and all-inclusive outreach of the powerful congeries of autonomous, objective, and impersonal functional associations within which he must operate, the average American is bound to feel that the scope of his personal choices and moral responsibilities is becoming progressively restricted since so much of his existence is being shaped by impersonal forces beyond his control. This pervasive sense of helplessness is further enforced by awareness that the development of comprehensive responses to modern society's crucial needs is beset by serious structural as well as value problems. Within the overall system or its major institutions it is becoming increasingly difficult to uncover the true *locus* of authority or decision-making power and consequently to determine the nature and extent of the moral responsibility incurred by those who are involved in various decision-making processes.

Moreover, the satisfactory development of policy decisions designed to deal with any major twentieth-century problem obviously requires a comprehensive view of relevant factors, trends, and consequences. Yet given the present state of the arts and the evolving complexity of the social system, this essential requirement can seldom be met. A review of the policy-making process in current programs designed to deal, for example, with poverty, integration, urbanism, education, or involvement in Vietnam shows that successive decisions are based on a strategy which is sequential and incremental rather than comprehensive in scope. Although policy-makers are unable or have not attempted to develop a comprehensive view of the problem, they uniformly decide to continue to do more and more of the same (escalation), until they run out of funds or the administration changes. Frustration with the limited results of this problem-solving procedure leads many Americans to question whether their society, as currently constructed, is capable of solving any of its major problems.

SUMMARY

The issues raised by massive population-shifts resulting in problems of unregulated urban growth, the concentration of minority power in central cities, the drastic reduction of family size, and changing sexual roles; by the erosion of the Protestant establishment and the eclipse of WASP ascendancy; by the public manifestations of pluralism, challenging the popular myths of a common value-system and the reducibility of all social conflicts to conflicts of interests; by a growing sense of helplessness and restriction of freedom; and by an acute public awareness of vast unsolved problems, together with uneasy doubts about the present social system's capacity to provide comprehensive responses—all these, to name only the basic ones, have contributed to the development of a general climate of opinion which is difficult to characterize. Thus there are pervasive currents of heightened anxiety, uncertainty, moral confusion, sensitivity to social evils, and disillusionment with science, organized religion, and existing authority structures.

More important, the majority of the people, apart from the limited number who have completely withdrawn from the system or dedicated themselves to its destruction, have the vague uneasy feeling that their entire "world" is beginning to fall apart at the seams. Among the faithful, the old beliefs, values, and structures are still present, but they seem to have lost their former power to motivate, inspire, and assure. The suddenness with which this has happened—the contrast between the 'fifties and 'sixties is truly amazing—only increases the shock. Under these conditions, people tend to be edgy, receptive to rumors, novelties, and fads, distrustful of lasting or long-range commitments, and primarily concerned with the present. How deeply basic traditional beliefs, attitudes, and practice are being affected is not yet clear; but, judging from the information available, general awareness of the transcendental dimensions of life is not likely to increase, and to the extent that this is true, any meaningful discussion of alienation in the immediate future appears questionable.

REFERENCES

Dean, D. G. Alienation: Its meaning and measurement. *American Sociological Review,* 1961, *26,* 753–758.

Fromm, E. *Escape from freedom.* New York: Rinehart, 1941.

Fromm, E. *The sane society.* New York: Rinehart, 1955.

Fromm, E. *Marx's concept of man.* New York: Rinehart, 1961.

Gabel, J. *Sociologie de l'aliénation.* Paris: Presses Universitaires de France, 1970.

Israel, J. *Alienation from Marx to modern sociology: A macrosociological analysis.* Boston: Allyn & Bacon, 1971.

James, W. *The varieties of religious experience.* New York: Longman, Green, 1902.

Keniston, K. *The uncommitted: Alienated youth in American society.* New York: Harcourt, Brace, 1965.

Lang, R. D. *The politics of experience.* New York: Pantheon, 1967.

Nettler, G. A measure of alienation. *American Sociological Review,* 1957, *22,* 670–677.

Regin, D. *Sources of cultural estrangement.* The Hague: Mouton, 1969.

Schacht, R. *Alienation.* Garden City, N.Y.: Doubleday, 1970.

Seeman, M. On the meaning of alienation. *American Sociological Review,* 1959, *24,* 783–793.

Seeman, M. On the personal consequences of alienation in work. *American Sociological Review,* 1967, *32,* 273–285.

Thomas, J. L. (s.j.) *Religion and the American people.* Paramus, N.J.: Newman, 1963.

Response to Alienation
from Religion*

WILLIAM J. BYRON, S.J.

Father William J. Byron, S.J., received his A.B. degree from St. Louis University in 1955, and his M.A. from the same institution in 1959. He also has an S.T.L. (1962) from Woodstock College, and a Ph.D. (1969) from the University of Maryland. Currently, Father Byron is director of field education and associate professor of social ethics at Woodstock College. He is also rector of the Woodstock Jesuit Community, now located in New York City. A member of the American Economic Association, and the American Society of Christian Ethics, Father Byron is a contributor to such diversified periodicals as America, Catholic Mind, Worship, Social Order, Federal Probation, *and the* Harvard Business Review.

If religion says anything at all to man it tells him that he is not alone. He is tied back to (*religare*) Something or Someone who transcends the limitations of space and time, who speaks to him, who gives ultimate meaning to his life, who is accessible through prayer, ritual, and the happenings of life.

If alienation says anything at all to man, it says that he is alone—estranged, lost, unconnected, incomplete. Religion, then, may well be considered as holding an antidotal position to alienation.

* An earlier draft of this paper was read by my Woodstock colleague, Rev. Avery Dulles, S.J. The present version benefited from his helpful criticisms.

I shall use the term alienation to cover four situations: (1) alienation from God (theological alienation); (2) alienation from self (psychological alienation); (3) alienation from the group or community (sociological alienation); (4) alienation from work (technological alienation). Included in technological alienation is the alienation of man from nature. To each of these conditions of man, I shall propose a response from religion, which I understand as an organized response to revelation involving both belief and practice.

In stating my understanding of the concept of alienation, I would want first to agree with Walter Kaufman's view that "alienation is neither a disease nor a blessing but, for better or worse, a central feature of human existence" (Kaufman, 1970, p. xv). Our individual and collective failure to adapt creatively to this central feature of human existence is, however, an evil, a disease which might be characterized as "unconnected self-interest." * In the unconnected state, self-interest can become destructive of the individual or collective self (the community). Our failure to connect ourselves to God, to group, to self, to work, and to nature is a failure of the creative, connective imagination and, at bottom, a failure of man to respond to grace. I understand alienation to be a sense of estrangement from God, from self, from fellow-man, from work, or from nature. One or all of these reference points may be the appropriate "whom" or "what" from which an individual or group is alienated.

THEOLOGICAL ALIENATION

Alienation from God is sin. The response from religion to this problem of theological alienation is put simply and clearly by St. Paul: "It is all God's work. It was God who reconciled us to himself through Christ. . . . For our sake God made the sinless one into sin, so that in him we might become the goodness of God" (2 Cor. 5:18,21). This, of course, is the work of grace. It is gratuitous. In St. Augustine's happy phrase, "We were fooled by the wisdom of the serpent, but saved by the foolishness of God." Religion, therefore, speaks to sinful man and tells him that his God is divinely foolish, loving, and generous. Religion pleads with man to believe that he is reconciled. But man may not believe. He may refuse to believe at all, and thus choose to remain alienated from God. Or, he may find himself saying with the man in Mark's gospel, "I do have faith. Help the little

---

* As will become clear later in this paper, I am indebted to Bernard Murchland's insistence throughout *The age of alienation* (Murchland, 1971) that the imagination is man's connective as well as his creative faculty. In a prenote to his book, Murchland quotes Kierkegaard's remark that "all burrowing into existence consists in establishing connections." If man's private pursuit of self-interest works against him by closing off connections, it is my view that this "unconnected self-interest" is in fact a disease threatening his existence. Religion speaks to this disease by reminding man that he must lose his life in order to find it (Mt. 16:26).

faith I have!" (Mk. 9:25). The varieties of unbelief are too numerous to catalogue here. The point to note would be that even for the believer who accepts reconciliation with the Father through Christ, there will be elements of estrangement as he finds himself wondering, from time to time, not whether God exists or has power to save, but whether God is here with him in a caring capacity at this hour, in this place. Doubt does not disqualify him from the community of believers; it does however leave him in a partially unconnected, partially alienated state. Religious belief and practice assist man in managing the problem of his alienated part, his unbelief.

PSYCHOLOGICAL ALIENATION

Alienation from self is a complicated psychological phenomenon. The Christian religion has been speaking to the issue for centuries as it ponders the meaning of St. Paul's expression of our double-mindedness: "I cannot understand my own behavior. I fail to carry out the things I want to do, and I find myself doing the very things I hate" (Rom. 7:15).

Among the alienated today there is, to an alarming degree, evidence of self-hatred. This is something beyond self-doubt, self-distrust, and a conviction of personal inadequacy. Moreover, it is something not limited to youth and the drug culture.* We speak too facilely of "alienated youth" and assert that "they" are alienated from "us." We fail to note that there are in both groups—the "they" and the "us"—countless self-alienated people, people who are separated from themselves by self-doubt, self-distrust, and self-hatred. It was chilling for me to listen recently to a young man refer to himself as "a walking graveyard." It is even more frightening to realize that many men two or three times his age say the same thing almost daily, but they say it to themselves. What is the response of religion?

One of the most difficult tasks for the Church and churchmen is to convince people that God loves them and that they are indeed lovable. "For our sake God made the sinless one into sin, so that in him we might become the goodness of God" (2 Cor. 5:21). Religion should assist man in celebrating the fact of his redemption. It should assure the individual that he can assimilate within himself the Paschal mystery, the doctrine of death *and resurrection*. It should assure him that he is or can become "the goodness of God."

---

* The complexities of psychological alienation seem to have been overlooked by President Nixon recently when he urged a visiting group of clergymen at the White House to give youth "some sense of faith" as the best alternative to a life ruined by drugs. "In the final analysis, if there is an answer to the drug problem, you have it," the President told the churchmen (Nixon, 1971). More than faith will be required to offset the forces of self-hatred and self-denigration which lead to self-destruction through drug abuse. It is true, however, that faith, if it is really deep, can transform a man so that he loves himself in Christ and hates his life only in the way commitment to Christ requires.

If I may use religion in a sense broad enough to include faith and theology, I would say that religion must respond to self-alienated man with a theology of human worth, a theology of failure, and a moral theology imaginative enough to bind the Christian to use his connective imagination to come to terms with his own doublemindedness. Thus integrated, the Christian is ready for the next stages of responsible growth and social obligation—connection of himself to a group and connection of one community to another.

There is an important implication for the pastoral counselor in this issue of alienation from self. The counselor has discovered in recent years that the young will often speak openly, frankly, and with apparent ease about highly personal, intimate problems. The fact that they do so without embarrassment might signal the presence of self-alienation. They speak about themselves impersonally because they regard themselves impersonally, as objects. The personal, intimate problem revealed in this self-disclosure may not be the problem which requires the counselor's attention. The client regards himself not only as an object, but possibly as an object of hatred as well. Similar clues may be discovered in the disclosures or silences of those who are no longer young. Under "the problem" there may well be the cavity of self-hatred.

SOCIOLOGICAL ALIENATION

Alienation from the group or community invites a response from religion. Kenneth Keniston sees in alienation from society "an explicit rejection, 'freely' chosen by the individual, of what he perceives as the dominant norms or values of his society" (Keniston, 1965, p. 455). Thus a person or group can be in society but not of it.

In one sense, the Christian tradition has always encouraged this. The monk rejects many of society's dominant values. James, "the brother of the Lord" and leader of the Judaeo-Christian community in Jerusalem, wrote around A.D. 50 to Jewish-Christians in the Graeco-Roman world in rather stern language: "You are as unfaithful as adulterous wives; don't you realize that making the world your friend is making God your enemy? Anyone who chooses the world for his friend turns himself into God's enemy" (Jm. 4:4). As used here, and also in Paul and John, "world" means opposition to God.

If we leave aside the Christian tradition just noted and assume a non-opposition to God in the dominant norms and values of our society, we would then say that those who reject these norms and values alienate themselves from society. Call them the "actively alienated." Someone could accept the dominant values but reject the dominant behavioral norms of a society. I would call such a person deviant rather than alienated.

If we assume, on the other hand, an admixture of opposition-to-God elements in the dominant norms and values of our society (I am thinking at the moment of racism and materialism), then those who are rejected by the society in function of these opposition-to-God values are also alienated, although not by choice. Call them the "passively alienated."

Among the actively alienated in our society, the young hold center stage. One of the lessons of the 1960s is that the cultural gap between generations can be as great as the cultural gap between nations. In America, therefore, the religious response to the alienated young might well be a missionary response. But a contemporary missionary response is called for. This means going when and where you are invited, and listening once you get there. Just as the missioner must be a transcultural intermediary avoiding triumphalism, imperialism, and unenlightened nationalism, the religious agent of transgenerational reconciliation must avoid the mindless excesses of missioners of another era. He must also understand what conversion really means today.*

I think the meeting ground for transgenerational reconciliation is in the area of commitment. Keniston (1965) calls his study of alienated youth in American society *The uncommitted*. The actively alienated young reject social norms and values which they regard as false, or thin, or constrictive of human potential. They quest for something worth committing their lives to, but they all too often give up the quest without finding a cause and settle for some*one* to cling to. Whether in a counterculture, a subculture, or a commune, the actively alienated youth removes himself from the negotiating table where a transgenerational shared search for commitment (a quest for a cause worth giving your life to) might have been possible. The President's Commission on Campus Unrest (the Scranton Commission), speaking of American youth-culture in the 1960s, reported that

> The tools of the workaday institutional world—hierarchy, discipline, rules, self-interest, self-defence, power—it [the youth culture] considered mad and tyrannical. It proclaimed instead the liberation of the individual to feel, to experience, to express whatever his unique humanity prompted. And its perceptions of the world grew ever more distant from the perceptions of the existing culture: what most called "justice" or "peace" or "accomplishment," the new culture envisioned as "enslavement" or "hysteria" or "meaninglessness." As this diversion of values and of vision proceeded, the new youth culture became increasingly oppositional [Scranton, 1970, p. 62].

The work of reconciliation is the work of religion. Man was reconciled to God in a poor and broken Christ. Perhaps a renewed commitment to

---

* In *Mid-Stream*, the Journal of the Council on Christian Unity, for Spring 1969 (Vol. 8, No. 3), there is a collection of papers on The meanings and practices of conversion, originally presented at the National Faith and Order Colloquium in Chicago in 1966.

poverty, simplicity, and self-sacrifice is the meeting ground for man and man, group and group, in our fragmented Christian society.

Religious institutions (and those who tend and attend them) must be authentically Christian—free, flexible, poor, and powerless. Young Christians, who accept the Christian faith while rejecting the institutionalized Christian religion, must confront themselves with radical gospel-principles and ask themselves whether their present alienation is leading to narcissism or to the Christian ideal of life through death to self.

Perhaps a mission, in the name of religion, to the passively alienated (the subordinated blacks, the rejected aged, the excluded poor and powerless, the unconnected loners) is the way to fill the gaps which divide institutional religion from the actively alienated young in America today. The prospect, however, is not promising. And when one's view is broadened to include the passively alienated in an international perspective, the prospect is less promising still.

It must not be forgotten that religion in the cultic sense, through its liturgical actions and celebrations, has a definite response to alienation. At the altar of sacrifice, Christians celebrate together the fact of their reconciliation with God, the fact that alienation from God through sin is healed in Christ's redeeming sacrifice. Today, however, it should be noted that at the same altar, viewed more as a table of communion than an altar of sacrifice, man's estrangement from his fellow-man can be reduced as he comes together with others, summoned out of his isolation into a community of love—a worshipping, celebrating community of believers united in the Eucharist.

Our Catholic-Christian failure to build community in this context is our great sin of omission in this age of alienation. Our "religious" concern for rubrics and regularity has been more evident than our Christian concern to minister to the alienated. True religion, the Epistle of James tells us, is "coming to the help of orphans and widows when they need it" (Jm. 1:27). For us, the "orphans and widows" are the alienated. Our sin of omission has been capitulation to the evil of "unconnected self-interest" through individual and collective failure to act imaginatively in the de-alienation of society. In this regard, we have displayed neither creative leadership nor creative followership in the Church.

> The imagination is man's connective as well as his creative faculty. This is to say that man must create his meanings; the kind of link between self and world we are talking about is not something given; nor is it something discovered; it is literally something made [Murchland, 1971, p. 188].

We have been seeking a better world as if it were "out there" waiting to be discovered, instead of realizing—as we must—that it is quite literally something "in here" waiting to be made. The American environment presents formidable cultural impediments to the kind of religious response which would foster the creative, connective formation of community. For, as Philip Slater puts it:

> Americans attempt to minimize, circumvent or deny the interdependence upon which all human societies are based. We need a private house, a private means of transportation, a private laundry, self service stores and do-it-yourself skills of every kind. An enormous technology seems to have set itself the task of making it unnecessary for one human being to ask anything of another in the course of going about his daily business. Even within the family Americans are unique in their feeling that each member should have a separate room, and even a separate telephone, television and car, when economically possible. We seek more and more privacy, and feel more and more alienated and lonely when we get it [Slater, 1970, p. 7].

Human experience verifies an inward and an outward impulse in all of us. In both directions we can find God; religion supports the quest in either direction. There is the inwardness of reflective solitude and the outwardness of community. The man who avoids either impulse is at best a part-time human being. In either direction the impulse can be impeded, even thwarted, by alienation from self or from the group. Moreover, in either direction God can be touched, so to speak, but not possessed. Hence the incompleteness of even the most unalienated of men. Religion, however, supports him in his incompleteness. And faith, of course, supports him too. "Only faith can guarantee the blessings that we hope for, or prove the existence of the realities that at present remain unseen," writes the author of the Letter to the Hebrews to his discouraged Jewish-Christian audience (Heb. 11:1).

At this point in the progress of my argument, a mid-course correction may be necessary. I would not want to give the impression that Christianity should fit into the mainstream of contemporary culture. Quite the contrary: Christianity is in fact a counterculture. Whether or not it can transform (convert?) the dominant culture to the point at which gospel values predominate is another question. Some theologians would say that the Church will always be a "remnant," a small community set apart. My personal view is that the "community of believers," however large or small, may well be contemporary man's best hope for an answer to the problem of sociological as well as theological alienation.

TECHNOLOGICAL ALIENATION

Let me turn now to technological alienation, or the alienation of man from work and nature. For Karl Marx, alienation meant "separation through surrender"; man involuntarily surrenders his right to the product of his labor (Schacht, 1970, p. 83). The economic roots of the concept of alienation are traceable to Marx and relate primarily to the economic order and the world of work. With the accelerated advance of technology in the twentieth century, men have been separated not only from the products of their labor but from their jobs as well through what has become known as technological unemployment. Moreover, work is organized in impersonal ways. Men at work have less and less contact with nature and with each other. The young postpone their entry into the labor force by taking technical education for work in a technological world. The very complexity of this world prompts some of the young to "drop out" of the preparation process; or, having completed their education, many reject the occupations for which they have been trained. Faced with the stepped-up competition and complexity of life, the alienated young display a hostility toward the instrumentalization of man and to industrial society's

> emphasis on effort, disciplined work, and the mechanisms that encourage it and reward it. This is seen in the insistence that everyone should do "his own thing" and more that he should not suffer for it.
> It would be an illusion to see this as being directed simply against some of the errors of this kind of society. This attack is directed as strongly— even *more* strongly—against those features of this kind of society that most of us consider virtues: its capacity to improve the material condition of people; its dependence on democracy and tolerance; its capacity to evoke work and effort and to reward work and effort.
> Thus, the possibility cannot be overlooked that the true causes of the events we today characterize as "campus unrest" lie deep in the social and economic patterns that have been building in Western industrial society for a hundred years or more. It is at least remarkable that so many of the themes of the new international youth culture appear to revolve in one way or another about the human costs of technology and urban life, and how often they seem to echo a yearning to return to an ancient and simpler day [Scranton, 1970, p. 87].

The contemporary "back-to-nature" impulse on the part of the alienated young poses a threat to institutional religion. This is unfortunate and unfair because the impulse is misdirected. It substitutes a reverence for nature for a reverence through nature, putting us on the road toward what Willis Elliott of New York Theological Seminary has called "poetic naturalism," a label which, he predicted in a recent conversation with me, will be descriptive of the dominant American "religion" in the year 2000.

Chapter Two of the Book of Wisdom portrays life as the godless see it —"they say to themselves, with their misguided reasoning":

> Our life is short and dreary. . . .
> By chance we came to birth. . . .

Our life will pass away like wisps of cloud. . . .
Yes, our days are the passing of a shadow,
from our death there is no turning back,
the seal is set: no one returns.
Come then, let us enjoy what good things there are,
use this creation with the zest of youth:
take our fill of the dearest wines and perfumes,
let not one flower of springtime pass us by,
before they wither crown ourselves with roses.
Let none of us forgo his part in our orgy,
let us leave the signs of our revelry everywhere,
this is our portion, this the lot assigned us [Wis. 2:1–9].

Institutional religion must raise up another Jeremiah who can say to the poetic naturalists:

What a brood you are! Listen, this is the word
of Yahweh:
Have I been a desert for Israel
or a land of deepest gloom?
Then why do my people say,
"We will go our own way,
we will no longer come to you"?
Does a girl forget her ornaments,
a bride her sash?
And yet my people have forgotten me,
for days beyond number [Jer. 2:31–32].

The contemporary countercultural return to nature and the simple life is an adaptation to the separation of contemporary man from work and nature. It displays a disturbing potential for fostering an alienation from God for future "days beyond number."

Those who are alienated in a Marxian sense are not free because they are captives of an alienating economic system. Religion in its contemporary concern for "orphans and widows" must challenge the alienating elements in the world of work. Just as Christ became man so that He could be where the alienation was in order to heal it, now the Christian seems called to the secular world of work to heal the technological alienation which is there. Once there, what does he do differently from anyone else? Nothing that immediately meets the eye. However, his motivation for being there should be different. It should be Christological and therefore reconciliatory, grounded in the New Commandment, and thus apostolic. Moreover, the results of his having been there may eventually become visible if through his creative and connective faculty, the imagination, he has discovered meaning in work; if he has under the impulse of Christian love designed a more human organization of the world of work; and if the witness of his Christian commitment has drawn a response from the connective imaginations of other workers, enabling them together to weave the fabric of community. But here again, incompleteness, unconnectedness, and some estrangement will admittedly remain despite the best efforts of the most creative intellects. After nudging him on in his vocation to make a better world, religion will remind the inhabitant of the world of work that he has no lasting city here (Heb. 13:14), but will sustain him through prayer, belief, and ritual as he lives with the difference between the present reality and the New Jerusalem.

REFERENCES

Kaufman, W. The inevitability of alienation. Introductory essay in R. Schacht. *Alienation*. Garden City, N.Y.: Doubleday, 1970. Pp. xiii–lvi.

Keniston, K. *The uncommitted: Alienated youth in American society*. New York: Harcourt, Brace, 1965.

Murchland, B. *The age of alienation*. New York: Random House, 1971.

Nixon, R. M. *New York Times*, March 27, 1971.

Schacht, R. *Alienation*. Garden City, N.Y.: Doubleday, 1970.

Scranton, W. W. (Chm.) *Report of the President's Commission on Campus Unrest*. Washington, D.C.: Government Printing Office, 1970.

Slater, P. E. *The pursuit of loneliness*. Boston: Beacon, 1970.